Psychological Perspectives on Intervention

Psychological Perspectives on Intervention

A Case Study Approach to Prescriptions for Change

Rik Carl D'Amato
University of Northern Colorado

Barbara A. Rothlisberg
Ball State University

WAVELAND PRESS, INC.
Prospect Heights, Illinois

For information about this book, write or call:
Waveland Press, Inc.
P.O. Box 400
Prospect Heights, Illinois 60070
847/634-0081

Love. Honor. Faith. Devotion. Pride. These are gifts that, when freely given, will be returned in full measure. For all that they have given to us, we dedicate this text to our parents, Ione D. D'Amato, Lawrence S. D'Amato, John K. Rothlisberg, and Ruth P. D. Rothlisberg.

Contents

Foreword

Jack I. Bardon

Two fundamental aspects of the human condition are the processes by which we come to know anything and the interplay between the consistencies and changes in behaviors, characteristics, and environmental circumstances throughout life. It is the enviable task of psychology to try to understand these aspects of the human condition. It is the awesome task of those whom the editors of this book call child service providers or practitioners to apply knowledge from psychology and related disciplines to the understanding of particular persons who are having difficulty dealing with their lives, or whose problems are bothersome to others.

What do we need to know to understand another person? What information should be collected? How do we order, evaluate, and give priority to the many pieces of the puzzle that contribute to the life of a person? How do we know when we know enough? And, most important of all, when what is known is collected and organized, what do we do with it? How do we relate information gathered to doing something to effect positive change in that person? And, ultimately, how do we know that what we do is the correct thing to do and the best thing to do? These critical questions, articulated or not, are those that form the bases for child and youth service provision, whether the service be formal education or intensive psychotherapy, or something in between.

Given the enormous complexity of these questions, it is not surprising that practitioners are tempted to find less complex answers and to seek out already organized and popular approaches that provide understandable frameworks for sorting out and reorganizing information that leads to readily available intervention methods and techniques, based on the frameworks adopted. Yet, it is my best guess that most practitioners of child services, over time, find that they must adapt their preconceived ideas about what works to different situations and different clients, students, or patients. Working with their own talents, with norms developed through actual experience, and with findings that do not conform to the theories or models taught them when they were learning to become child service providers, they make modifications in their ways of thinking, acting, and advising. Often, such modifications in assumptions made and procedures used occur in the absence of knowledge of other frameworks that might better suit practitioner inclinations and purposes.

This inevitable integration of what is taught, what is learned through experience, and what is the "best fit" to professional style is a life-long professional struggle. It offers testimony to the fact that there are many ways to know and many ways to be a helping professional. Every person we seek to help is not exactly like any other person we have sought to help in the past. Our knowledge-base and our theoretical assumptions often are only guideposts along the way toward our becoming change-agents.

When I was a graduate student, long ago, I was exposed to a limited variety of ways of knowing and was denied access to still other ways of knowing, based, presumably, on the premise that some were more correct than others and that one was, in truth, the best way to know. My getting a doctoral degree depended, in part, on my knowing this best way very well. Time and experience and resultant professional maturity gave me license to learn that all I was taught in graduate school was not all there was to know. If this book had been given to me to read and to discuss with my fellow students and faculty, much needless agony and guilt about my subsequent professional performance might have been avoided. But, of course, this book could not have been written then. We are both more sophisticated and more open to ideas now than we were when I was in graduate school. Similarly, if this book had been available to me during my early years of professional practice, I believe I would have been more of a risk-taker than I was and might have been more useful than I was in moving from data to action in many of the school-related problems referred to me.

This book is, to my knowledge, unique. It is a resource of excellent information and references about many of the major theoretical positions applicable to helping others who are having difficulty dealing with life events. It offers a comparative basis for understanding how different points of view lead to deciding what interventions are most likely to be efficacious. It offers insight into the thought processes by which experts in human services come to their conclusions about what is helpful to know in order to do what is best to help another.

If you think you already know the answers to the questions I posed earlier, if you are already convinced that there is only one approach to intervention, if you are not knowledgeable about other approaches, if you are satisfied that you know the truth, then prepare for dissonance and temporary confusion. But, if you are also prepared to think seriously about the approaches so well described and about the information provided and how it is used selectively by each contributor to this volume, then you have come to the right book. You can engage in a process of discovery about human service provision that could move you toward greater tolerance for ways to know and, perhaps, to a personal integration of your own experiences with the view of the change process you have learned to espouse.

On the other hand, if you are already confused, dissatisfied with what you have learned, and seek to understand the many ways information can be utilized toward the common goal of helping people (children and youth) change, you also have come to the right book. To me, this volume is like a good detective story with many endings provided. Given the plot (the case of Vince Chandler) and all the clues (the information gathered), how do you (the reader-detective) come to know the solution (the best interventions)?

What makes sense to you? Why does it make sense? What would *you* do with the information given?

Over the past several decades we have gradually learned that intervention does not flow naturally and easily from diagnosis, or, more broadly, assessment. We must work at bridging the large gap between data and intervention. We have learned that intervention is the reason for assessment. What is the use of describing if we can't do something to help, based on what we have learned or inferred from the information collected and analyzed?

This is a book to reflect upon and to discuss with others. It doesn't let you rest content; at the same time it informs and entertains. Enjoy yourself while you learn from experts. Learn that experts do not think alike and that there are many ways of coming to help others. Learn more about what you think and why. This is a book that can help you grow professionally, if you let it.

J. I. B.
Excellence Foundation Professor Emeritus
The University of North Carolina at Greensboro

Acknowledgments

We have been fortunate enough to assemble and work with a group of talented authors and wish to express our appreciation to them for the commitment they have shown to this volume. They have helped us to demonstrate the promise of psychology for intervention. We also want to thank our families, who have shown patience, especially when we had to work and they did not, and extend a special thanks to Naomi Silverman, our editor at Longman. We have been fortunate to have a number of individuals who provided continued support and encouragement.

We hope this book will serve as an inspiration for students. We met as graduate students in school psychology at the University of Wisconsin–Madison. We made lofty plans then, although such planning was not easy with heavy study demands. We discussed how the field of psychology would change, and which procedures or techniques would be needed for the many expanded opportunities that we envisioned for our specialty. At that time we were interested in various therapeutic techniques and quipped about directing school psychology training programs and contributing to the field. Students be warned: Be careful what you plan—you may have the opportunity to make your plans come true. We did.

RIK CARL D'AMATO
BARBARA A. ROTHLISBERG

Contributors

Jack I. Bardon, Ph.D.
Excellence Foundation Professor
  Emeritus
University of North Carolina–Greensboro

Mary Mathai Chittooran, Ph.D.
Infant and Child Development Clinic
University of Mississippi Medical Center

Jane Close Conoley, Ph.D.
Buros Institute of Mental Measurements
  and Chair, Department of Educational
  Psychology
University of Nebraska–Lincoln

Rik Carl D'Amato, Ph.D.
Director, Programs in School Psychology
  and Associate Professor of School
  Psychology
Division of Professional Psychology
University of Northern Colorado

Robert D. Enright, Ph.D.
Professor, Human Development Area
Department of Educational Psychology
University of Wisconsin–Madison

Suzanne Freedman, Ph.D.
Department of Educational Psychology
University of Wisconsin–Madison

Gladys Haynes, Ph.D.
School Psychology Program
Department of Educational Psychology
University of Nebraska–Lincoln

Jan N. Hughes, Ph.D.
Director, School Psychology Program
  and Professor, Department
  of Educational Psychology
College of Education
Texas A&M University

Sylvia M. Kemenoff, Ph.D.
School Psychology Program
Department of Educational Psychology
College of Education
Texas A&M University

Radhi Al-Mabuk, Ph.D.
Department of Educational Psychology
University of Wisconsin–Madison

Richard J. Morris, Ph.D.
Director, School Psychology Program
and Professor, Division of Educational
Psychology
College of Education
University of Arizona

Yvonne P. Morris, Ph.D.
School Psychology Program
Division of Educational Psychology
College of Education
University of Arizona

Barbara A. Rothlisberg, Ph.D.
Director, School Psychology I Program
and Associate Professor of Educational
Psychology
Ball State University

Avis J. Ruthven, Ed.D.
Director of Graduate Education and
Professor of Educational Psychology
College of Education
Mississippi State University

Issidoros Sarinopoulos, Ph.D.
Department of Educational Psychology
University of Wisconsin–Madison

Agnes E. Shine, Ph.D.
Director, Programs in School Psychology
and Assistant Professor of Educational
Psychology
Mississippi State University

Susan C. Warshaw, Ed.D.
Associate Professor
Ferkauf Graduate School of Psychology
Yeshiva University

Janice Campbell Whitten, Ph.D.
Assistant Director, Neuropsychology
Laboratory for Evaluation and Therapy
Programs in School Psychology
Department of Educational Psychology
Mississippi State University

Psychological Perspectives on Intervention

CHAPTER 1

Introduction: Foundations of Psychological Intervention

Rik Carl D'Amato
University of Northern Colorado

Barbara A. Rothlisberg
Ball State University

The history of applied psychology has been marked by philosophical diversity and theoretical movements devoted to the investigation of individual differences. For example, the supremacy enjoyed by the psychoanalytic perspective early in this century was eclipsed by behaviorism when it was touted as the best method of providing for individual description and change (Corsini & Wedding, 1989; Leahey, 1980). Now, no single diagnostic paradigm seems sufficient to explain the vagaries of behavior. Psychoanalytically, behaviorally, and biologically based as well as other theoretical positions have been challenged not only to describe behavior but also to provide effective intervention with their client populations (D'Amato & Dean, 1989a; Gutkin & Reynolds, 1990; Maher & Zins, 1987).

Early on, identification and classification of individuals—especially children—was seen as the critical enterprise of psychology based on the supposition that appropriate diagnosis leads directly to appropriate treatment (Bardon & Bennett, 1974; D'Amato & Dean, 1989b; Gray, 1963). Sadly, this supposition was in error because diagnostic considerations tended to be emphasized at the expense of intervention. While the reasons for this imbalance are numerous (e.g., lack of psychological technology and sophistication in intervention procedures, a need to understand patients' etiology to offer prevention), it now seems that the field of psychology is ready to focus on the issue of intervention (Hughes, 1988; Kratochwill & Morris, 1991; Sandoval, 1988)—thus, the publication of this book.

THE NEED FOR MULTIPLE INTERVENTION APPROACHES

To address the growing need for information on and procedures for intervention, numerous treatment techniques have evolved (Bellack & Hersen, 1988; D'Amato, 1985, 1990;

Greenwald, 1984; Kazdin, 1988; Schaefer & Millman, 1977). However, most training methods (and thus most textbooks) fall into one of two general categories: the study of the application of a single paradigm or the study of a potpourri of prescriptive options. The process of concentrating on and mastering a single treatment approach has been popular for many years and stresses a highly specialized expert-based philosophy. Use of a single paradigm invokes a sense of continuity across varied client requirements and offers clear guidelines for the practitioner. Common expert paradigms have included behaviorism, consulting, and clinical neuropsychology and have been reflected in texts such as Wolpe's (1990) *The Practice of Behavior Therapy*, Brown, Pryzwansky, and Schulte's (1987) *Psychological Consultation* and Lezak's (1983) *Neuropsychological Assessment*.

Although it seems easier to train individuals in a single approach rather than in a variety of techniques, it is clear that no one theoretical model is preeminent in terms of intervention (Blau, 1988; Corsini, 1991; Loevinger, 1987; Prout & Brown, 1983). Instead, practitioners have been charged with selecting paradigms to meet the unique needs of individual clients. Consequently, practitioners and researchers have begun to address the complex issues associated with matching treatments to clients to obtain the best long-term benefit (D'Amato & Dean, 1989b; Sandoval, 1988; Wolfgang & Glickman, 1986). At the risk of advocating the creation of generalists rather than masters of specific procedures, it would seem logical that practitioners avail themselves of the information currently known on a variety of psychological philosophies. The purpose of this text is to bring together in a comprehensive volume a number of divergent views on psychological treatments.

THE CASE STUDY APPROACH

This text uses a unique approach to highlight the benefits of and potential problems with major theoretical perspectives on evaluation and intervention. The experts representing the major paradigms must deal with the use of a single case study. The case is offered as the unifying element running across the several paradigms. The elegance of this approach is that it allows the reader to compare how various perspectives utilize the same data set in developing a picture of the individual client. The intent of the single case study format was not to prove or disprove the relative merits of contrasting positions but simply to provide a forum from which the unique elements of the approaches can be seen. Some psychological approaches reach a consensus on treatment issues but do so by different routes; other positions address common issues yet arrive at disparate conclusions. In either case, the purpose of the text—to highlight the perspectives that attempt to facilitate change in human behavior—will have been served.

To accomplish the task of contrasting different perspectives on psychological intervention, a common data set was necessary. It should be noted that, by including data purportedly of use to varying positions, the case information will of necessity have covered areas that a single position would find excessive. However, it should prove instructional to the reader to see the value that different perspectives give to the information provided. To offer the reader diversity in theory yet to sample effectively among the multitude of psychological approaches commonly encountered, eight different positions will be reviewed in this volume:

a behavioral approach

a psychoanalytic approach

a psychoeducational approach

a person-centered/humanistic approach

a neuropsychological approach

a moral developmental approach

a cognitive-behavioral approach

an ecological approach

The case study is of a 13-year-old adolescent male named Vince Chandler. As the reader makes his or her way through the various chapters, it is expected that the reader will become intimately acquainted with Vince and will recognize some of the common issues with which he struggles.

ANTICIPATED AUDIENCE FOR THIS BOOK

This volume has been designed for individuals who work with children. They may be employed in a variety of positions such as school psychologists, clinical child psychologists, counseling psychologists, neuropsychologists, psychotherapists, counselors, social workers, child psychiatrists, counselor educators, special educators, family therapists, pastors, or teachers, and they most probably serve in such different settings as schools, hospitals, residential treatment facilities, community mental health centers and the like. Whatever they are called or wherever they work—this book is for people who want to help children. It is not setting specific or employee/position specific (D'Amato & Dean, 1989a). Therefore, whenever possible we have called these child service providers *practitioners.*

It is hoped that the treatment of Vince's case will provide even a reader uninitiated to topics of assessment and intervention some insight into the way in which various theoretical approaches synthesize and judge information. As such, the text should be seen as a useful tool for trainers or faculty in psychology and related disciplines who need to offer undergraduate and graduate students comparisons of the given theoretical positions. Similarly, it is hoped that practitioners will gain increased understanding of different orientations and insight into potential treatment options.

SUMMARY

Psychology may be described as a discipline that endeavors to interpret and modify behavior. Since its inception practitioners have attempted to explain actions on the basis of their favored theoretical perspectives. Many times, different approaches have seemed to take diametrically opposing viewpoints in attempting to explain the same phenomenon (e.g., psychoanalytic versus behavioral views of a situation). The variation in perception, coupled with the infinite array of human differences in possible behavior, has made the description and modification of behavior a daunting task at best. Justifiably, one single approach to behavioral interpretation has not evolved. Instead, multiple approaches to explain behavior, each with its own perception and perspective exist. Diagnostic or descriptive paradigms are no longer sufficient to maintain a theoretical position. Now the issue of prescriptive effectiveness has come to the forefront and challenges psychological paradigms to provide evidence that they are effective in both analyzing and intervening in problem situations. This book is viewed as an attempt to offer practitioners an integration of many of the intervention techniques available today. We hope practitioners will be able to use these practices to assist the many children who critically need help. If even one child's life is positively affected then this volume will have been a success.

REFERENCES

Bardon, J. I., & Bennett, V. C. (1974). *School psychology.* Englewood Cliffs, NJ: Prentice-Hall.

Bellack, A. S., & Hersen, M. (1988). *Behavioral assessment: A practical handbook* (3rd ed.). New York: Pergamon.

Blau, T. H. (1988). *Psychotherapy tradecraft: The technique and style of doing therapy.* New York: Brunner/Mazel.

Brown, D., Pryzwansky, W. B., & Schulte, A. C. (1987). *Psychological consultation: Introduction to theory and practice.* Boston: Allyn & Bacon.

Corsini, R. J. (1991). *Five therapists and one client.* Itasca, IL: F. E. Peacock.

Corsini, R. J., & Wedding, D. (1989). *Current psychotherapies* (4th ed.). Itasca, IL: F. E. Peacock.

D'Amato, R. C. (1985). Teacher assistance teams: A problem solving system that creates intervention. *Proceedings of the 17th annual convention of the National Association of School Psychologists,* Las Vegas, NV. Washington, DC: NASP.

D'Amato, R. C. (1990). A neuropsychological approach to school psychology. *School Psychology Quarterly, 5,* 141–160.

D'Amato, R. C., & Dean, R. S. (Eds.). (1989a). *The school psychologist in nontraditional settings: Integrating clients, services, and settings.* Hillsdale, NJ: Erlbaum.

D'Amato, R. C., & Dean, R. S. (1989b). The past, present, and future of school psychology in nontraditional settings. In R. C. D'Amato & R. S. Dean (Eds.), *The school psychologist in nontraditional settings: Integrating clients, services, and settings* (pp. 185–209). Hillsdale, NJ: Erlbaum.

Gray, S. W. (1963). *The psychologist in the schools.* New York: Holt, Rinehart and Winston.

Greenwald, H. (1984). *Active psychotherapy.* New York: Jason Aronson.

Gutkin, T. B., & Reynolds, C. R. (Eds.). (1990). *The handbook of school psychology* (2nd ed.). New York: Wiley.

Hughes, J. N. (1988). *Cognitive behavior therapy with children in schools.* New York: Pergamon.

Kazdin, A. E. (1988). *Child psychotherapy: Developing and identifying effective treatments.* New York: Pergamon.

Kratochwill, T. R., & Morris R. J. (1991). *The practice of child therapy* (2nd ed.). New York: Pergamon.

Leahey, T. H., (1980). *A history of psychology.* Englewood Cliffs, NJ: Prentice-Hall.

Lezak, M. D. (1983). *Neuropsychological assessment* (2nd ed.). New York: Oxford University Press.

Loevinger, J. (1987). *Paradigms of personality.* New York: W. H. Freeman.

Maher, C. A., & Zins, J. E. (1987). *Psychoeducational interventions in the schools: Methods and procedures for enhancing student competence.* New York: Pergamon.

Prout, H. T., & Brown, D. T. (1983). *Counseling and psychotherapy with children and adolescents: Theory and practice for school and clinic settings.* Tampa, FL: Mariner.

Sandoval, J. (Ed.). (1988). *Crisis counseling, intervention and prevention in the schools.* Hillsdale, NJ: Erlbaum.

Schaefer, C. E., & Millman, H. L. (1977). *Therapies for children.* San Francisco, CA: Jossey-Bass.

Wolfgang, C. H., & Glickman, C. D. (1986). *Solving discipline problems: Strategies for classroom teachers.* Boston: Allyn & Bacon.

Wolpe, J. (1990). *The practice of behavior therapy* (4th ed.). New York: Pergamon.

CHAPTER 2

The Case of Vince Chandler

Rik Carl D'Amato
University of Northern Colorado

Barbara A. Rothlisberg
Ball State University

PSYCHOLOGICAL EVALUATION

Name:	Vince Chandler
School:	Brookline Middle
Grade:	Seventh
Chronological Age:	13–9
Parents:	Mr. and Mrs. Todd Kirk (Chandler)

Referral Information

Vince was referred for evaluation by his parents and teachers after a progressive decline in school performance. During a series of parent-teacher conferences, Vince's parents expressed concern over his current report card, which showed Vince to be performing at a D or F level in the content areas of English, mathematics, science, and social studies. Associated with this drop in academic performance has been an increase in problem behavior. Vince has displayed a low frustration tolerance, excitability, and an inability to relate appropriately to adults and peers.

Evaluation Procedures

   Wechsler Intelligence Scale for Children–Revised (WISC–R)

   Halstead–Reitan Neuropsychological Battery (HRNB)

   Test of Nonverbal Intelligence (TONI)

   Woodcock–Johnson Psychoeducational Battery, Part Two: Tests of Achievement (WJTA)

Piers–Harris Children's Self-Concept Scale (Piers–Harris)

Vineland Adaptive Behavior Scales (Vineland)

Thematic Apperception Test (TAT)

Behavior Evaluation Scale (BES)

Bender Visual–Motor Gestalt Test (Bender)

Peabody Picture Vocabulary Test–Revised (PPVT–R)

Revised Children's Manifest Anxiety Scale (RCMAS)

Sentence Completion Test

Three Wishes Interview

Interviews with Parents, Teachers, and Vince

Medical History

Mrs. Kirk reported no difficulties during pregnancy and could recall no perinatal complications. Vince was full term. Vince's mother stated that he enjoyed normal health and development until he was 16 months of age. At that point he developed severe ear infections. The high fever associated with these infections caused three instances of febrile convulsions. At 19 months, it became necessary to place Vince on phenobarbital to prevent future convulsions.

Mrs. Kirk reported that, as a result of the ear infections, Vince developed hearing problems and subsequent articulation difficulties that slowed language development. Between the ages of 3 and 4, the difficulties appeared to diminish with cessation of infections. Medication was discontinued and Vince has since had two reoccurrences of infection, one at age 7 and one at age 9. Residual hearing loss is not perceived as a problem.

Vince was placed on Ritalin by his pediatrician when he was 8 years of age after Mrs. Kirk and Vince's teachers complained of his high activity level. At that time, Vince was described as excitable and unable to inhibit his behavior when frustrated. For instance, he would rip his clothes, throw things, or kick and hit objects. He remained on this medication for three years, but it was discontinued because he experienced difficulty sleeping and had bad dreams. Mrs. Kirk reported that she had used the antihistamine diphenhydramine to help calm Vince when he was between the ages of 10 and 11. This antihistamine was never used more than once a day, or administered more than a few times a week. When Vince began maturing the medication was discontinued. His activity level is now reported to be within normal limits.

The school nurse completed vision screening with results within the average range. The speech teacher/audiologist completed hearing screening with results also falling within the average range. Dr. Husman, the family physician, completed a physical examination and reported unremarkable results for a maturing male.

Family/Social Interactions

Current Status.   Vince lives with his mother and stepfather. His parents were divorced some five years ago. Since that time, Vince's interactions with his father have decreased from several times per year to a brief summer visit and intermittent phone conversations. Mr. Chandler relocated to another state about 18 months ago. A telephone conversation with Mr. Chandler regarding Vince's academic and behavioral difficulties established that Mr. Chandler is interested in his son. However, Mr. Chandler reported that he will soon be remarrying and will be unable to provide additional support for Vince. Vince's mother remarried two years ago. Mr. Kirk, Vince's stepfather, stated that he and Vince "get along" but that Vince increasingly questions his authority in setting behavioral guidelines. Vince will argue with his stepfather and will dare him to do things. For example, Vince will say, *"That's not fair. You can't make me do that! I don't see why I should listen to you."* Mr. Kirk said that the confrontations make him so angry that he typically withdraws until he calms down. This pattern of behavior has occurred regularly. Mrs. Kirk agreed with her husband's statements and added that she felt somewhat "powerless" in controlling Vince's actions, especially since he has begun to mature. His parents have tried to discipline Vince using the withdrawal of reinforcers (e.g., loss of television privileges, grounding), but they report limited success. Vince continually challenges the rules and comments about the unfairness of the restrictions or contends that he does not mind the punishment. Vince's attitude is of concern to Mrs. Kirk since Vince does not appear to see his parents' viewpoint regarding his behavior. Mrs. Kirk did report, however, that Vince gets along "exceptionally well" with his 9-year-old stepsister, Beatrice, for whom he often baby-sits. During these times, Vince was described as well behaved and a real gentleman.

Family History.   During Vince's preschool years, the Chandler family lived in a rural setting. Mrs. Kirk reported that Vince had limited access to age mates at this time but, when social gatherings occurred, Vince appeared to interact in an appropriate manner once he became used to the visitors. Mrs. Kirk had remained at home during Vince's early childhood. Mr. Chandler had been employed as a personnel manager for a small manufacturing company.

Mrs. Kirk expressed some guilt as to the degree of isolation Vince experienced during these early years. She reported that the family did not engage in a lot of social activities and that Mr. Chandler devoted a great deal of his time to his career. Consequently, it did not seem that Vince got to spend much time with his father. When conflicts between his job and family events occurred, Mr. Chandler typically chose to fulfill his job requirements. Mr. Chandler was said to express regret over his absences and promised to attend or participate in the next event, but promises were seldom kept. Eventually, Mrs. Kirk did not plan on her ex-husband's participation in anything. For example, she reported that she attended all Vince's school functions alone.

Mrs. Kirk felt that she may have overcompensated for Vince's "absent" father (her phrase). While Vince got along well with his Dad when they were together, the chances for them to spend time talking or playing were few. To counteract this, Mrs. Kirk said she used to stress the importance of her ex-husband's contribution to the family and downplay his absences from family outings. For instance, she tried to see that Vince had the toys he wanted and reinforced her ex-husband's role in providing the support for them. She said she tried to build up Mr. Chandler as having a very important job and as being someone on whom many people were depending. Mrs. Kirk also admitted that she was not as strict as she should have been with Vince. When Vince would throw a tantrum,

Mrs. Kirk said she tried to ignore the behavior or punish Vince for it, but often would end up comforting him instead. Given Vince's early articulation problems and lack of companionship, Mrs. Kirk believed that his outbursts were just evidence of his frustration either at being alone or at being unable to communicate his wants effectively. Seldom did Vince's mother seek his father's intervention. Mr. Chandler was said to believe in spanking or "switching" as the most effective means of behavioral control.

When Vince was about 5 years of age, Mr. Chandler received a promotion and the family moved with him to a nearby city. At this time, Mrs. Kirk returned to work as a secretary. Mrs. Kirk reported that Vince seemed to adjust fairly well, although there was a brief period when enuresis was a problem. She suggested that Vince's sudden change in residence was the contributing factor since he was restricted to the home and the company of a neighborhood baby-sitter. Before he had been able to spend more time out-of-doors. Mrs. Olson, the sitter, took care of Vince the year before he attended school and subsequently continued to provide after-school care.

When asked about the events leading up to the Chandlers' divorce and their effect on Vince, Mrs. Kirk stated that the family's *breakup* was more a gradual thing than the consequence of a single event. She reported that Mr. Chandler simply spent more and more time away from the rest of the family as his position changed in his company. Mrs. Kirk stated that the separation and divorce were amicable. She said that she had tried to communicate to Vince that both his parents still cared about him; she did not think that Vince was traumatized by the situation. In fact, Mrs. Kirk characterized the period between her divorce and remarriage as a relatively quiet one. Vince had some school difficulties (e.g., acting out, difficulty following rules) but his home life seemed calm. Mrs. Kirk said that she and Vince had depended on one another and so clashes of will were few.

When Mrs. Kirk remarried, Vince was 11 years old. Mrs. Kirk stated that Vince seemed ambivalent about having a stepfather but enjoyed playing *big brother* to his stepsister, Beatrice. His stepfather, Mr. Kirk, owns a small store in the community and participates in local activities. Mrs. Kirk reported that her husband has not had much time to devote to Vince but is concerned about Vince's latest school problems.

Social History.   Vince's history of friendships appeared unremarkable. Although a hesitant child during preschool and early elementary years, Vince was reported as having at least several friends during his elementary school years. Mrs. Kirk did not characterize Vince as an overly popular child but as "normal." She recalled that boys used to come to the house and that Vince participated in neighborhood activities, often excelling in sports. Mrs. Kirk reported that Vince did appear to become less outgoing after his parents' divorce and more negative when his mother dated and remarried.

Vince's Perspective.   Vince was asked about his views concerning his friends and the members of his family. Currently, Vince perceives himself as socially competent and reported that he has a group of "*guys he hangs out with.*" They play basketball, attend school activities, and generally spend time together. Vince has begun to become interested in girls, concomitantly with some girls' becoming interested in him. He stated that there are several girls who have called him or have hung around when he and his friends are playing ball. Vince appeared to be rather proud of the fact that he is being pursued in this fashion. He stated that now he has to consider his *"reputation"* more than in the past since he has been getting special attention from *"chicks."* In fact, he expressed some frustration that he had to be evaluated, because *"the guys ask me what I did and joke that I'm going to have to go to the dummy class."* Vince explained that he has *"had to set them straight on how I'm doing. They won't be talking about the dummy class anymore."*

Vince reported that he has always had friends and considers a friend someone you could do things with and someone whom you could count on. He dismissed the idea that he did not get along well with peers or adults. *"I'm basically real easygoing. I get mad at people sometimes but I don't know why they can't take a joke. I don't hold a grudge. If I don't like something I let people know. I've never really hit anyone or given them trouble. It's all exaggerated."*

Even though Mr. Chandler was characterized by Mrs. Kirk as being uninvolved with Vince, he reported looking up to his father and wanting to make him proud. Vince cannot understand why his Dad has disengaged as much as he has. Vince remembered his father as working hard for the family so that the family could live well. Vince said that after his father had *"made it"* he expected that things could have changed and *"everything could've worked out."* Vince seemed to place blame on his stepfather for interfering with Mr. Chandler's visits and plans. *"My Dad is a great guy with an important job. It's just that he's so busy that he hasn't been able to see me lately. If my stepdad would let her, my Mom would let me visit Dad more often. He used to invite me all the time; it's just that he got tired of asking. I see him one weekend a month and more during vacation time."* Vince seemed to think highly of his mother. *"Mom has been there for me. She's worked really hard. We used to help each other a lot, but I guess things change. I won't always be around and she needed him* (referring to his stepdad). *She is pretty easy on me too. If I want anything, I know she'll be easier to convince than my stepdad or real Dad."*

Vince mentioned that one of his favorite people is his stepsister, Beatrice. *"She's a neat little kid; the best part of my Mom remarrying."* Vince said that Bea depends on him and always does what he asks. *"Sometimes she can get in the way when I want to do something with my friends, but I know she's on my side when there is trouble, so I don't mind her much. She stands by me and I'll protect her."* He claimed that he did not mind having to look after Bea when his parents were out; however, some of his friends did not seem to think that baby-sitting was a normal thing to do. Consequently, Vince tended to keep his family relationships separate from his friendships. He reported that most of his friends had not met his parents.

Vince appeared ambivalent about his stepfather. *"He's O.K. when he's not telling me what to do. I got along before he came on the scene and I could do it again. As long as he stays off my back about things* (like school) *we'll get along. He's not my Dad and he isn't around much so he's not a big deal. He is for Mom, not for me."*

Educational History

Vince attended a private, parochial school from kindergarten through fourth grade. Mrs. Kirk stated that his progress seemed to be acceptable, except for minor social disturbances. It was reported that Vince was sensitive about his articulation difficulties; therefore, he resisted communicating with children and adults he did not know. He seemed especially sensitive about class recitations and would typically act out when he was asked to respond before the entire class. Vince's parents believed that the school's procedure of continuing to require this speaking was a good one; Vince seemed to adjust to the requirements by second grade. Speech and language services were not available to Vince.

Interviews with Vince's early elementary teachers showed Vince to be remembered as an active boy who worked hard but who had difficulty controlling frustration when tasks became difficult. They recalled that Vince was an average pupil who seemed to respond well to social reinforcement. Vince's early report cards suggest adequate performance in the basic skill areas, although reading and spelling grades were lower than math and science. Recitation or memory work was least satisfactory. Vince was characterized as having low tolerance for any activity that presented problems for him. He would comment that the activity was not important and that he did not need to do it if he did not want to do it. Vince also would divert attention by acting out in class (e.g., teasing classmates, throwing paper, talking out of turn). Vince's acting out appeared to increase as he moved through the various grade levels.

Mrs. Kirk explained that at the end of fourth grade, Vince was asked to leave the school because his *"reactions to and defiance of the rules could no longer be tolerated."* Specific reasons for expulsion were listed as inappropriate classroom behavior, not following rules and directions, not completing homework, gum chewing, and student harassment. The parents stated that they had been surprised by this action and would give no further background to the incident.

Vince was asked about his early school years and what precipitated his move to public school. He stated that his teachers in first and second grade were "O.K." and that they seemed to do a good job. Vince recalled that memory work had been his least favorite thing but that his first- and second-grade teachers would sometimes allow him to say his passages to them without having to stand in front of the entire class. Vince was less positive about his third-grade teacher and seemed to openly dislike his fourth-grade teacher, Mr. Millberger. Vince stated that Mr. Millberger used to spank students who did not finish their work or would belittle them in front of the class. Vince remembered that on one occasion he had to stand in front of the entire class for over an hour because he had not completed a reading assignment. He could remember Mr. Millberger telling him that he was lazy and stupid for not doing his work well. Further discussions with Vince suggested that the core reason for the school's request for him to leave involved an incident when he was "caught" masturbating in the boy's bathroom. In relaying this information, Vince seemed to be embarrassed about the whole situation and claimed that he had never done anything like that since. He seemed to think the school had *"stupid rules and stupid teachers and I didn't like it anyway."*

Vince attended Jefferson School in fifth grade. Mrs. Kirk said that Vince seemed to adjust to the new environment fairly well. Vince's teacher, Mr. Angelo seemed to have a more relaxed attitude toward discipline but still appeared interested in student progress. Vince seemed to do above average work and even became interested in school sports. Vince was on the basketball team and also tried out for track. When Vince was asked about fifth grade, he remembered it as his best year. He said he had really liked the school and had fit in.

In sixth grade, Vince attended Brookline Middle School. Mrs. Kirk reported that this change seemed more difficult for Vince. In Brookline, Vince had different teachers for each of the academic subjects. He was also expected to take more responsibility for his work habits and be more self-directed. Vince appeared to be able to do well in sixth-grade mathematics, but had difficulty diagramming sentences and understanding grammatical relationships. He also experienced difficulty in writing activities. His sixth-grade teacher described Vince's writing as "egocentric"; Vince had difficulty writing for an audience and seemed to give limited information to explain himself to others. In addition to content, Vince's format left much to be desired; spelling and sentence structure were marginal.

Presently, Vince appears to be having difficulty in all subject areas except art and physical education. His schedule for the year includes American government, English composition/literature, mathematics, physical (earth) science, family living, art, and physical education. Vince's teachers have reported that he seems to lack writing skills, particularly in organizing his ideas. Lack of organization in planning his assignments and in his study skills also seems to be a problem. Vince typically does not hand in written work and does his reading only sporadically. When teachers question him on his lack of performance, he tends to become defensive and may argue. His teachers fear that his disrespectful behavior will spread to the rest of the class; Vince already is a member of a clique of students who do not seem interested in academic achievement.

School Observations

Before Vince was aware of the psychologist and the evaluation, he was observed in two of his classes: English composition and mathematics. Observations took place over the course of several days with two sessions occurring in each subject area. Informal as well as formal behavioral charting was undertaken in each case. Vince's behavior was compared to another student who was reported to be an "average" member of the class.

English Composition.   Vince has this class third hour (morning). He is seated in the third seat of the first row of students as one enters the room. As the teacher described the assignment for the day, a short essay about current events, Vince was observed to sit with his eyes downward, focused on the doodles he was making on his paper. His posture appeared to be relaxed as he slouched down in his chair with his elbows resting on his desk. The comparison student exhibited a more upright posture and appeared to have his attention on the teacher. Questions from the class as to what would be acceptable topics seemed to awaken Vince's interest—especially when one boy asked about sporting events. The male students then began to banter about their favorite teams and Vince participated by putting down another student's choice. The teacher took several moments to reestablish her control.

During nondirected seatwork time, Vince exhibited restless behavior. Initially, Vince seemed to work on the essay assignment. He sat up straighter in his chair and leaned over his notebook while writing. Writing movements persisted for two minutes, after which Vince threw down his pencil and closed his notebook. He then crossed his arms and leaned back in his seat. He looked around and began to speak to the boy across from him in the next row. They appeared to be sharing anecdotes and laughing. The teacher spoke to Vince three times about getting back to work. Vince responded that he was finished and did not feel like doing anything else. The comparison student worked for the full 10 minutes of nondirected time on his assignment.

During the second observational time in English, the teacher had asked students to read their essays to the class. Volunteers were requested. As the students read their essays, Vince was observed talking to other students in his immediate vicinity. The students seemed to be commenting on the oral work of their classmates and laughing about it. After asking for quiet, the teacher requested that Vince read his essay to the class. Vince responded that he couldn't as he had left his essay at home. The teacher responded by suggesting that Vince would be able to finish it after school that day. Vince sat back in his seat and stared at the teacher. Interestingly, Vince did not report for his after-school session, and his teacher did not follow up.

Mathematics.   Vince has this class fifth hour (afternoon). He is seated in the first row of seats almost directly in front of his teacher. Class began this day with a surprise computational quiz. Vince took the paper and seemed to concentrate on figuring out the answers. He sat hunched over his paper with one hand propping up his head. Vince was one of the last in the class to hand in his paper. He was heard to state to another student as he walked by that the quiz was *"no problem."* The lecture for the day involved word problems in which the students would have to structure a mathematical statement to discover an unknown. Vince appeared to be attentive to the examples as they were presented on the board. He asked one question about a particular equation but did not volunteer to do an example himself. About ten minutes of work time was given and Vince seemed to attend to the problems that were part of the assignment. There was no communication with other class members during this work period.

During the second observational session, the quizzes were returned to the students. Vince took a look at his and then crumpled up the paper. He mumbled to himself and appeared to angrily respond to a classmate who asked him about his performance. Vince spent the remainder of the class period leaning back in his seat with his arms crossed over his chest, staring straight ahead. He did not respond to teacher inquiries or instructions. His books and notes remained closed and on his desk. It was later learned that Vince had received a "C" on this quiz.

Lunch.   Vince was observed for a brief period of time during two school lunch breaks. After eating with a group of boys, he was observed leaving the cafeteria with the same group. On both days, the boys ate rapidly, left the building, and on their way out, stopped and engaged groups of girls in conversation. The boys then stood outside the school by one of the entrances and appeared to talk among themselves. Vince appears to be a popular member of this group.

Evaluation Observations

Vince is a well-built, maturing adolescent. His muscular appearance suggests that he is maturing early and that he is committed to physical fitness. Vince appeared to be at ease during the evaluation situation although he did not appear convinced that testing was necessary. Vince suggested that he was doing just fine and that he did not see the usefulness of his classes. Furthermore, he explained that since he figured he could get a job in his stepfather's business, academic achievement was not important. Vince communicated that he could *"do a good job in school if he wanted,"* but in his case, it was basically a waste of time. He would rather concentrate on peer group activities and sports. Although his grade point average currently precludes him from being on any of the junior varsity teams, Vince claimed this was not important. Again, he asserted that, if he wished to have better grades, he could achieve them.

Once the assessment started, Vince appeared to give his full attention to the tasks presented. Vince seemed to become increasingly anxious as the questions became more difficult. He made statements, such as, *"Who made up these questions? They're stupid!"* Vince displayed an impulsive approach to problem-solving situations. He would attack tasks as soon as they were presented but without apparent regard for strategy development. For instance, on a picture sequencing task, Vince quickly moved the pictures into an alternate pattern seemingly without attending to details in each of the pictures. Consequently, Vince appeared to work for a quicker solution rather than a correct one. If the question or task seemed too difficult for him, Vince gave up and did not persist with the problem.

Evaluation Results

***Wechsler Intelligence Scale for Children–Revised* (WISC-R).**   Vince was administered the WISC–R (Wechsler, 1974). This test is a nationally standardized measure of overall general ability. It is broken down into a number of subtests that relate to specific abilities. Scaled scores of 7 to 13 on these subtests define an average range.

Subtest	*Scaled Scores*	*Ranges*
Information	10	Average
Similarities	16	Very superior
Arithmetic	12	Average
Vocabulary	12	Average
Comprehension	15	Superior
Digit Span	14	Superior
Picture Completion	9	Average
Picture Arrangement	11	Average
Block Design	10	Average
Object Assembly	8	Average
Coding	9	Average
VIQ	118	High average
PIQ	96	Average
FSIQ	108	Average

***Woodcock–Johnson Tests of Achievement* (WJTA).**   The WJTA (Woodcock & Johnson, 1977) is a nationally standardized test of academic achievement. It includes subtests that measure decoding, work attack, and comprehension in reading; calculations and applications in mathematics; dictation and proofing skills in written language and content areas like science, social studies and the humanities in the knowledge area. Standard scores from 85–115 are considered to fall in the average range.

Reading	94
Mathematics	100
Written Language	80
Knowledge	87

Peabody Picture Vocabulary Test–Revised (**PPVT–R**).   The PPVT–R (Dunn & Dunn, 1981) was administered to evaluate Vince's language development and receptive vocabulary. The test does not require extensive verbal interactions and is often used as an estimate of language abilities because no reading or written language abilities are needed. Often the test is related to scholastic aptitude because word usage and language development are important predictors of school success.

On the Peabody, Vince achieved a standard score of 119. Average scores are usually seen as 85–115.

Test of Nonverbal Intelligence (**TONI**).   The TONI (Brown, Sherbenou, & Johnsen, 1982) is a language-free measure of cognitive abilities. This measure evaluates nonverbal problem solving. Items require subjects to solve problems by identifying relationships among abstract figures. Each item consists of a set of figures in which one or more of the figures is missing. The examinee completes the set by selecting the correct figure from either four or six response alternatives. Items cover the concept areas of simple matching, matching analogies, adding analogies, subtracting analogies, alternated analogies, progressive analogies, figure classification, understanding intersections, and object progressions. Vince obtained a TONI standard score of 99 which falls in the average range of functioning.

Bender Visual–Motor Gestalt Test (**Bender, 1946**).   The Bender addresses an examinee's skills in terms of visual–motor and personality development. It requires the examinee to copy nine geometric designs. The child's productions relate to visual perception, motor coordination, and visual–motor integration skills. The Bender can be scored both developmentally and emotionally. While Vince obtained no developmental errors, emotional indicators suggested poor planning abilities, explosiveness, anxiety, impulsiveness, and aggressiveness.

Sentence Completion Test.   Sentence completion tests (see Haak, 1990) can be used to collect information from the student concerning his or her view of various areas of functioning. Vince appeared to have a difficult time on this task. He seemed unable to formulate thoughts easily and put them on paper. If direct attention was not paid to keeping him on task, he tended to daydream and not complete the sentences. Vince's answers were difficult to read. Some samples of Vince's answers are reported below:

1. When I feel like mouthing off in class *I let it rip*.
2. If someone plays a practical joke on me *I get even*.

3. Girls often *enjoy looking at my body*.
4. My family *is not a real family*.
5. The best thing I like to do is *have a good time*.
6. School is *bad*.
7. Playing jokes on other people *is what I like to do*.
8. When people pressure me *it pisses me off*.
9. If I feel I am not good at something (left blank).
10. I wish I could be *Ozzy Osbourne*.

Additionally, Vince reported enjoyment with selected home activities and especially with spending time with his father. He indicated significant interests in many outdoor sports and girls. Vince indicated little enjoyment at school, except lifting weights and interacting during lunch. While relationships did not appear overly important to Vince in the past, currently, he seems pleased that a number of girls are interested in him.

Revised Children's Manifest Anxiety Scale (RCMAS). The RCMAS (Reynolds & Richmond, 1985) is a thirty-seven question test that asks students to report how they feel about questions that purport to measure total anxiety and three additional areas: Worry and Oversensitivity, Physiological Anxiety, and Concentration/Social Concerns.

Vince scored 14 in the Total Anxiety area, achieving a T-score of 58, which fell in the 40 to 60 average range. Average scores for the remaining scales range from 7 to 13, with a mean of 10. In the 11-item Worry and Oversensitivity area, Vince obtained a scaled score of 11, which falls in the average range. In the 10-item Physiological Anxiety area, Vince achieved a scaled score of 10. This score falls in the average range for students his age. Vince scored 6 in the Social Concerns/ Concentration area, receiving a standard score of 15. This high score suggests anxiety in this area. The Social Concerns/Concentration subscale scale covers seven questions that relate to the student's ability to remain attentive, be task oriented, and be somewhat socially accepted. The final scale is a lie scale that indicates if the student has been truthful when completing this test. Vince achieved a scaled score of 11, suggesting that he had been truthful when completing this test.

Piers–Harris Children's Self-Concept Scale. Vince completed the Piers–Harris (Piers, 1984), a self-report measure of self-concept ratings in the six areas of:

Behavior	Intellectual and School Status
Popularity	Physical Appearance and Attributes
Anxiety	Happiness and Satisfaction

Vince received a T-score of 50 with a corresponding percentile rank of 49. Average T-scores are usually seen as ranging from 40 to 60. These scores fell within the average range and suggested that Vince equals or exceeds 49 percent of his normative group in self-concept ratings. Of interest were Vince's percentile ranks indicating potential difficulties in the areas of Behavior and Intellectual and School Status which both fell at about the 7th percentile rank level. Vince's scores in the areas of Popularity, Anxiety, and Happiness and Satisfaction were all in the average range, with Physical Appearance and Attributes clearly a strength at the 84th percentile.

Thematic Apperception Test (**TAT**).   The TAT (Murray & Bellack, 1943) is an apperception test that requires the individual to make up a story about each of ten pictures. Vince completed the TAT, but was hesitant at the beginning of the series. Although most of his stories tended to be short, he appeared to enjoy the test as it progressed. Sample stories can be found below:

Card 4 (A man turning away from an embrace with a woman—with the woman clutching the shoulder of the man.)

"It's a man and he is with another woman. He is thinking of going with this woman and leaving his wife. She has been trying to seduce him. But he says no—this time. He goes home to his wife."

Card 13 (A young man with his head resting on his arm. Behind him is a woman lying in bed.)

"This guy had a night better than he ever believed he could have. Now it's morning. Time for work—and this guy is tired. But the night was worth it. He made it in life without his parents' help. Before this picture he got a good job. Then he married a beautiful girl. In the future they will be happy together—forever."

Card 14 (A man sitting on the ledge of a bright window in a darkened room.)

"This one is me watching chicks go by. When I see someone I want to be with, I'll jump down and go off with them to party. I'll probably have a good time."

Card 17 BM (A muscular man climbing a rope.)

"This old guy works out at the gym. You can see he is in good shape. He feels good because he is in good shape. People are amazed at this old guy's body. He will keep working out and live a long healthy life."

Card 20 (A man standing alone in the night on a dimly lit street.)

"It's a man going for a walk. He has come here often in the past. He is trying to decide if he should leave his wife. Tonight he made the decision—he will leave her. His family will be unhappy about the divorce. But they will be O.K."

Vince's stories offered realistic themes that were frequently related to material gain or sexual conquests. Many stories were typical of teenage boys. It seems that Vince places great importance on unambiguous male/female roles. In his stories, men most were seen as aggressive, strong, dominant, and protective of females. Women were seen as feminine, caring, staying home with children, partaking in domestic activities, and meeting the needs of men. In addition, most women were viewed as intelligent and highly competent.

Overall, families were portrayed as either fighting or living together harmoniously. Elements of discord were frequently related to divorce—and divorce was seen as the cause of great tension. Parents who stayed married were seen as content and fulfilled. Stories revealed no bizarre or unusual thoughts, desires, or feelings. Most stories centered on individuals who wanted to succeed, be popular, or please others. Environments were rational and offered clear consequences for the actions displayed in the stories.

Three Wishes Interview.   Vince seemed to consider the three wishes interview seriously. After much thought he put forth the following three wishes:

1. his father would remarry his mother
2. he would be out of school
3. he would win $1 million

Behavior Evaluation Scale (**BES**).   Four of Vince's teachers completed the BES (McCarney, Leigh, & Cornbleet, 1983), a 52-question inventory that assesses behavior in five major areas. Scores from 85 to 115 are considered to be average or normal. Scores less than 85 indicate that the student exhibits negative or inappropriate behaviors frequently enough to indicate concern. Scores awarded to Vince by his four teachers are displayed below and arranged according to subject area and subscale of the BES.

1. The inability to learn that cannot be explained by intellectual, sensory, or health factors.

English Composition (5)	75
Family Living (3)	65
Mathematics (7)	85
Physical Education (13)	115

2. An inability to build or maintain satisfactory interpersonal relationships with peers and teachers.

English Composition (7)	85
Family Living (4)	70
Mathematics (8)	90
Physical Education (11)	105

3. Inappropriate types of behavior or feelings under normal circumstances.

English Composition (9)	95
Family Living (7)	85
Mathematics (8)	90
Physical Education (10)	100

4. A general pervasive mood of unhappiness or depression.

English Composition (10)	100
Family Living (6)	80
Mathematics (9)	95
Physical Education (12)	110

5. A tendency to develop physical symptoms or fears associated with personal or school problems.

English Composition (9)	95
Family Living (8)	90
Mathematics (11)	105
Physical Education (15)	125

6. Overall behavior quotients.

English Composition (40)	86
Family Living (28)	69
Mathematics (43)	90
Physical Education (61)	115

Vineland Adaptive Behavior Scales. The Vineland (Sparrow, Balla, & Cicchetti, 1984) represents a comprehensive estimate of Vince's individual level of personal and social sufficiency. Information was collected from Vince's mother concerning his behavior using the Vineland. Average scores are seen as falling within the 85 to 115 range. Vince achieved the following scores in the following areas:

Areas	*Standard Scores*
Communication Domain	99
Receptive Subdomain	
Expressive Subdomain	
Written Subdomain	
Daily Living Skills Domain	107
Personal Subdomain	
Domestic Subdomain	
Community Subdomain	
Socialization Domain	98
Interpersonal Relationship Subdomain	
Play and Leisure Time Subdomain	
Coping Skills Subdomain	
Adaptive Behavior Composite	98

Halstead–Reitan Neuropsychological Battery **(HRNB).** Neuropsychological examinations include the collection of information from sensory, motor, cognitive and achievement areas, as well as data relating to emotional/control systems. The seven tests that compose the HRNB (Reitan, 1969) have been seen as measures of nonverbal abstract reasoning, tactual discrimination, spatial memory, verbal–auditory discrimination, nonverbal auditory discrimination, conceptual flexibility, academic achievement, and manual dexterity. Such data are usually considered in relationship to the overall integrity of the brain.

Measures	*Score*	*Ranges*
Category Test	55	Mild impairment
Seashore Rhythm	5	Adequate
Speech-Sounds Perception	8	Moderate impairment
TPT–Dominant	3.9	Mild impairment
TPT–Nondominant	1.8	Adequate
TPT–Both Hands	.9	Adequate
TPT–Location	6	Excellent
TPT–Memory	6	Excellent

Trail Making A	17	Adequate
Trail Making B	60	Moderate impairment
Aphasia Errors	9	Mild impairment
Tapping–Dominant	48	Adequate
Tapping–Nondominant	44	Adequate

TEST REFERENCES

Bender, L. (1946). *A Visual Motor Gestalt Test*. New York: American Orthopsychiatry Association.

Brown, L., Sherbenou, R. J., & Johnsen, S. K. (1982). *Test of Nonverbal Intelligence*. Austin, TX: Pro-Ed.

Dunn, L. M., & Dunn, L. M. (1981). *Peabody Picture Vocabulary Test—Revised*. Circle Pines, MN: American Guidance Service.

Haak, R. A. (1990). Using the sentence completion to assess emotional disturbance. In C. R. Reynolds & R. W. Kamphaus (Eds.), *Handbook of psychological and educational assessment of children: Personality, behavior, & context* (pp. 147–167). New York: Guilford.

McCarney, S. B., Leigh, J. E., & Cornbleet, J. A. (1983). *Behavior Evaluation Scale*. Austin, TX: Pro-Ed.

Murray, H. A., & Bellack, L. (1943). *Thematic Apperception Test*. Cambridge, MA: Harvard University Press.

Piers, E. V. (1984). *A manual for the Piers-Harris Children's Self-Concept Scale*. Nashville, TN: Counselor Recordings and Tests.

Reitan, R. M. (1969). *Manual for administration of neuropsychological test batteries for adults and children*. Indianapolis: Author.

Reynolds, C. R., & Richmond, B. O. (1985). *Revised Children's Manifest Anxiety Scale (RCMAS)*. Los Angeles: Western Psychological Services.

Sparrow, S. S., Balla, D. A., & Cicchetti, D. V. (1984). *Vineland Adaptive Behavior Scales*. Circle Pines, MN: American Guidance Service.

Wechsler, D. (1974). *The Wechsler Intelligence Scale for Children—Revised*. New York: Psychological Corporation.

Woodcock, R. W., & Johnson, M. B. (1977). *Woodcock-Johnson Psychoeducational Battery*. Hingham, MA: Teaching Resources Corporation.

CHAPTER **3**

A Behavioral Approach to Intervention

Richard J. Morris
and Yvonne P. Morris
University of Arizona

A behavioral approach is derived from theories of learning and conditioning and is based on the premise that procedures developed from these theories can be utilized to effect positive behavior change. The main assumptions underlying this approach are that behavior is learned, unless empirical data are presented to the contrary, and that behavioral or learning problems are caused by the environment. The emphasis of this approach is on identifying specific target behaviors in need of change, as well as the antecedent and consequent factors that contribute to behavior maintenance and change.

In order to understand the basis of our behavioral approach regarding the assessment and treatment recommendations involving this most interesting case, it is first necessary to present a brief overview of the historical roots, general assumptions, assessment considerations, and ethical practices associated with a behavioral approach.

HISTORICAL OVERVIEW AND GENERAL ASSUMPTIONS

Behavioral conceptualizations of the development, assessment and treatment of behavior disorders in children and adolescents have their roots in the learning theory positions of Pavlov (1927), Skinner (1938, 1953), Hull (1943), Mowrer (1939, 1960), and Bandura (1969, 1977a, 1977b; Bandura & Walters, 1963).

One of the first learning theory positions was that of Pavlov (1927, 1928), called classical conditioning. According to this view, certain physical stimuli in one's environment such as food, light, and noise, elicit specific reflex or unlearned responses—such as salivation in the case of food placed in a person's mouth, or an eyeblink in the case of a puff of air blown in one's eye. The stimulus part of this reflex pattern is called an unconditioned stimulus (UCS) whereas the response component of this reflex is called an unconditioned response (UCR). Pavlov further observed that at times a neutral stimulus that was paired in time with a particular UCS could produce a response like that of the UCR in a UCS–UCR reflex pattern, even though (1) the neutral stimulus was not a natural part of the particular UCS–UCR reflex pattern and (2) the UCS did not occur when the neutral stimulus was presented. The neutral stimulus in this case was called a conditioned stimulus (CS) because it was associated in time with the UCS, and the response that was similar to the UCR was called a conditioned response (CR) since the organism produced this response because of the previous pairing in time of the CS and UCS. This learning paradigm is diagrammed in Figure 3.1.

Thus, through this conditioning paradigm, an organism can be taught to produce a response (CR) to a stimulus (CS) that is not the original stimulus (UCS) but that automatically produces or elicits a similar response (UCR).

Perhaps the most famous study in behavior modification that demonstrated the application of classical conditioning to children was performed by Watson and Reyner (1920) with an eleven-month-old child called Little Albert. These investigators reported that through classical conditioning they could teach Little Albert to become afraid of a live white rat, and that this conditioned fear could be generalized to a fear of other animals and furry objects (e.g., a white rabbit, dog, and piece of cotton). Initially, it was reported that the rat (CS) did not elicit any fear or startle reaction (UCR) from the child, but after its presence was paired several times with a loud noise (UCS), it produced fear responses (CR) from Little Albert (Morris & Kratochwill, 1983).

Another learning theory position is Skinner's (1938, 1953) operant conditioning in which it is assumed that a major component of human learning involves the performance of responses that are controlled primarily by their consequences. Thus, a person's responses or behaviors are assumed to operate on his or her environment and therefore

Figure 3.1 Learning Paradigm

Note: CS = conditioned stimulus; CR = conditioned response; UCS = unconditioned stimulus; UCR = unconditioned response.

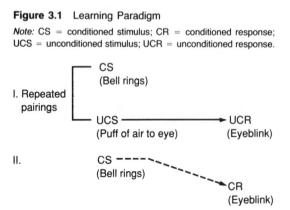

will produce certain consequences (Skinner, 1953). These consequences will then result in either an increase or decrease in the frequency of occurrence of the responses. Although Skinner (1938) acknowledged the existence of reflexes and classical conditioning, he maintained that most learning in organisms occurred through operant conditioning. This approach operates primarily on only those behaviors or activities that can be observed directly by the behavior modifier, and is oriented toward modifying the relationships that exist between particular observable behaviors and their consequences.

An extension of the operant conditioning position to applied settings has been called applied behavior analysis (Baer, Wolf, & Risley, 1968). In particular, this approach utilized operant procedures to modify behavior of social and personal importance. A great deal of literature has been published over the years on applied behavior analysis and the use of operant conditioning procedures with exceptional children (e.g., Graziano, 1975; Harris, 1976; Kazdin, 1980; Mash & Terdal, 1981; Matson & Mulick, 1983; Morris & Kratochwill, 1983; Ollendick & Cerny, 1981; Ross, 1980), and it is this approach that forms the basis for much of the present chapter.

A third theoretical position combines elements of both classical and operant conditioning, and is associated with Mowrer's (1939, 1960) two-factor learning or S–R mediational learning theory approach. This approach has many components in common with operant conditioning such as the contribution of reinforcement to conditioning and learning. The major difference between this position and operant conditioning is the emphasis on underlying drives such as anxiety that are presumed to motivate a person's observable behavior, and the view that behavior is both classically and operantly conditioned. For example, a child's avoidance of a feared stimulus, activity, or event is assumed to be motivated by anxiety which, in turn, was classically conditioned in the child through the pairing of a neutral CS and an aversive UCS (e.g., Morris & Kratochwill, 1983). Thus, the anxiety mediates the operant response of avoidance behavior.

Two popular behavior modification procedures have their roots in two-factor learning theory. The first method has to do with bladder control (enuresis) and bowel control (encopresis). In each case, we teach the child to associate a neutral stimulus (CS; toilet) with the unconditioned reflex pattern of defecation or urination—for example, pressure on the bladder (UCS) elicits urination (UCR). The child is then reinforced for his or her successes in eliminating in the toilet.

The second procedure derived from two-factor learning is called systematic desensitization (Wolpe, 1958; Wolpe & Lazarus, 1966). This procedure is used mainly to reduce the frequency and intensity of fear reactions in people by substituting an activity (in the actual or imagined presence of the feared stimulus) which is antagonistic to the fear response (Morris & Kratochwill, 1983).

The fourth theoretical position is the social learning theory approach of Bandura (e.g., Bandura, 1969, 1977b; Bandura & Walters, 1963). This view involves the development of behavior through vicarious learning. Here the person acquires a response by directly observing a model perform the behavior and acquiring a symbolic representation of the modeled event. As Bandura (1977b) states, "Social learning theory . . . assumes that modeling influences operate principally through their informative function, and that observers acquire mainly symbolic representations of modeled events rather than specific stimulus–response connections" (p. 16). Modeling, according to Bandura, is governed by four subprocesses: observer attentional processes, observer retention processes, observer motoric reproduction processes, and reinforcement and motivational processes to regulate the observer's performance of the modeled behavior. Bandura (1977a) has also emphasized the notion of "reciprocal determinism," in which a person's behavior involves a reciprocal interaction between his or her behavior, cognitive processes, and environmental influences. In addition, Bandura has noted that behavioral procedures may serve the function of creating and strengthening "personal efficacy." A distinction is made here between outcome expectations that relate to whether a behavior will result in a certain consequence and efficacy expectations that relate to one's personal conviction that he or she can perform a particular behavior.

These different theories of learning have been tested and refined in scientific laboratories over the past several decades. Three general assumptions that were repeatedly supported by this early research were that people and animals behave in predictable ways, there are principles that explain the manner in which people and animals learn to do things, and procedures based on various theories of learning can be developed to change the behavior of people and animals (Morris, 1985). Following this largely laboratory-based research, psychologists and other behaviorally oriented professionals began in the 1960s to apply the knowledge gained from this early literature to more practical research areas that focused on the development, assessment, and treatment of behavior and learning problems in children and adolescents (see, for example, Bandura, 1969; Bandura & Walters, 1963; Bijou & Baer, 1966; Eysenck, 1964; Franks, 1969; Gardner, 1971; Kanfer & Phillips, 1970; O'Leary & O'Leary, 1972; Ullmann & Krasner, 1965; Ulrich, Stachnik, & Mabry, 1966; Wolpe & Lazarus, 1963).

The findings from these more applied—although still highly controlled—laboratory studies continued to be encouraging and led investigators to expand their research to work with a variety of behavior and learning problems in various child populations (e.g., children having different mental, physical, and emotional handicapping conditions), in various settings (e.g., classroom, home, clinic, and residential treatment settings), and using different types of behavior change agents (e.g., parents, teachers, aides, peers, etc.) (see, for example, Kazdin, 1978, 1980; Mash & Terdal, 1981; Morris & Blatt, 1986; Morris & Kratochwill, 1983).

Behaviorally oriented assessment and intervention studies follow a set of general working assumptions regarding behavior and learning problems in children and adolescents. These general assumptions regarding the etiology, assessment, and treatment of behavior and learning problems in children and adolescents can be summarized in the following manner (adapted from Kazdin, 1980; Morris, 1976; Morris & Kratochwill, 1983; Rimm & Masters, 1979):

Behavior is learned. This assumption maintains that a child's particular behavior or learning problem has been learned, unless there is genetic or biological evidence to suggest the contrary.

Behavior problems are learned separately. This assumption maintains that each behavior or learning problem demonstrated by a child is learned separately from and independently of the other problem(s) that the child manifests, unless there is genetic or biological evidence or other objective data that show that these behaviors are interconnected and occur together.

The behavior or learning problems that a child shows in a particular situation indicate only how he or she typically behaves in that situation. This assumption maintains, unless there is contradictory evidence, that a child's particular behavior or learning problem is specific to the conditions under which it occurs and does not generalize to other situations. This is an important assumption because it forces the professional to look within the environmental setting where the behavior or learning problem occurs for possible reasons that a student, for example, talks out of turn in one classroom but does not show this behavior in another classroom setting.

Emphasis is placed on changing the child's behavior or learning problem in the here and now. This assumption focuses the intervention strategy on what is presently contributing to the child's behavior or learning problem, as well as what can presently be done within the particular environmental setting in which the problem occurs. The past history of the child is important only to (1) assist in determining which procedures have been effective/ineffective in changing the child's behavior in previous similar settings, (2) determine the chronicity of the problem and/or whether its frequency, duration, and intensity have gotten better or worse over time, and, (3) assess whether a pattern has developed over time of the type(s) of settings in which the problem occurs on a regular basis. Behaviorally oriented persons do not deny that historical events may have contributed to the child's present behavior or learning problems, but maintain that these events cannot presently be manipulated and, therefore, are of low importance to the treatment plan. Historical conditioning events are emphasized only if they are also presently contributing to the child's problem.

The goals of a behavioral intervention are specific. Because proponents of a behavioral approach assume that behavior and learning problems are situation specific, under the control of environmental factors, and learned independently of other problems, they view the goals of therapy as being very specific (e.g., the reduction of a particular behavior problem within a particular setting).

Behavior or learning problems are caused by the environment; unconscious or unobservable factors play no essential role. Given the previous assumptions that have been presented, it follows that from a behavioral perspective an "unconscious" or other not directly observable factor does not contribute to the development, assessment, maintenance, or treatment of children's learning and behavior problems. The emphasis of the behavioral approach is on those environmental circumstances that might contribute to an increase or decrease in the frequency of the problem.

Insight is not necessary for changing a child's learning or behavior problem. Since the proponents of a behavioral approach do not accept the belief that there are underlying unconscious factors responsible for a child's learning or behavior problems, it follows that they do not assume that insight is a necessary condition for effecting positive behavior change.

These assumptions represent a somewhat ideal position regarding a behavioral approach. In actual practice, however, not all proponents of a behavioral perspective agree with each of these assumptions. Their disagreements with particular assumptions, however, do not prevent practitioners from using the various behavioral assessment and behavior modification procedures.

OVERVIEW OF BEHAVIORAL ASSESSMENT

Major advances have occurred in the development of behavioral approaches to the assessment of children's and adolescents' behavior and learning problems (see, for example, Bellack & Hersen, 1988; Frame & Matson, 1987; Mash & Terdal, 1988; Ollendick & Hersen, 1984). Behavioral assessment has been used in four major areas: problem classification or selection, research, treatment program development, and monitoring of treatment outcome. It is the latter two areas that are of concern here.

Response Channels

Behavioral assessment of children's behavior and learning problems represents a diverse set of procedures and techniques. An increasingly popular conceptualization of the assessment of learning and behavior problems in children and adolescents has been variously labeled the "triple response mode" (e.g., Cone, 1979) or "multiple response components" (e.g., Nietzel & Bernstein, 1981). This refers to the view that a learning or behavior problem is a complex multichannel response pattern that includes motoric, cognitive and physiological components. These response patterns are not always highly correlated, but they are often related to some extent (see, for example, Barrios & O'Dell, 1989).

Motoric Channel.   This channel focuses on the overt behavior that the child or adolescent demonstrates. Measurement here involves the observation of the person and the recording of his or her behavior either at the time of the occurrence of the behavior or recorded in questionnaire format in which the observer reflects on a previous time(s) when the target behavior occurred.

Cognitive Channel.   This channel is regarded as a subjective system in that it depends upon the self-report of the person to validate its existence. The self-report data may come through direct statements made to the clinician or recorded at the moment the response occurs, or the data can be gathered through a questionnaire format in which the person reflects on a previous period of time when the response occurred. Behaviorally oriented professionals vary with respect to their emphasis of the use of this channel in their work (see the chapter by Hughes & Kemenoff for a more detailed description of the cognitive-behavioral approach).

Physiological Channel.   This channel focuses on measurement of the sympathetic portion of the autonomic nervous system (e.g., Nietzel & Bernstein, 1981). The target behavior or learning problem is therefore assessed by a variety of measures such as heart rate, blood pressure, and galvanic skin response. Although this channel has been used increasingly with children and adolescents who exhibit anxiety and fear as part of their behavior or learning problems, it has not been used a great deal with children and adolescents who manifest externalizing behavior problems (e.g., Kratochwill & Morris, 1991).

Changes in one response mode or channel may not always be reflected by or lead to changes in another mode. The implication of this, at least theoretically, is that the behavioral clinician needs to take measures of the child's or adolescent's target behavior across each of the three modes. Moreover, consistent with the assumption of the situational specificity of behavior, the clinician should take these multimodal measures across the various settings in which the target behavior occurs. Finally, the clinician should make sure that he or she is utilizing a behavior modification procedure that is directed toward the specific mode that the child or adolescent finds especially troublesome rather than only toward the mode that is of interest to the clinician. The reason for this is that we cannot, at least at this point, assume that a procedure that is used successfully, for example, in the motoric mode will transfer its effects to the cognitive or physiological modes associated with the target behavior (e.g., Morris & Kratochwill, 1983, 1991).

Assessment Methods

The assessment methods that are used within a behavioral assessment framework can be ordered according to the extent to which they measure a target behavior at the time and place of its occurrence (Cone, 1979). Within this framework, interviews, behavior checklists, behavior rating scales, and self-report questionnaires, are each considered as indirect measures because the behavior being recorded occurred at an earlier time and/or place. In addition, data derived from "traditional" norm-referenced psychological tests (e.g., WISC–R, Woodcock–Johnson Psychoeducational Battery, PPVT, etc.) also are seen as indirect measures since the computed scores are representations or summarizations of responses that occurred at an earlier time. On the other hand, self-monitoring observations, direct observations, and physiological measures are considered to be direct measures because the behavior is being recorded at the time when the behavior naturally occurs.

The assumption underlying the use of each of these methods is that they meet the psychometric properties of a "good" measure (see, for example, Anastasi, 1988; Cone, 1988), and provide the clinician with both reliable and valid scores.

ETHICAL PRACTICES

The focus of many discussions of the use of behaviorally oriented procedures to treat children's and adolescents' behavior and learning problems often centers on (1) the issue of controlling people and (2) the value or belief that the procedures are being used in the "best interests" of the person to help him or her progress socially, emotionally, academically, or developmentally (Morris, 1985; Morris & Brown, 1983). In addition, concerns have been raised regarding the possible misapplication and misuse of these procedures, the level of aversiveness/restrictiveness of the procedures being used, and whether there is an infringement on the rights of persons receiving these intervention procedures (e.g., Kazdin, 1980; Morris & McReynolds, in press). These issues revolve around the concept of *behavioral control*—that is, the manipulation of a person's behavior through the modification of the environment in order to achieve a particular goal.

Much has been written in recent years about ethical practices in the use of these procedures (see, for example, Bernstein, 1989; Braun, 1975; Griffith & Spreat, 1989; Kazdin, 1980, 1989; Morris, 1985; Roos, 1977; Spreat & Lanzi, 1989; Van Houten, Axelrod, Bailey, Favell, Foxx, Iwata, & Lovaas, 1988). It would be beyond the scope of this chapter to discuss these issues in detail. Suffice to say that writers in this area maintain that behavior modification procedures must follow sound ethical practices and, wherever and whenever possible, programming that utilizes reinforcement procedures and other positive practices should be first exhausted before any aversive programming is initiated.

By "ethical practices," we mean that the practitioner using behavior modification procedures agrees to follow a particular set of standards, policies, and/or guidelines established by particular professional groups, organizations, or societies of which he or she is a member (or with which he or she identifies) regarding how one should carry out behavior modification procedures. For example, the Association for Advancement of Behavior Therapy has published the following guidelines for the ethical use of behavior modification procedures with adults and children in a variety of settings. Professionals who are unfamiliar with these and other guidelines (e.g., Accreditation Council for Services for Mentally Retarded and Other Developmentally Disabled Persons, 1978), as well as other discussions on ethical and legal issues in the use of behavior modification procedures (e.g., Bernstein, 1989; Braun, 1975; Roos, 1977; Spreat & Lanzi, 1989), should take the time to carefully study this material and its implications for practice.

Association for Advancement of Behavior Therapy—Ethical Guidelines

A. Have the goals of treatment been adequately considered?
  1. To insure that the goals are explicit, are they written?
  2. Has the client's understanding of the goals been assured by having the client restate them orally or in writing?
  3. Have the therapist and client agreed on the goals of therapy?
  4. Will serving the client's interests be contrary to the interests of other persons?
  5. Will serving the client's immediate interests be contrary to the client's long-term interest?
B. Has the choice of treatment methods been adequately considered?
  1. Does the published literature show the procedure to be the best one available for that problem?
  2. If no literature exists regarding the treatment method, is the method consistent with generally accepted practice?
  3. Has the client been told of alternative procedures that might be preferred by the client on the basis of significant differences in discomfort, treatment time, cost, or degree of demonstrated effectiveness?
  4. If a treatment procedure is publicly, legally, or professionally controversial, has formal professional consultation been obtained, has the reaction of the affected segment of the public been adequately considered, and have the alternative treatment methods been more closely reexamined and reconsidered?
C. Is the client's participation voluntary?
  1. Have possible sources of coercion on the client's participation been considered?
  2. If treatment is legally mandated, has the available range of treatments and therapists been offered?

3. Can the client withdraw from treatment without a penalty or financial loss that exceeds actual clinical costs?

D. When another person or an agency is empowered to arrange for therapy, have the interests of the subordinated client been sufficiently considered?
  1. Has the subordinated client been informed of the treatment objectives and participated in the choice of treatment procedures?
  2. Where the subordinated client's competence to decide is limited, has the client as well as the guardian participated in the treatment discussions to the extent that the client's abilities permit?
  3. If the interests of the subordinated person and the superordinate persons or agency conflict, have attempts been made to reduce the conflict by dealing with both interests?

E. Has the adequacy of treatment been evaluated?
  1. Have quantitative measures of the problem and its progress been obtained?
  2. Have the measures of the problem and its progress been made available to the client during treatment?

F. Has the confidentiality of the treatment relationship been protected?
  1. Has the client been told who has access to the records?
  2. Are records available only to authorized persons?

G. Does the therapist refer the clients to other therapists when necessary?
  1. If treatment is unsuccessful, is the client referred to other therapists?
  2. Has the client been told that if dissatisfied with the treatment, referral will be made?

H. Is the therapist qualified to provide treatment?
  1. Has the therapist had training or experience in treating problems like the client's?
  2. If deficits exist in the therapist's qualifications, has the client been informed?
  3. If the therapist is not adequately qualified, is the client referred to other therapists, or has supervision by a qualified therapist been provided? Is the client informed of the supervisory relation?
  4. If the treatment is administered by mediators, have the mediators been adequately supervised by a qualified therapist?

SOURCE: Copyright 1977 by the Association for Advancement of Behavior Therapy. Ethical issues for human services. *Behavior Therapy*. 1977, p. v–vi. Reprinted with permission.

One issue in the ethical application of behavior modification treatment programs that has recently been addressed in the literature involves the notion of "acceptability of treatment" in the behavior modification treatment of a child or adolescent (e.g., Bernstein, 1989; Elliott, 1988; Kazdin, 1989). This issue is multifaceted and involves the level of acceptance (and, in turn, degree of willingness to participate in the implementation) of the behavior modification procedure(s) on the part of the parents, teachers, and others who are involved in the treatment program. Discussions regarding "acceptability" range from the rights of children and the level of aversiveness/restrictiveness of the procedure(s) being used to the "work effort" needed on the part of these persons to assist in the program's implementation. Our position is that no matter which behavior modification procedure is planned for a child or adolescent, data must be gathered from all of the participants—both before and during the use of the procedure—indicating their acceptance of the program plan and their willingness to participate and/or continue participating in its implementation.

CASE ANALYSIS[1]

Medical Information

One of the key assumptions of the behavioral approach is that a child's particular behavior or learning problem has been learned, unless there is genetic or biological evidence to suggest the contrary. As a consequence, one of the first steps in a behavior analysis is to determine whether there are any genetic or biological factors that have influenced or can influence learning. A careful review of Vince's case suggests that medically significant biological factors may have played a role in his early learning and behavior developmental history, but that these factors no longer appear to be contributing to his present learning and behavior problems. This conclusion is based on the history that is provided in the case report.

We were informed in Vince's case history of severe ear infections and hearing problems (beginning at about 16 months of age). It is possible that the articulation difficulties and slow language development noted at this point in his life were related to his hearing difficulties. In addition, it was noted that Vince had three febrile convulsions, and was subsequently placed on phenobarbital, an antiseizure medication. However, there are no data or other information provided that suggest that the seizures or phenobarbital affected Vince's behavior or learning in any way. In addition, no other seizures were noted, and phenobarbital was discontinued by the time Vince was 3 to 4 years of age. The frequency and severity of his ear infections had also decreased by this age—with his residual hearing loss being described as "minimal" and not identified as being a problem. His articulation difficulties were reported to have decreased, too.

Other than a brief period of enuresis at 5 years of age that abated without intervention—and for which no medical basis was reported in the material provided—no other medically significant features were noted in the case report until Vince was 7 to 8 years of age. At that time, Vince was noted to have had an ear infection, but school hearing and vision screening revealed that his hearing and vision were within the normal range. At 8 years of age Vince was placed on Ritalin following teacher reports of increased activity level. It was also noted that Vince was excitable and unable to inhibit his behaviors when frustrated (e.g., he ripped his clothes, threw things, and kicked or hit objects). Although these and related behaviors may be observed in children with Attention Deficit Hyperactivity Disorder (ADHD)—for which Ritalin is often prescribed—the age at onset of these behaviors in Vince is relatively late for an ADHD child, and Vince's history of social development and peer relationships is not typical of ADHD children (see, for example, Barkley, 1990; Dupaul, Guevremont, & Barkley, 1991). The case report also notes that Ritalin was discontinued when Vince was 11 years of age because he had sleeping difficulties and bad dreams. The report does not state, however, whether the treatment regimen of Ritalin had any other impact on Vince's social, emotional, or academic behavior. The report indicates that Vince's mother used the antihistamine diphenhydramine to help calm Vince when he was between the ages of 10 and 11, with this being discontinued when Vince began to mature. As was the case for Ritalin, we do not know whether this treatment regimen had any impact on Vince's social, emotional, or academic behavior. The case history states only that by 13 years of age Vince's activity level was in the normal range, and that no physical problems were present.

Our conclusion from this medical history is that there are no genetic or biological conditions that are contributing to Vince's current behavior and learning problems, and our assumption, therefore, is that such problems are learned.

Assessment Information

Assessment information that can be useful in a behaviorally based case analysis can be found in interview data, behavior checklists and rating scales, self-report data, self-monitoring data, direct observation information, and physiological measures (see, for example, Bellack & Hersen, 1988; Kratochwill, 1982; Morris & Kratochwill, 1983).

These materials provide a wealth of information that can be used to develop hypotheses regarding what is presently contributing to Vince's behavior and/or learning problems, as well as what can presently be done within the particular setting(s) in which the problem(s) occur. In addition, information on Vince's past history can help identify: (1) procedures that have been effective or ineffective in changing his behavior in previous or similar settings, (2) the chronicity of the problem and/or whether its frequency, duration and intensity have improved or gotten worse over time, and (3) whether a pattern has developed over time of the type(s) of settings in which the problem(s) occurs or does not occur on a regular basis (e.g., Morris, 1985). This information is critical for the development of a behaviorally based treatment plan.

Interview Data.   Interview data form the basis for much of what is presented in the Family and Social History section of the case history, with interviews with Mrs. Kirk, Vince's mother, Mr. Kirk, Vince's stepfather, Vince, and a telephone interview with Vince's biological father, Mr. Chandler, being cited. The interviews with Vince and Mrs. Kirk indicate that she has a close and supportive relationship with Vince, and that she has been inconsistent and ineffective in her efforts to discipline him (e.g., she stated that she feels "powerless" to control Vince). Her descriptions of Vince's relationship with his biological father reveal that Mr. Chandler has a history of putting career activities ahead of family activities. She stated that she accounted for Mr. Chandler's "absence" from the home and from family activities by emphasizing his importance to the family and to others who were depending on him. Although Mrs. Kirk described her divorce from Mr. Chandler as "amicable," she indicated that Vince became increasingly "negative" following the divorce, when he was 8 years of age, and during the time that his mother was dating and when she remarried.

It was mentioned that Mr. Chandler's contacts with Vince have grown more infrequent, especially since he moved to another state 18 months ago. Nevertheless, Vince perceives his relationship with his biological father as strong—looking up to his father and wanting to make his father proud of him. Vince also blamed his stepfather for his father's declining contact with him. Mr. Kirk stated that he and Vince get along, but that Vince questions his authority in setting behavioral guidelines. Vince was also described as feeling ambivalent about his stepfather. In response to Vince's oppositional behaviors, Mr. Kirk stated that he gets angry and withdraws. Mr. Kirk maintains that he is interested in Vince's school problems, but he does not have much time to devote to Vince. Attempts to discipline Vince by withdrawal of television watching or grounding have only met with limited success.

In terms of Vince's relationship with his sibling, Mrs. Kirk stated that Vince gets along "exceptionally well" with his nine-year-old stepsister. He was described as very courteous and responsible in his relationship with her. Vince described his stepsister as a "neat little kid," and indicated that he believes she depends on him and he feels protective of her.

In terms of peer relationships, interview data indicate that Vince has a long history of positive peer relationships. Although he was described as being less outgoing following his parent's divorce, his mother described his pattern of peer relationships as "normal." Currently, Vince is described as having a group of friends with whom he spends time and engages in sports. He is sought after by girls ("chicks") and he feels positive about his peer relationships. Thus, in contrast to these parent-child relationships, Vince's peer relationships are consistently described as being positive, as is his relationship with his stepsister.

In terms of Vince's behavior and academic achievement at school, interview data indicate that he attended a private, parochial school for grades kindergarten through fourth. His progress was described as "acceptable except for minor social disturbances." For example, Vince's mother reported that when he entered school he avoided communication with adults and peers whom he did not know. She felt that this was because of articulation difficulties. It was noted that he was uncomfortable with class recitation, and would "act out" when asked to respond in front of the class. His parents supported this public speaking requirement, and he "adjusted" to this by the second grade. Elementary school teachers were reported to have described Vince as someone who worked hard, was active, and who had difficulty controlling frustration when tasks became difficult. They described Vince as an "average pupil," and noted that he responded well to social reinforcement.

Case notes further state that his relationship with his third grade teacher was somewhat problematic. Vince stated that he did not like his fourth grade teacher, and described an episode in which he had humiliated Vince in front of other students. Vince was asked to leave the parochial school following fourth grade, but the reasons for this are unclear, with Vince, his mother, and case records presenting different reasons for this action. Academically, Vince was described as an average student who did better in math and science than in reading and spelling. Vince's own interview data concurred with this, stating that his areas of greatest difficulty in elementary school were recitation and memory work. He was described as becoming frustrated when tasks became difficult, and it was reported that at these times he would say that the work or activity was not important and that he didn't need to do it.

Vince attended a different school for fifth grade. His teacher was described as having a less strict approach to discipline, and Vince described fifth grade as "my best year." In the sixth grade he transferred to a middle school. Vince's mother described this transition as difficult for him, and noted that he did well in math but had difficulty in grammar, writing, and spelling. These were the same subjects that Vince perceived as difficult in the lower grades. In the absence of teacher interview data for fifth and sixth grades, it is not possible to determine why these areas were not problematic for Vince in the fifth grade.

In his current seventh grade, Vince's mother reports that he is having difficulty in all subject areas except art and physical education. Organization and planning of assignments, study skills, not handing in written work, and not reading regularly are mentioned as problem areas. He is also reported to have become defensive and argumentative when teachers ask about any decline in his school performance. Interview data with teachers concerning this or other behaviors were not available in the case report.

In summary, what emerges from this interview information is a contrast between Vince's strong relationship with his mother—supported historically by her physical presence and availability—and Vince's perceived strong relationship with his biological father—supported historically by his very limited and inconsistent physical presence and availability. This contrast may have led Vince to feel that his father was rejecting him (cognitive mode) as well as to the perceived loss (cognitive mode) of the secondary reinforcement value of being associated with his biological father. These feelings of rejection could, in turn, have negatively affected Vince's interactions with his stepfather, who also has limited time for Vince and who withdraws in the face of Vince's oppositional behavior (motoric mode).

An analysis of Vince's school activities reveals that from kindergarten to fourth grade Vince was in an academic setting that was becoming increasingly negative for him, with positive reinforcement being decreasingly available to him for his academic performance and school-based interactions with his teachers. Moreover, this was occurring at a time when his parents were divorcing and when the time that he was spending with his biological father was also decreasing. Moreover, what emerges from this interview information is a picture of intermittent difficulty in writing and spelling, as well as acting out behaviors and/or argumentativeness in response to pressures for performance.

On the basis of the interview, the following target behaviors need to be addressed: (1) decrease in Vince's oppositional behaviors (motoric mode) at home, (2) increase in the consistency with which his parents discipline Vince (motoric mode), (3) discuss Vince's feelings (cognitive mode) about his father and its impact on his behavior (motoric mode) in various settings, (4) increase his academic performance and skills (motoric mode) at school, and (5) decrease his argumentativeness (motoric mode) at school.

Checklists and Rating Scales.   Case files provide information on self-report checklists and rating scales that have been completed by Vince (*Revised Children's Manifest Anxiety Scale, Piers–Harris Children's Self-Concept Scale*). Four of Vince's teachers also filled out a behavior checklist on him (*Behavior Evaluation Scale*). Interpretation of the responses on these measures assumes that they are psychometrically sound, they are tied to behavioral referents, and Vince's demographic characteristics are representative of those found in the normative sample.

Vince's answers on the Revised Children's Manifest Anxiety Scale indicate that the overall number of ideas associated with anxiety endorsed by Vince is not significantly different from that of other students. He endorsed an average number of statements describing the physiological responses associated with the presence of anxiety as well as expressing worry and sensitivity. In contrast, he endorsed a higher percentage of items expressing social concerns and concentration issues.

Vince's answers on the Piers–Harris Children's Self-Concept Scale place his overall self-concept score in the average range. He endorsed more positive statements than average on the Physical Appearance and Attributes subscale suggesting that he views his physical appearance positively. On the Behavior and on the Intellectual and School Status subscales he endorsed fewer than average positive statements, suggesting that he does not see others as viewing his behavior positively and he does not see himself doing well academically.

Vince's answers on these checklists and rating scales suggest that while his overall view of himself is positive, there are specific areas of concern. In particular, Vince is concerned about his social position, and about his school academic performance. He views his physical appearance as a strength.

When the ratings of the four teachers are compared, Vince is seen the most positively by his physical education teacher, who does not identify any problem areas, and most negatively by the teacher in his family living class, who sees him as having problems in learning and also in interpersonal relationships, and who sees Vince as being depressed. No ratings are provided by Vince's other teachers. Thus, we do not know the extent to which similar behavior categories may be problematic for him in these other classroom environments.

In summary, on the basis of the self-report and teacher report data, we conclude that the following target behaviors need to be addressed: (1) Vince's feelings and views (cognitive mode) of his overall academic performance should be increased, and (2) his academic performance in his family living class, as well as in his other classes, needs to be increased.

Direct Observation Data.   The behavioral observations made of Vince during the psychological testing sessions are helpful in providing us with information regarding how Vince behaves when confronted with a structured situation in which challenging questions are asked that vary in their level of difficulty (e.g., WISC–R questions) and/or ambiguity (e.g., TAT instructions and cards). For example, we are told that he paid attention to the tasks that were presented to him, but that he became increasingly "anxious" as questions became more difficult, saying, "Who made up these questions? They're stupid!" The case report also indicates that Vince often worked for a quick solution rather than an accurate answer on the problem-solving tasks. Moreover, on difficult tasks, he evidently gave up and did not persist in solving the problem or question.

The information provided about his performance on the Sentence Completion test is also helpful as a direct observation measure. For example, we are told in the report that Vince had to be kept on task; otherwise he would daydream. In addition, the report states that his answers were difficult to read because of his poor handwriting.

Last, the responses that Vince gave on the Three Wishes test also provided direct observation data. Specifically, he said that he wished his father would remarry his mother, that he would be out of school, and that he would win a million dollars.

Vince was also observed twice in his English and math classes, and was compared to an "average" student in these classes. He was also observed at lunch. In his English class he was observed engaging in off-task behaviors, in contrast to the comparison student, who was attentive.

He was also restless during an unstructured writing activity, and did not complete that assignment. Teacher attempts to discipline him following disruptive behavior were ignored by Vince, and the teacher did not follow up with any disciplinary action. In the math class Vince was on task and attentive during lecture and quiz periods. He responded to a "C" grade on the quiz by "crumpling" his paper and not responding to teacher inquiries, suggesting that he looks for positive feedback and dislikes negative feedback in those academic areas in which he feels competent.

During lunch Vince appeared to be a "popular" member of a peer group that ate and socialized together during "free time."

In summary, on the basis of the direct observation data that were available, we conclude that the following target behaviors need to be addressed: (1) improve his handwriting skill (motoric mode) to a level that is consistent with those of same age and same sex peers, (2) discuss with a therapist his feelings (cognitive mode) about his biological father and mother remarrying (and, originally obtaining a divorce), (3) discuss with a therapist his feelings (cognitive mode) concerning what about the school environment contributes to his statement that he wants to be out of school, (4) increase his completion of in-class assignments (motoric mode), (5) increase his time on task (motoric mode) during structured task assignments, and (6) decrease his talking and disruptive behavior (motoric mode) in class.

Self-monitoring Data. No self-monitoring data were available in this case report; therefore, no target behaviors can be identified.

Physiological Data. No physiological data were available in this case report; therefore, no target behaviors can be identified.

Indirect Measures. Vince's WISC–R IQ scores, as well as his PPVT–R score, Woodcock–Johnson Tests of Achievement Cluster scores, and scores on neuropsychological tests (such as those included in the Halstead–Reitan Neuropsychological Battery) are indirect measures that can provide information helpful in designing a behavioral program for Vince—assuming that these measures are psychometrically sound, the scores are tied to behavioral referents, and Vince's demographic characteristics are representative of those of the normative samples associated with these tests. His scores on these tests allow us to compare his performance on a variety of measures with the performance of his peers, as well as to identify his individual cognitive and academic achievement strengths and weaknesses.

Following the assumption that the scores on these tests are tied directly to behavioral referents, we can conclude that Vince is generally able to perform academically and cognitively at an "acceptable" level relative to his peers. His performance on some of the neuropsychological tests (e.g., Category Test, Trails B, Aphasia Screening Test), and on the Written Language component of the Woodcock–Johnson Psychoeducational Battery Tests of Achievement, however, suggests that a modification of Vince's "traditional" curriculum may help him to experience greater success in organizing his approach to academic materials and in working with such materials—especially those dealing directly with written language. Given these curriculum issues, we would request a consultation with those school officials who are knowledgeable in the areas of cognitive retraining, as well as in developing a special education curriculum for Vince in spelling and written language so that we can help remediate these "deficit" areas (see, for example, Deutsch Smith & Robinson, 1986; Hynd & Obrzut, 1981).

Assessment Information Not Used
in the Present Case Analysis

Consistent with the overview of behavioral assessment presented earlier, some of the assessment information provided in the case report is not of a great deal of use in behaviorally oriented approaches. In particular, the information provided by the Bender Visual-Motor Gestalt Test regarding his low planning ability, explosiveness, anxiety, impulsiveness, and aggressiveness is stated in very general terms with none of the latter constructs tied to either specific situations (other than the copying of particular designs in response to a specific set of instructions) or behavioral referents. Similarly, the answers that he provided on the Sentence Completion test and Thematic Apperception Test are not useful since there are no data provided to suggest that the sentences or stories that he produced are tied to any observable behavioral referents.

Additional Assessment Information That Is Missing
and That Would Be Helpful in the Case Analysis

Biological father interview (motoric and cognitive channels) to determine his commitment to his relationship with Vince and willingness to participate in the therapy process (e.g., return to town on a regular basis for visits with Vince)

Teacher interview comments (motoric channel) from his fifth through seventh grade classes—teacher comments stopped at fourth grade

Classroom observations (motoric channel) in each of his present classes—not just English Composition and Math

Behavior checklists (motoric channel) filled out by each of his present teachers—not just four

Self-report behavior checklists (cognitive and motoric channels) regarding "depression" (e.g., *Reynolds Adolescent Depression Scale*)

Behavior checklists and rating scales (cognitive and motoric channels) completed by mother (e.g., *Personality Inventory for Children–Revised; Conners Parent Questionnaire*)

Physiological measures of his responsiveness in the classroom when he is not doing his work versus when he is doing his work, as well as when he is talking about his relationship with his stepfather and biological father, and interacting with his parents

Types of reinforcers, social (e.g., praise, smile, hug, etc.) and tangible (e.g., activities, events, etc.), that are attractive to him

TREATMENT PLAN AND RECOMMENDATIONS

On the assumption that the behavior and/or learning problems that a child shows in particular situations indicate how he or she typically behaves in that situation, we discuss the treatment recommendations.

Parent Counseling/Consultation

Initial Session. Vince's parents should receive regular, one-hour-per-week parent counseling/consultation sessions that emphasize child behavior management skills. These counseling sessions should first emphasize a review of the findings of Vince's psychological assessment and answer any questions that his parents might have regarding the assessment. The therapist should provide the parents with an overview of the target behaviors to be changed and the treatment recommendations and strategies. The parents should then be asked to make additions or deletions in the overall plan, followed by a request to sign "Release of Information" forms in order for the therapist to share information with (and receive information from) Vince's teachers.

The parents should also be informed about confidentiality between them and the therapist, as well as between Vince and the therapist (see, for example, DeKraai & Sales, 1991; Gustafson & McNamara, 1987). Before embarking on this discussion the therapist should review the laws of his or her state regarding legally protected privileged communication for adults and/or children in psychotherapy. In those instances where a therapist does not enjoy legally protected privileged communication with a child, he or she should ask the parents to grant "moral" (i.e., not legally binding) confidentiality between the therapist and the child, with the parents being requested to respect the therapist's moral confidentiality with their child and, therefore, not ask the therapist to reveal information about his or her sessions with Vince—unless Vince presents to the therapist issues of legal concern or matters pertaining to potentially dangerous activities.

Baseline Information. Following the initial session, and assuming that Vince's parents have agreed with the treatment plan, they should be asked to rate Vince on a number of variables, with these ratings taking place on a daily basis, until their next appointment. Vince and his teachers will be asked to make similar daily ratings on other variables. Physiological channel measures, however, will not be used in the treatment plan because of the difficulty associated with obtaining these measures (e.g., Morris & Kratochwill, 1983). Specifically, the following variables will be rated:[2]

1. Mother and stepfather will be asked to each independently rate Vince on a five-point rating scale ("Not at All," "Occasionally," "A Moderate Amount," "Often," "Very Often") on his Level of Compliance to parental requests.
2. Mother and stepfather will be asked to each independently rate Vince on the same five-point rating scale as above, except they will rate him on Level of Aggressiveness/Anger in the presence of that parent doing the rating.
3. Mother and stepfather will be asked to each independently rate Vince on a five-point rating scale ("Poor," "Not Very Good," "Good," "Very Good," "Excellent") on his relationship with his biological father.
4. Mother and stepfather will be asked to each independently rate Vince on a five-point rating scale ("Poor," "Not Very Good," "Good," "Very Good," "Excellent") on his overall academic performance in school.

Training in Child Behavior Management. Following the initial session, the counseling sessions should emphasize the teaching of basic behavior modification procedures and principles such as identification of target behavior(s), contingencies of reinforcement, shaping, prompting, extinction, differential reinforcement of other behavior (DRO), and token economy programs (see, for example, Kazdin, 1989; Morris, 1985). In addition, the parents should be given a parent guide to behavior management such as Becker (1971) and Patterson (1976), or selections from such parent training programs as those used by Barkley (1987a, 1987b).

In addition to learning behavior management procedures, these sessions would also be oriented toward teaching the parents to (1) recognize the "negative" comments and/or criticisms that they may make to Vince, as well as identify those circumstances and situations in which they are likely to make such comments, (2) rephrase their negative comments and/or criticisms towards Vince so that when such comments are made they are phrased in a "positive" manner, and (3) make sure that they "catch Vince being good" and reward him with social praise and/or a tangible reward. Homework assignments should also be given to the parents to facilitate practicing these skills and procedures in the home environment.

The parents should also be encouraged to keep a daily log (self-monitoring) of the behaviors and/or situations in which they are "not sure" or "do not know" what to say or how to act toward Vince. Similarly, comments should be written down concerning those situations in which they are especially proud and happy about the manner in which they handled themselves with Vince. The log should then be reviewed during the weekly session, and recommendations made accordingly.

It might also be helpful to the parent consultation process to ask the parents to place an audiotape recorder in an unobtrusive location during the family dinner hour each day as well as during other times when Vince is likely to be interacting with one or both parents. The resulting tape(s) should then be brought to the next parent counseling/training session so that the clinician can review the verbal interactions among various family members. The therapist should give the parents feedback regarding these latter interactions and role-play, where necessary, alternative verbal interactions between them and Vince (see, for example, Goldstein, Sprafkin, Gershaw & Klein, 1980). An alternative approach would involve having Vince and his parents come to the therapist's office where their interactions (while each is alone with Vince as well as when they both are together with him) would be videotaped unobtrusively (e.g., through a one-way glass or by remote control) in the play therapy room under both structured and unstructured play conditions. The therapist should then review the videotape with both Vince and his parents—seeing them either together or separately from Vince—and provide them with feedback regarding their various interactional patterns. Role playing should then follow, where it is appropriate, to teach alternative ways Vince and his parents can more positively interact with each other.

Another alternative could be to have both Vince and his parents make up a list of problematic interactions that they experience between themselves. They could then be asked to come to the office where the therapist would follow Goldstein's structured learning therapy approach (e.g., Goldstein, 1974; Goldstein et al., 1980) and rehearse various alternative interactional strategies and tactics in order to enhance the number of positive interactions between Vince and his parents.

Last, the therapist should work with the parents and school in establishing a home-based reinforcement program (see, for example, Kelley & Carper, 1988; Morris, 1985). The therapist should work out with the teachers the specifics as to which behaviors will be monitored, and he or she should work out with the parents and Vince the specifics regarding the kinds of rewards that would be offered to him as well as the number of points needed to earn each of the rewards.

School Consultation and Behavioral Programming

Baseline Information.   Before the initial meeting with Vince's teachers, they should be asked to rate Vince on a number of variables (many on a daily basis) for three to five consecutive days. Specifically, the following variables should be rated:[3]

  1. Present grade in each school subject area as determined by each teacher
  2. Daily monitoring sheets on each of the following variables for each "Subject/Class":
     a. Completion of in-class work
     b. Handing in of homework assignments
     c. Level of organization and planning of assignments today
     d. Level of study skills today
     e. Grade in school "Subject/Class" today
     f. Grade in classroom "Behavior Today" category

The behavioral clinician should have a meeting with each of Vince's teachers to: (1) learn about his strengths and needs in both the academic and behavior areas, (2) inform them of the results of the psychological assessment and answer any questions that they might have, (3) determine in which classes Vince is behaving—both academically and/or socially—in an "acceptable" versus "unacceptable" manner based on the norms that each teacher has established for his or her class, (4) encourage teachers in those classes where his social and/or academic behavior is acceptable to make sure that they are informing him about how well he is doing and to use social rewards on a regular basis to maintain his level of performance, (5) encourage teachers in those classes where his social and/or academic behavior is often at an unacceptable level to make sure that they are socially rewarding him whenever his social and/or academic behavior is at an acceptable level, and (6) set up a home-based reinforcement program for Vince in each of his classes for the first three weeks to determine specifically for the therapist, Vince, his parents and teachers those classes in which he is having behavior and/or academic difficulties on a regular basis.

A tentative "Daily Monitoring Sheet" is presented in Figure 3.2. The teachers should be asked to fill out the section for their particular class and then initial it. The sheets will be tallied each evening by Vince's parents and appropriate reinforcers delivered after dinner each Friday evening. The particular rewards and point schedule for each teacher rating will be worked out in the parent counseling sessions with the therapist, Vince, and his parents. After the three-week period is over, a reevaluation should be made of which classes should have the daily monitoring continued. Those classes that are continued on the home-based reinforcement program should have the daily monitoring continued until Vince achieves the three-week criterion of success outlined above. Once this is achieved, the monitoring should be reduced to two times per week (i.e., Wednes-

Figure 3.2 Sample Daily Monitoring Sheet

DAILY MONITORING SHEET

Student: Vince Chandler   Today's Date:_____

Subject: ENGLISH COMP	In-Class Work Comp'd Y N	Homework Handed in? Y N	Academic Grade: A B C D F	Org/Plan'g Level Today? A B C D F
Teacher Comments	Behavior Today? A B C D F	Level of Skill Today? Acc. Unacc.		Teacher Sig.

Subject: MATH	In-Class Work Comp'd Y N	Homework Handed in? Y N	Academic Grade: A B C D F	Org/Plan'g Level Today? A B C D F
Teacher Comments	Behavior Today? A B C D F	Level of Skill Today? Acc. Unacc.		Teacher Sig.

Subject: PHYSICAL ED.	In-Class Work Comp'd Y N	Homework Handed in? Y N	Academic Grade: A B C D F	Org/Plan'g Level Today? A B C D F
Teacher Comments	Behavior Today? A B C D F	Level of Skill Today? Acc. Unacc.		Teacher Sig.

Subject: ART	In-Class Work Comp'd Y N	Homework Handed in? Y N	Academic Grade: A B C D F	Org/Plan'g Level Today? A B C D F
Teacher Comments	Behavior Today? A B C D F	Level of Skill Today? Acc. Unacc.		Teacher Sig.

Subject: AM. GOVERNMENT	In-Class Work Comp'd Y N	Homework Handed in? Y N	Academic Grade: A B C D F	Org/Plan'g Level Today? A B C D F
Teacher Comments	Behavior Today? A B C D F	Level of Skill Today? Acc. Unacc.		Teacher Sig.

Subject: FAMILY LIVING	In-Class Work Comp'd Y N	Homework Handed in? Y N	Academic Grade: A B C D F	Org/Plan'g Level Today? A B C D F
Teacher Comments	Behavior Today? A B C D F	Level of Skill Today? Acc. Unacc.		Teacher Sig.

Subject: EARTH SCI.	In-Class Work Comp'd Y N	Homework Handed in? Y N	Academic Grade: A B C D F	Org/Plan'g Level Today? A B C D F
Teacher Comments	Behavior Today? A B C D F	Level of Skill Today? Acc. Unacc.		Teacher Sig.

days and Fridays) until the three-week criterion is again reached. Following this achievement the monitoring should be reduced to one time each week (i.e., Fridays) until the three-week criterion is met. When each criterion change occurs, the therapist should discuss with Vince and his parents an associated change in the points needed to receive the designated reinforcers in the home-based program.

In addition to the above focus, a behavioral school consultation approach (e.g., Bergan, 1977; Bergan & Kratochwill, 1990) should be established with those teachers who feel they need assistance in developing classroom behavior management programs to assist Vince in managing either his social behavior or specific academic content areas. The behavioral clinician should be available to the teachers on a regular basis to help him or her meet their goals and objectives regarding the management of Vince's academic and/ or social behavior.

Individual Therapy Sessions with Vince

Initial Session. Vince should receive regular, one-hour-per-week individual therapy sessions that emphasize relationship enhancement procedures and aggression/anger replacement approaches in both the home and school setting, as well as with his biological father. The first session, however, should emphasize a review of the findings of the psychological assessment and to answer any questions that Vince might have regarding the testing. Next, an overview of the target behaviors to be changed, treatment recommendations and strategies should be discussed, with input solicited from the child regarding additions or deletions that he would like to make in the overall plan. He should also be told that on occasion he will meet with his parents and the therapist to work out certain problems and issues that might arise.

Vince should also be informed about confidentiality between the therapist and client, and informed, where necessary, about what his parents agreed to in terms of "moral" confidentiality. He should also be told about the intended school visits and his permission should be obtained to allow the therapist to meet with his teachers.

Baseline Information. Following the initial therapy session, Vince should be asked to rate himself on a daily basis on a number of variables until he returns for the next therapy session. Specifically, the following variables should be rated:[4]

1. Vince will be asked to rate himself on a five-point rating scale ("Not at All," "Occasionally," "A Moderate Amount," "Often," "Very Often") on Level of Compliance to (a) requests by mother and (b) requests by stepfather.
2. Vince will be asked to rate himself on a five-point rating scale ("Not at All," "Occasionally," "A Moderate Amount," "Often," "Very Often") on Level of Anger in the presence of (a) mother and (b) stepfather.
3. Vince will be asked to rate himself on a five-point rating scale ("Poor," "Not Very Good," "Good," "Very Good," "Excellent") on his relationship with his (a) biological father and (b) stepfather.
4. Vince will be asked to rate himself on a five-point rating scale ("Poor," "Not Very Good," "Good," "Very Good," "Excellent") on his academic performance in school.

Subsequent Therapy Sessions.   The remaining therapy sessions should focus first on establishing a positive therapeutic relationship between Vince and the therapist (see, for example, Goldfried & Davison, 1975; Goldstein & Myers, 1986; Morris & Nicholson, in press). Following this, the therapist should examine with Vince the strengths and weaknesses of his relationship with his biological father, as well as what aspects of the relationship are a problem for him. Wherever possible, these latter problem areas should be role-played and solutions worked out in a cooperative manner between Vince and the clinician.

The therapist should also bring Vince into the play therapy room to interact with him in a variety of structured and unstructured games (e.g., checkers, computer games like "Space Invaders" or "Frog," darts, hide-and-seek, card tricks, gin rummy) and activities (e.g., basketball, boxing, "cops and robbers," drawing, etc.). In this way, the therapist can learn more about Vince's strategies when confronted with frustrating situations in the presence of an adult. In addition, these interactions between Vince and the therapist will set the occasion for the therapist to become a secondary reinforcing male model for Vince—someone whose meetings with Vince are predictable, stable, and consistent (i.e., regular weekly meetings with an adult who provides Vince with his undivided attention, in a room that is always available to Vince when he arrives for his appointment, with the repeated opportunity to engage in many interesting and attractive activities).

The information gained from these play activities and interactions with the therapist should be used to identify appropriate behaviors that Vince needs to learn as replacement behaviors for his current undesirable target behaviors and/or interactional patterns with his parents and teachers—with role playing and performance feedback established with Vince by the therapist in order for Vince to practice these new replacement behaviors (see, for example, Goldstein & Glick, 1987; Goldstein et al., 1980).

As the therapy sessions progress and the positive relationship between Vince and the therapist further develops, the therapist should model for Vince socially appropriate adult–child interactional patterns in order for Vince and the therapist to discuss the differences between these interactional patterns with those that Vince has experienced with his biological father, mother, stepfather, and teachers. Vince should then be encouraged to practice these positive interactional patterns with his stepfather, mother, teachers, and, if possible, his biological father. If the performance of such behaviors is not rewarding for Vince, this matter should be presented by Vince at the next therapy session and both he and the therapist should role-play alternative approaches (e.g., assertiveness training) to assist Vince in interacting with each parent (or other person) in a successful manner. Vince should then be encouraged to practice these new approaches at home and at school and report his successes and/or difficulties at the next session.

This "feedback to therapist; role play alternative approaches in play therapy; practice in the natural environment; feedback to therapist" loop should continue until Vince, his parents, and his relevant teachers rate him on the outcome measures as achieving at least 50% of the "criteria for success." At this time, Vince should be asked for his permission to allow his stepfather and mother and, where possible in separate sessions, selected teachers to sit in and observe the play therapy sessions. The purpose here is to gradually transfer the positive interactional behaviors that Vince has learned with the therapist to each of his parents and selected teachers (see, for example, Goldstein & Kanfer, 1979; Morris, 1985).

At this time, Vince should also be asked whether he would like to have his biological father visit with him and the therapist in order to resolve any behavior difficulties that Vince may have with his father. If Vince agrees, then a number of preliminary sessions should be held between Vince and the therapist in which the two: (1) identify the problem behavior(s) that Vince feels exist(s) in the relationship between him and his father, (2) brainstorm possible intervention strategies to change these problem behaviors, and (3) role-play the chosen intervention strategies in the play therapy room—with the therapist providing feedback to Vince regarding his performance. An intervention strategy should also be developed for the possibility—especially given the father's past performance—of the father declining to come or "finding an excuse" as to why he is not able to come after his initial agreement to come. The biological father should then be invited to travel to the city and meet with Vince and the therapist to discuss the targeted problem behaviors, and for Vince to begin to implement the intervention strategies in the office and during the time that the father remains in the city.

In summary, as therapy progresses toward reaching the "criteria for success," significant people in the child's various learning environments should be incorporated into the therapy sessions in order to maximize treatment effectiveness. These people should be increasingly encouraged to participate and interact with Vince, with the therapist first directing the sessions and then gradually decreasing his or her active involvement. It should be pointed out, however, that *generalization is not a required outcome of a successful behavior modification program* (Bijou & Baer, 1979), but rather is a preferred outcome. The reason for this relates to the assumptions of a behavioral approach that we presented earlier in this chapter. Thus, we should not expect generalization to just take place as a result of therapy being successful. Generalization needs to be programmed into the child's play therapy treatment plan in order to maximize the treatment effects.

During-Treatment Assessment

Once every four weeks throughout the therapy period, Vince, his parents, and teachers should be asked to fill out the "criteria for success" measures (except the "Daily Monitoring Sheet," which is on a different assessment schedule). Each rater should be asked to return the forms to the therapist for his or her review. After reviewing these forms, the therapist should discuss the findings with each of the therapy participants and suggestions elicited about whether any changes should be made in the treatment plan.

Posttreatment Assessment Phase

Following the completion of the generalization portion of the treatment plan, Vince, his parents, and his teachers should each be asked to fill out a final set of "criteria of success" rating forms. They should be asked to return them to the therapist who will review them and set up a final appointment for Vince and his parents. At this meeting the results will be reviewed and Vince and his parents will be asked to identify the various points that they learned in therapy as well as discuss what they are now doing differently from what they did before therapy began. The therapist should verbally reinforce these responses, where it is appropriate, and outline for them the "Follow-up Assessment Phase" of the treatment plan.

Follow-Up Assessment Phase

After the successful completion of this treatment program, a follow-up assessment/review schedule should be established with Vince and his parents and teachers. Specifically, three weeks following the termination of treatment, a phone call should be made to Vince's parents and to Vince to determine if any issues or problems have occurred since the last visit and to problem solve with them possible solutions. If the problems/issues are judged to be serious, then Vince and/or his parents should be asked to come back to the office for an appointment. Similarly, Vince's teachers should be contacted by telephone to determine if there are any problems or issues that need to be addressed and/or whether a school consultation is necessary.

Six weeks later Vince, his parents, and each of his teachers should be given the rating forms that were used to determine the "criteria for success" of treatment. They should be asked to fill them out and returned to the therapist for evaluation. Vince and his parents should be asked to return to the office following the therapist's review of the various forms. At this time, all of the information that has been gathered should be reviewed with Vince and his parents and any other issues or problems should be discussed. If the ratings have dropped below the success criteria, then "booster" sessions should be scheduled with Vince, his parents, and, if necessary, relevant teachers. At this time target behaviors should be identified and the framework of therapy described above should be initiated until the "criteria for success" are again achieved. If, on the other hand, the ratings have been maintained at their posttreatment levels, then an appointment should be scheduled three months later and then one year posttreatment to again review the rating forms that should be sent out to Vince, his parents, and, where appropriate, his teachers.

NOTES

1. The case analysis and subsequent treatment recommendations that are discussed in this chapter represent the behavioral approach followed by the authors. For a more complete discussion of the authors' approach, the reader is referred to Morris (1976, 1985), Morris and Kratochwill (1983), Morris and McReynolds (in press), and Morris and Morris (1989).
2. The variables that are listed in this section should be construed as tentative since some assessment information that is necessary for a final determination of the target behaviors is missing from the case report (see section on "Additional Assessment Information That Is Missing and That Would Be Helpful in the Case Analysis").
3. See note 2.
4. See note 2.

REFERENCES

Accreditation Council for Services for Mentally Retarded and Other Developmentally Disabled Persons (1978). *Standards for services for developmentally disabled individuals.* Chicago: Joint Commission on Accreditation of Hospitals.

Anastasi, A. (1988). *Psychological testing* (6th ed.). New York: Macmillan Publishing Co.

Baer, D. M., Wolf, M., & Risley, T. R. (1968). Some current dimensions of applied behavior analysis. *Journal of Applied Behavior Analysis, 1*, 91–97.

Bandura, A. (1969). *Principles of behavior modification*. New York: Holt, Rinehart & Winston.

Bandura, A. (1977a). Self-efficacy: Towards a unifying theory of behavior change. *Psychological Review, 84*, 191–215.

Bandura, A. (1977b). *Social learning theory*. Englewood Cliffs, NJ: Prentice Hall.

Bandura, A., & Walters, R. H. (1963). *Social learning and personality*. New York: Holt, Rinehart & Winston.

Barkley, R. A. (1987a) *Defiant children: A clinician's manual for parent training*. New York: Guilford.

Barkley, R. A. (1987b). *Defiant children: Parent-teacher assignments*. New York: Guilford.

Barkley R. A. (1990). *Attention deficit hyperactivity disorder: A handbook for diagnosis and treatment*. New York: Guilford.

Barrios, B. A., & O'Dell, S. L. (1989). Fears and anxieties. In E. J. Mash & R. A. Barkley (Eds.), *Treatment of childhood disorders* (pp. 167–221). New York: Guilford.

Becker, W. C. (1971). *Parents are teachers*. Champaign, IL: Research Press.

Bellack, A. S., & Hersen, M. (Eds.). (1988). *Behavioral assessment*. New York: Pergamon.

Bergan, J. R. (1977). *Behavioral consultation*. Columbus, OH: Merrill.

Bergan, J. R., & Kratochwill, T. R. (1990). *Behavioral school consultation*. New York: Plenum.

Bernstein, G. S. (1989). Social validity and the debate over use of aversive/ intrusive procedures. *The Behavior Therapist, 12*, 123–125.

Bijou, S. B., & Baer, D. M. (1966). Operant methods in child behavior and development. In W. K. Honig (Ed.), *Operant behavior* (pp. 718–189). New York: Appleton-Century-Crofts.

Bijou, S. B., & Baer, D. M. (1979). *Behavior analysis of child development*. Englewood Cliffs, NJ: Prentice Hall.

Braun, S. H. (1975). Ethical issues in behavior modification. *Behavior Therapy, 6*, 51–62.

Cone, J. D. (1979). Confounded comparisons in triple response mode assessment research. *Behavioral Assessment, 1*, 85–95.

Cone, J. D. (1988). Psychometric considerations and the multiple models of behavioral assessment. In A. S. Bellack & M. Hersen (Eds.), *Behavioral assessment* (pp. 42–66). New York: Pergamon.

DeKraai, M. B., & Sales, B. (1991). Legal issues in the conduct of child therapy. In T. R. Kratochwill & R. J. Morris (Eds.), *The practice of child therapy* (pp. 441–458). New York: Pergamon.

Deutsch Smith, D., & Robinson, S. (1986). Educating the learning disabled. In R. J. Morris & B. Blatt (Eds.), *Special education: Research and trends* (pp. 222–248). New York: Pergamon.

Dupaul, G. J., Guevremont, D. C., & Barkley, R. A. (1991). Hyperactivity. In T. R. Kratochwill & R. J. Morris (Eds.), *The practice of child therapy* (2nd ed.) (pp. 115–144). New York: Pergamon.

Elliott, S. N. (1988). Acceptability of behavioral treatments in educational settings. In J. C. Witt, S. N. Elliott, & F. M. Gresham (Eds.), *Handbook of behavior therapy in education* (pp. 121–150). New York: Plenum.

Eysenck, H. J. (Ed.). (1964). *Experiments in behaviour therapy*. Oxford: Pergamon.

Frame, C. L., & Matson, J. L. (Eds.). (1987). *Handbook of assessment in childhood psychopathology*. New York: Plenum.

Franks, C. M. (Ed.). (1969). *Behavior therapy: Appraisal and status*. New York: McGraw-Hill.

Gardner, W. I. (1971). *Behavior modification: Applications in mental retardation*. Chicago: Aldine.

Goldfried, M. R., & Davison, G. (1975). *Clinical behavior therapy*. New York: Holt, Rinehart & Winston.

Goldstein, A. P. (1974). *Structured learning therapy: Toward a psychotherapy for the poor*. New York: Academic.

Goldstein, A. P., & Glick, B. (1987). *Aggression replacement training: A comprehensive intervention for aggressive youth*. Champaign, IL: Research Press.

Goldstein, A. P., & Kanfer, F. H. (Eds.). (1979). *Maximizing treatment gains*. New York: Academic.

Goldstein, A. P., & Myers, C. R. (1986). Relationship-enhancement methods. In F. H. Kanfer & A. P. Goldstein (Eds.), *Helping people change* (3rd Ed.) (pp. 19–65). New York: Pergamon.

Goldstein, A. P., Sprafkin, R. P., Gershaw, N. J., & Klein, P. (1980). *Skillstreaming the adolescent*. Champaign, IL: Research Press.

Graziano, A. M. (Ed.). (1975). *Behavior therapy with children II*. Chicago: Aldine Publishing Co.

Griffith, R., & Spreat, S. (1989). Aversive behavior modification procedures and the use of professional judgement. *The Behavior Therapist, 12*, 143–146.

Gustafson, K. E., & McNamara, J. R. (1987). Confidentiality with minor clients: Issues and guidelines for therapists. *Professional Psychology; Research and Practice, 18*, 503–508.

Harris, S. B. (1976). *Teaching speech to the nonverbal child*. Lawrence, KS: H & H Enterprises.

Hull, C. (1943). *Principles of behavior*. New York: Appleton-Century.

Hynd, G. W., & Obrzut, J. E. (1981). *Neuropsychological assessment and the school-age child: Issues and procedures*. New York: Grune & Stratton.

Kanfer, F. H., & Phillips, J. S. (1970). *Learning foundations of behavior therapy*. New York: Wiley.

Kazdin, A. E. (1978). *History of behavior modification: Experimental foundations of contemporary research*. Baltimore: University Park Press.

Kazdin, A. E. (1980). *Behavior modification in applied settings* (Rev. ed.). Homewood, IL: Dorsey.

Kazdin, A. E. (1989). *Behavior modification in applied settings* (4th Ed.). Pacific Grove, CA: Brooks/Cole.

Kelley, M. L., & Carper, L. B. (1988). Home-based reinforcement procedures. In J. C. Witt, S. N. Elliott, & F. M. Gresham (Eds.), *Handbook of behavior therapy in education* (pp. 419–438). New York: Plenum.

Kratochwill, T. R. (1982). Advances in behavioral assessment. In C. R. Reynolds & T. B. Gutkin (Eds.), *Handbook of school psychology* (pp. 314–350). New York: Wiley.

Kratochwill, T. R., & Morris, R. J. (Eds.). (1991). *The practice of child therapy* (2nd ed.). New York: Pergamon.

Mash, E. J., & Terdal, L. G. (Eds.). (1981). *Behavior therapy assessment of childhood disorders*. New York: Guilford.

Mash, E. J., & Terdal, L. G. (Eds.). (1988). *Behavior therapy assessment of childhood disorders* (2nd ed.). New York: Guilford.

Matson, J. L., & Mulick, J. A. (Eds.). (1983). *Handbook of mental retardation*. New York: Pergamon.

Morris, R. J. (1976). *Behavior modification with children: A systematic guide*. Cambridge, MA: Winthrop Publishers.

Morris, R. J. (1985). *Behavior modification with exceptional children: Principles and practices*. Glenview, IL: Scott, Foresman.

Morris, R. J., & Blatt, B. (1986). *Special education: Research and trends*. New York: Pergamon.

Morris, R. J., & Brown, D. K. (1983). Legal and ethical issues in behavior modification with mentally retarded persons. In J. L. Matson & F. Andrasik (Eds.), *Treatment issues and innovations in mental retardation* (pp. 120–168). New York: Plenum.

Morris, R. J., & Kratochwill, T. R. (1983). *Treating fears and phobias in children: A behavioral perspective*. New York: Pergamon.

Morris, R. J., & Kratochwill, T. R. (1991). Fears and phobias. In T. R. Kratochwill & R. J. Morris, (Eds.), *The practice of child therapy* (2nd ed.) (pp. 76–114). New York: Pergamon.

Morris, R. J., & McReynolds, R. A. (in press). *Managing aggressive and disruptive behavior in children and adolescents.* Champaign, IL: Research Press.

Morris, R. J., & Morris, Y. P. (1989). School psychology in residential treatment facilities. In R. C. D'Amato & R. S. Dean (Eds.), *The school psychologist in nontraditional settings: Integrating clients, services, and settings* (pp. 159–184). Hillsdale, NJ: Erlbaum.

Morris, R. J., & Nicholson, J. (in press). The therapeutic relationship in child therapy. In T. R. Kratochwill & R. J. Morris (Eds.), *Handbook of child and adolescent psychotherapy.* New York: Pergamon.

Mowrer, O. H. (1939). A stimulus-response analysis of anxiety and its role as a reinforcing agent. *Psychological Review, 46,* 553–65.

Mowrer, O. H. (1960). *Learning theory and behavior.* New York: Wiley.

Nietzel, M. T., & Bernstein, D. A. (1981). Assessment of anxiety and fear. In M. Hersen & A. S. Bellack (Eds.), *Behavioral assessment: A practical handbook* (pp. 215–245). New York: Pergamon.

O'Leary, K. D., & O'Leary, S. G. (1972). *Classroom management.* New York: Pergamon.

Ollendick, T. H., & Cerny, J. A. (1981). *Clinical behavior therapy with children.* New York: Plenum.

Ollendick, T. H., & Hersen, M. (Eds.). (1984). *Child behavioral assessment; Principles and procedures.* New York: Pergamon.

Patterson, G. R. (1976). *Living with children.* (Rev.). Champaign, IL: Research Press.

Pavlov, I. P. (1927). *Conditioned reflexes.* Translated by G. V. Anrep. London, England: Oxford University Press.

Pavlov, I. P., (1928). *Lectures on conditioned reflexes.* Translated by W. H. Gantt. New York: International Publishers.

Rimm, D. C., & Masters, J. C. (1979). *Behavior therapy: Techniques and empirical findings* (2nd ed.). New York: Academic Press.

Roos, P. (1977). Issues and implications of establishing guidelines for the use of behavior modification. *Journal of Applied Behavior Analysis, 10,* 531–540.

Ross, A. O. (1980). *Psychological disorders of children: A behavioral approach to theory, research, and therapy* (2nd ed.). New York: McGraw-Hill.

Skinner, B. F. (1938). *Behavior of organisms.* New York: Appleton-Century-Crofts, Inc.

Skinner, B. F. (1953). *Science and human behavior.* New York: Macmillan.

Spreat, S., & Lanzi, F. (1989). Role of human rights committees in the review of restrictive/ aversive behavior modification procedures: A national survey. *Mental Retardation, 27,* 375–382.

Ullmann, L., & Krasner, L. (Eds.). (1965). *Case studies in behavior modification.* New York: Holt.

Ulrich, R., Stachnik, T., & Mabry, J. (Eds.). (1966). *Control of human behavior.* Glenview, IL: Scott, Foresman.

Van Houten, R., Axelrod, S., Bailey, J. S., Favell, J. E., Foxx, R. M., Iwata, B. A., & Lovaas, O. I. (1988). The right to effective behavioral treatment. *Journal of Applied Behavior Analysis, 21,* 381–384.

Watson, J. B., & Reyner, R. (1920). Conditioned emotional reactions. *Journal of Experimental Psychology, 3,* 1–14.

Wolpe, J. (1958). *Reciprocal inhibition therapy.* Stanford, CA: Stanford University Press.

Wolpe, J., & Lazarus, A. (1966). *Behavior therapy techniques.* New York: Pergamon.

CHAPTER 4

A Psychoanalytic Approach to Intervention

Susan C. Warshaw
Yeshiva University

There are a variety of treatment approaches that consider themselves to be psychoanalytic. This chapter attempts to provide a framework for understanding the similarities and differences among some of the major schools of psychoanalytic thought. Utilizing a historical approach, the author develops some key psychoanalytic concepts and lays the groundwork for the case analysis and intervention plan from one psychoanalytic perspective which can be considered essentially ego psychological/relational. Emphasizing assessment and intervention specifically tailored to the needs of the young adolescent, the chapter describes the way a psychodynamic formation leads to interventions.

Psychoanalytic perspectives on development and approaches to interventions with troubled children have had a major impact on the child mental health movement in this country and abroad. Despite the historical importance of these contributions to the fields of psychotherapy and education, psychoanalytic concepts are insufficiently understood by many who are in a position to develop interventions for children and youth. Among the factors contributing to this situation are the complexity of the material to be mastered, the evolutionary nature of the field, and the multiplicity of treatment approaches which consider themselves to be psychoanalytic. In addition, while having its roots in adult psychoanalysis, the field of child and adolescent psychoanalysis has developed its own body of knowledge derived from studying youngsters and their families. Within the fields of adult and child treatment one is confronted with several evolving theories of personality and its development, as well as their corresponding evolving theories of treatment techniques.

In order to assist the reader in understanding the author's theoretical perspective and its position within the body of psychoanalytic thought, a brief overview of some aspects of the evolution of psychoanalytic theories will be provided, including a discussion of the major models of psychoanalytic thinking. Then a framework for thinking about the case of Vince will be presented before the case analysis and treatment recommendations are discussed.

How one understands psychoanalytic theory depends in part on where one reads theory in historical time. Pine (1985) describes the evolution of psychoanalytic theories as occurring in three great waves: the first being the period in which *Drive Theory* was developed and elaborated, the second the era in which much of the focus was on the understanding of the functions and development of the *Ego*, and the third, which is still continuing, the period of elaboration of theories of *Object Relations* and *Self*. Object relations theories, simply stated, are those theories that concern themselves with the development and function of internal images or mental representations (in the mind) of the self and the other (the object). Greenberg and Mitchell (1983) state, "The term thus designates theories, or aspects of theories, concerned with exploring the relationship between real external people and internal images and residues of relations with them" (p. 12). Implicit in object relations theories is the belief that one's mental representations or perceptions of the self, the other, and the self in interaction with the other, will have an impact on one's functioning.

OVERVIEW OF PSYCHOANALYTIC THEORY

The psychoanalytic concepts that were developed and/or given greater focus in each of the eras of theory development need to be discussed in greater detail in order to understand the evolution of psychoanalytic thought. It is important to note that the model of the mind, as well as the motivational concepts inherent in drive theory, have been among the most controversial aspects of classical Freudian theory. These controversies were the impetus for the development of alternative models of the mind that led to numerous schisms within the psychoanalytic world. In the United States, interpersonal psychoanalysts (followers of Sullivan) were among the early analysts who not only disavowed important aspects of drive theory, but overtly broke with the Freudians and established an entirely different school of psychoanalysis (Greenberg & Mitchell, 1983). Most contemporary psychoanalysts (including interpersonalists) utilize models of the mind that integrate insights about personality functioning derived from each of the three eras, but differ about which of these models to build upon, to discard, or to rework.

Early Psychoanalytic Thinking: Drive Theory

Sigmund Freud, the earliest psychoanalytic theorist, thought of the mind as an energy system. According to Arlow and Brenner (1979), "Freud conceived of the psychic apparatus as an agency for the regulation and discharge of mental energy; the source of that energy was identified as the instinctual drives" (S. Freud, 1905, p. 6). Thus Freudian theory began to be referred to as Drive, or Instinct, Theory.

Freud began to develop his ideas about personality organization as a result of his work with adult patients, many of whom exhibited bizarre physical symptoms that could not be traced to any known neurological cause (hysterics). It became apparent that many patients developed such symptoms as a result of feelings, ideas, and experiences that were outside their awareness or consciousness. These were observed to be sexual in nature, and accounted significantly for Freud's preoccupation with the vicissitudes of the sexual instinct in his early writings.

Freud's first model of the mind, referred to as the "topographical" model (Arlow & Brenner, 1979), was an attempt to integrate the observation of the phenomena of "unconscious" experience, and the sexual nature of those experiences, into a theory of mental functioning. Freud theorized that the mind was composed of three systems: the *conscious*, the *preconscious*, and the *unconscious*.

The contents of the system "unconscious" were believed to be sexual, or more specifically, the mental representations of the primitive sexual instincts of early childhood and their derivatives. Between the unconscious and the conscious was the system preconscious, with one of its functions to prevent the emergence into the conscious those aspects of the unconscious that might be considered immoral or socially unacceptable. This censorial function was called *repression*. Should the censor fail to repress the objectionable aspects of the unconscious, the person would become symptomatic (Arlow & Brenner, 1964/1979). The symptom, containing aspects of the primitive unconscious wish, would reach the conscious in a disguised or "compromise" form. Thus the goal of psychoanalytic treatment was to bring into the conscious those unacceptable aspects of the unconscious, because it was believed that when the unconscious became conscious, the reason for the symptom would dissipate and therefore the symptom would disappear.

Freud described the process by which the unconscious functioned and called it the primary process, because it comes first and earliest in development. When one reads descriptions of the primary process, one has a sense of what Freud must have conceived of as the functioning of the infant mind. Primary process thinking refers, among other things, to thinking that is concrete, and in which instinctual wishes press for immediate gratification. In addition, primary process thinking has qualities which are most readily observed in dreams, where a single image may represent several different ideas, and where images may readily substitute for one another (Arlow & Brenner, 1964-1979).

Freud's observations on the reported childhood sexual experiences and preoccupations in the formation of his patients' symptoms contributed to the development of his interest in infantile sexuality and the promulgation of the psychosexual theory of development (S. Freud, 1905). The sexual drive and its derivatives was seen as one of the prime motivators of behavior. Later (S. Freud, 1920) he elaborated on the other primary motivator, the death instinct, which manifested itself in the aggressive drive. Freud believed that the individual was motivated primarily by the need for gratification of the instincts (the aim), a need that led the child to form relationships to the "Object," or the source of the gratification. Thus, this theory was one in which relationships to others—the Objects—evolved as a result of the necessity of gratifying the drives, or instincts. The relationship to the object was shaped by this need for instinctual gratification through various erotogenic zones that were believed to develop in stages. Early Freudian theory paid much attention to the description of the psychosexual stages and the kinds of object relationships and personality traits that developed during the oral, anal, and phallic stages of development.

The belief in the sexual and aggressive instincts as primary motivators, and the psychosexual theory of development, which charts the maturational course of the instincts, are among the most controversial aspects of classical Freudian theory. As mentioned earlier, numerous splits have occurred within the psychoanalytic world over the nature of drives and the place of the sexual and aggressive drives as the prime motivators of behavior. However, it is to this early period of psychoanalytic theorizing to which contemporary theory owes the origin of the concepts of the "unconscious," "repression," "primary process thinking," and the idea of the "object." These are terms that even non-Freudians tend to utilize freely, though not always with agreement as to meaning.

Because of dissatisfaction with the accuracy of the topographic model, Freud developed his second theory of psychic structure that has come to be known as the Structural Theory of the Mind (S. Freud, 1923). In this theory Freud divided the mind into three structures that relate to psychic function: the *Id*, the *Ego*, and the *Superego*. This is also a drive or instinct theory, and is the model of the mind used by contemporary Freudian psychoanalysts.

As conceptualized by Freud, the id is the source of all instinctual drives. It is present from birth, is entirely unconscious, and functions according to the primary process.

The second agency of the mind is the ego, originally conceived by Freud as growing out of the id. The ego develops because of the necessity of negotiating with the world to gratify instinctual needs. The ego is the agency of adaptation, facilitating the gratification of instinctual needs in conformance with the demands of reality. Freud talked of the ego as manifesting secondary process thinking—logical, coherent, reality oriented—in essence, manifesting a more mature form of coping. The ego's task is to mediate between the id and the external world, and between the id and the superego, the third agency of the mind.

The superego, an outgrowth of the ego, is conceived as having two parts, the conscience and the ego ideal. Forged from the ego, in identification with the parents, the superego is the internal representation of the child's perception of the idealized yet prohibiting parents. The superego is the upholder of the perfection and standards of the ideal to which people strive.

Conflict among the agencies of the mind, as well as between the inner world and external reality, is ever-present. In health, instinctual needs and their derivatives are gratified as a result of an appropriately functioning ego negotiating between the demands of external reality and the moral pressures of the superego. In pathology, there is a lack of balance within the structure. For example, there may be too great an expression of instinctual need and insufficient ego control. Alternatively, there may be excessive control, resulting in conflict within the person over gratification or expression of instincts, causing symptom formation. Pathology is described in terms of the functioning of the agencies of the mind, individually and in relation to each other.

Ego Psychology

Pine (1985) notes that early Freudian theory had a conceptual problem with respect to the origin of the ego. The ego was believed to grow out of the id, but this theory had its problems because the id was conceived as entirely unconscious and incapable of learning. However, researchers noted that some capacities of the ego were present from birth, seemed to follow their own developmental timetable, and developed other than only in response to the resolution of conflict between the id instincts and demands of the outside world. These were called the autonomous ego functions.

Hartmann (as cited in Pine, 1985), as well as Anna Freud (1966), were among the major theorists giving birth to the second great wave of psychoanalytic thinking, the era of Ego Psychology. It was in this era that analysts shifted their focus from the description of the evolution of the instincts to the study of the birth, evolution, and description of the functions of the ego. Psychoanalytic theory was increasingly enriched by data from allied disciplines and, beginning with the work of the early child analysts (A. Freud, 1966) expanded its own observational research with parents and children (Mahler, Pine & Bergman, 1975; Stern, 1985).

Ego psychologists have been concerned particularly with understanding those factors that facilitate or impede the development of the ego and superego functions. A healthy ego can evolve only in a physically intact child, because it relies on some inborn capacities of perception and cognition to perform its functions. For its development and evolution, the ego also requires the appropriate environmental supports that are provided by the caretaking parents in the context of an interpersonal relationship with the infant.

The ego, the facilitator of adaptation and the negotiator among the agencies of the mind, is responsible for maintaining inner equilibrium while mediating between the needs of the self and the demands of the external world, assuring the satisfaction of inner urges, all in conformance with outer reality. The ego must also evaluate the demands of the superego, assuring that its prohibitions and standards are realistic. It is the ego that defends against unacceptable thoughts and impulses, eventually differentiating between thought and deed. It is the ego that organizes and synthesizes perceptions of inner states and external experiences. The ego must have—and develop further—the capacity to distinguish between inner and outer reality (reality testing), to delay gratification (frustration tolerance), to develop awareness of the self and the other, and to reflect upon this awareness. The ego thus develops and maintains a sense of continuity of self in time as well as a continuity of relatedness to others. These functions evolve over time if given a normal endowment and a facilitating environment.

During the development of Ego Psychology, the theory of the development of the psychic structure moved from that based primarily on reconstruction from data derived during the analysis of adults, to one that relied upon direct observation of children. Observational research increased our understanding of ego development in general, and also provided a vast amount of information regarding the development of the self, which ego psychologists consider to be but one specific aspect of ego functioning (Mahler, Pine & Bergman, 1975). Failures or difficulties in the development of ego functions, in the sense of self, and in object relations were understood as important facets of a variety of forms of severe psychopathology (e.g., psychosis, borderline personality organization, narcissistic character pathology).

Object Relations Theories and Theories of the Self

The American ego psychologists were not alone in their belief that difficulties in the development of self and object relations were significant contributory factors to psychopathology. Psychoanalysts within the American interpersonal school (followers of Sullivan, 1953), as well as those within the British school of Object Relations (followers of

Klein, as cited in Pine, 1985; Fairbairn, 1952), evolved their own theories as to the causation of pathology. Their concerns with the ways in which the inner world of relationships develops, their interest in the development of the experience of self, and their beliefs that difficulties in these areas were of major importance in the development of pathology, seem to bear much resemblance to the concerns of the American ego psychologists. However, theorists within these schools differed in the degree to which they embraced the classical Freudian theory of the mind, which included Instinct Theory.

American ego psychologists, who are Freudians, describe their study of the development of object relations as supplementing the basic structural model, not supplanting it. In the classical frame, object relations develop as a result of the need for the gratification of instincts, and contemporary Freudians are careful to integrate the instincts into their understanding of the development of object relations (Mahler, Pine & Bergman, 1975). Similarly, Kleinian analysts of the British school maintain a belief in Instinct or Drive Theory.

Many non-Freudians, such as Bowlby (1969), posit a basic need for attachment to others, a need that is present from birth, and is not secondary to the sexual drive. They focus their study on the development of the mind in the context of relatedness to others (e.g., Sullivan, 1953; Fairbairn, 1952; Stern, 1985). "We are portrayed not as a conglomeration of physically based urges, but as being shaped by and inevitably embedded within a matrix of relationships with other people, struggling both to maintain our ties to others, and to differentiate ourselves from them" (Mitchell, 1988, p. 3). "Mind is composed of relational configurations" (Mitchell, 1988, p. 3). Thus while relational theories concern themselves with pathology of the self and the self in relation to others, they differ from the Freudian theories with respect to the models of the mind they utilize and their concepts of motivation, as well as their beliefs about how the sense of self and self in relation to others develops. They tend to disavow the classical Instinct Theory and perceive the mind as developing in the context of relatedness to others. Mother–infant interaction researchers (Stern, 1985) have been attempting to study the ways in which early parent–child interactions become encoded, and eventually represented as the inner, subjective world of the infant.

Greenberg and Mitchell (1983) suggest that it is of use to consider all these theories and partial theories, which focus on the development of representations of relationships within the mind, as falling within a broadly defined category of "Object Relations theories." However they make an important distinction between those theories that adhere to the basic drive/structure model and those that fall within the relational model. The author's own theoretical orientation aligns with the relational model.

PSYCHOANALYTIC THEORIES: COMMONALITIES

As mentioned in the early part of this chapter, psychoanalytic theory is ever-evolving and highly complex. Most contemporary psychoanalysts integrate insights about personality development and functioning derived from the historically early era of Drive Theory (Instinct Theory), from Ego Psychology, and from Object Relations theories and theories of the development of the self. Earlier conceptualizations either have been reworked, discarded, or integrated into an overall schema for the understanding of personality.

Complexity does not end here, however, because, depending on the analyst's theoretical orientation, the kinds of integrations made among ideas may differ. Certain understandings may be included and others, discarded. Despite the ferment in psychoanalysis, and theoretical disagreements over such issues as the primacy of the drives, all psychoanalytic approaches have the following commonalities:

1. Psychoanalysts believe that symptomatic behaviors serve a function for the individual and represent his or her best attempts at adaptation or coping with inner needs and external realities.
2. All similar external behaviors cannot be assumed to have the same or similar causes, and any given behavior may serve more than one need. Psychoanalysts thus attempt to conceptualize the meaning or function of behaviors for the adaptation of the individual. Delineating the kinds of needs the individual has, and understanding what he or she is attempting to cope with, are the first steps in understanding the behavior, and necessary prerequisites for initiating effective behavioral change.
3. Psychoanalysts are concerned with the subjective experiences of their clients. They do not assume that all individuals are affected in exactly the same way by similar experiences. For example, the way the client perceives an interpersonal event will significantly affect how he or she handles that event behaviorally. Analysts come to understand the subjective experiences of their clients in a variety of ways:
   a. Analysts explore their patients' subjective world both verbally and nonverbally. Beliefs, fantasies, and patterns of interpersonal interaction are both observed and discussed.
   b. Perception of experience is obviously colored by previous experiences. Thus, the life history of the individual, particularly the history of his or her most significant relationships, will provide important clues to understanding how the individual has developed his or her expectancies about, and patterns of interaction in, relationships.
   c. The most powerful tool to understanding the nature of the client's perceptions regarding relationships is through exploration of the nature of the evolving relationship between client and therapist. Psychoanalysts believe that individuals repeat patterns of relationships, many of which developed with early caretakers, and other significant persons in a person's life. There is a belief that early patterns of relatedness color later patterns, and that clues to both current patterns (displacements) and early patterns (transferences) of interaction are discernible in the client–therapist interaction.
   d. In addition to subjective experiences that are conscious, individuals have experiences of which they may not, or may never have been, consciously aware. Such experiences still motivate behavior. Some experiences are unconscious because they occurred at a time when the individual did not have the verbal or symbolic capacity to preserve them in language. Other experiences are rendered unconscious for defensive purposes. To know of them or to acknowledge them would pose a threat to some aspects of the functioning

of the individual. Defenses against threatening thoughts and feelings occur in all phases of the life cycle. Experiences that occurred in early periods of a person's life would have been processed cognitively and emotionally according to the child's level of development at that time. They represent the child's concepts of events and the child's best attempts at both regulating the self and adapting to the external world. Analysts are interested in both current anxieties and defenses, as well as the historical antecedents of current responses. Analysts of different orientations have different beliefs as to the reasons or motivations for experiences being maintained outside of awareness. For example, classical Freudian analysts tend to talk in terms of archaic (infantile) wishes, which are derived from the instincts, that were maintained outside of awareness because their expression would have caused either external conflicts with the environment, or internal conflicts with the ego and superego. Relational analysts tend to deemphasize or totally discard the idea of instinctual danger, and instead emphasize the need to maintain out of awareness, any idea, feeling or experience that threatens to disrupt the basic relationship with the parent.

4. Simply stated, the goals of the psychoanalytic treatment of adults are to clarify the individual's basic motivations and ways of coping, including both those of which the individual is subjectively aware and those of which the individual is unaware. The treatment model associated with classical theory is designed to facilitate bringing into awareness ideas, thoughts, and feelings that were rendered unconscious because of a need to defend against them in early childhood, but which still have motivational force. Once brought into awareness, the individual is in a position to evaluate his or her infantile needs, beliefs, anxieties, and ways of coping, discarding those that are no longer necessary or appropriate in adult life, and is then able to develop more appropriate adaptations.

In the early years of psychoanalysis, attempts were made to treat children with adaptations of the basic adult treatment model, but it became clear to many child analysts that the basic concepts and premises of adult psychoanalysis needed to be reevaluated with respect to appropriateness for use with children and adolescents.

PSYCHOANALYTIC TREATMENT APPROACHES: CHILDREN AND ADOLESCENTS

Treatment of children and adolescents differs in significant ways from treatment of adults. One very important difference between children or adolescents and adults is the fact that their personality organization is more fluid and in the process of development (A. Freud, 1965). Children or adolescents are not expected to have fully developed adaptive capacities (ego function), a completely developed moral sense (superego function), fully realistic perceptions and expectations of self and other, or a mature physiological system. In addition, changes are expected not only in basic biological givens and adaptive capacities, but in the basic stability of personality organization. For example, as the child matures, the emergence of increasingly reliable styles of adaptation and relatedness are expected (Pine, 1985). Children who are thus "in process" are needful of interventions in their development. They are in effect creating what, in the treatment of adults, will be talked about as history. Children and adolescents are also highly dependent upon their environment for the development of most ego and superego functions. They are intimately involved in the matrix of their families in which patterns of relatedness have both evolved and are evolving. Thus treatment techniques utilized with youngsters are significantly concerned with the facilitation of development of adaptive capacities. Where symptomatology is felt to be a result of environmental failure, the environment (parents, school, etc.) will be worked with. Whenever possible, work with important figures in the child's life will focus upon the development of a growth facilitating environment, including support for appropriate parenting skills, provision of information about developmental issues that underlie symptomatology, clarification of problematic parent–child interactions, and so forth.

In the psychoanalytically informed treatment of youngsters, a great deal of work involves support for the development of ego functions. Such support serves not only the purpose of facilitating adaptation to the external world, but also expedites the management of the psychological needs of the individual, some of which may be discernible only through exploration of the patient's subjective experience. There is thus a concern with both adaptation to the external environment and adaptation within the internal world of the child. With respect to work with parents and others in the environment, however, it is the belief of psychoanalysts that environmental change alone may not always be sufficient to alter the subjective world of the child. Children as well as adults may be operating on the basis of motivations that lie outside of awareness. Children in particular, may not be given to reflect on their own experiences. They may defend against anxiety-provoking thoughts and feelings, and develop symptoms and maladaptive behaviors, based on unconscious motivations. Patterns of relatedness established in early childhood, as well as archaic wishes and fears in relation to parental figures, may need to be reevaluated in the light of current reality. To accomplish this, techniques to facilitate expression and awareness had to be developed that gave due consideration to the developmental capacities of the child or adolescent.

Melanie Klein (as cited in Pine, 1985) and Anna Freud (1965) were among the early child psychoanalysts who recognized the developmental incapacity of children to engage in treatment in the same manner as adults. Klein was one of the first analysts to utilize play and fantasy material as a way of communicating with children. Through play, which is a natural means of both expression and communication in childhood, it has been observed that children represent their inner conflicts, reflect their subjective perceptions of relationships, and repeat significant aspects of their experiences, including those that are pleasurable as well as those that are traumatic. Through a sensitive attunement to a variety of forms of verbal as well as nonverbal communication, the analyst endeavors to help the youngster become aware of his or her feelings, including fear, conflicts, and wishes; in general, his or her experiences and motives. The analyst's task will be to enable the youngster to become more self-reflective, and less fearful of acknowledging a wide range of thoughts, feelings, and motives. In addition, the analyst will be concerned with increasing awareness of feelings, and so forth, which the youngster has not known, or has avoided knowing.

A THEORETICAL FRAMEWORK
FOR THE CASE ANALYSIS

Anna Freud (1965) was the first analyst to attempt to organize a profile by which to assess normality and pathology in child and adolescent development. She recognized and stated the now commonly held belief that childhood pathology cannot be assessed by adult criteria because of the continuing nature of the developmental process. In order to assess a developing youngster we must do so according to expected norms for that age and stage of development. Anna Freud's developmental profile reflects her psychoanalytic theory of personality structure as well as her beliefs regarding the causes of pathology or maladaptive functioning. She thus recommends an assessment of each component of the personality structure—the id, ego, and superego—according to norms for that developmental stage, as well as an assessment of the ways in which the component parts function in relation to one another. In other words, what is needed is an assessment of the child's capacities to regulate his or her basic needs to the extent that can be expected of a youngster at that stage.

When we talk in terms of the basic needs of the individual, we speak not only of the basic physiological needs that must be met (some of which are sexual), but also the psychological needs that are not all derivatives of the dual instincts (sexual and aggressive). We think in terms of the regulation of a full range of impulses and affects (for example, depressive feelings, sadness, loneliness, elation, anxiety). We also are concerned with establishing and maintaining a steady and clearly differentiated sense of self. Relational theories have expanded the description and understanding of the development of the self. Self is experienced in myriad ways—integrated or disorganized, agent of action or as totally under the control of others. An individual may feel in tune with others or detached, familiar to one's self or unfamiliar (e.g., "I don't feel like myself") (Stern, 1985). How we evaluate our self, positively or negatively (self-esteem), can have a significant impact upon our emotions, dropping us into despair, raising us to elation, or maintaining a calm self-satisfaction. These experiences of self are developed in relation to others (our objects). Thus in assessment, the age appropriateness of the development of the self, the sense of self, and the quality of the relationships of self to other must all be evaluated.

In addition to assessing these aspects of personality functioning, other individual characteristics must be explored. Anna Freud (1965, pp. 140–147) recommended assessing the kinds of conflicts an individual has (i.e., conflicts between the individual and the external world, or within the personality structure). Internal conflicts may occur when attempts at meeting basic needs or expressing certain feelings evoke guilt, or the anxiety of disapproval by internal representations of the parents (superego anxiety). Internal conflicts can also exist between love and hate for the same object. Both external and internal conflicts are often present. The youngster's general characteristics, such as ability to tolerate anxiety and master frustration as well as styles of coping with stress, must also be determined. Throughout the assessment process, the impact of physical illnesses and traumatic interpersonal and life experiences on personality development are considered as well.

We note in the case material that Vince has had life experiences that probably have had a significant impact upon his development (parental divorce and remarriage) and that he may have had some constitutional vulnerabilities, which perhaps have caused difficulty in both mastery of developmental tasks and the experience of self. His current difficulties have been shown to have a long history, the meaning of which will be discussed in greater detail in the case analysis section.

Before turning to the actual case data, we propose to explore two aspects of the case particularly meaningful to Vince's current situation: the stage of adolescence and the impact of divorce and remarriage on children. Adolescence has attached to it specific adaptational tasks with which every youngster must wrestle. The practitioner must understand normal development in order to evaluate a client's status. Concurrently, the impact of specific life events, such as divorce, must be assessed to determine their meaning for the youngster. Therefore, the following sections will offer detailed discussions of these aspects to familiarize the reader with the literature and offer a reference point for later case interpretation.

Adolescence

Peter Blos (1979), perhaps one of the best-known psychoanalysts specializing in the area of adolescence, divides the overall period into phases (preadolescence, early adolescence, adolescence proper, late adolescence, and postadolescence) for the purpose of understanding developmental issues and sequences (1979, pp. 101–102). Each phase is seen as having its own particular tasks and characteristic conflicts, the resolution of which contributes to the completion of the overall process of adolescent growth. Vince, at the age of 13 years, 9 months, can be described chronologically as in the phase of early adolescence.

Blos describes the central task of adolescence to be that of individuation. Throughout our development we grow and become who we are in part by identifying with significant people in our lives. We adopt their styles of being in the world and their styles of coping with strife; we incorporate their values and beliefs. Much of this occurs outside our awareness. In addition to identifying with the important people in our lives, we also must separate ourselves from them and come to know the ways in which we are different from them; in other words, we individuate. Our parents are necessary figures in our lives both because we grow by becoming like them and because we individuate, in part, by being recognized by them for our differences. "Individuation implies that the growing person takes increasing responsibility for what he does and what he is, rather than depositing this responsibility on the shoulders of those under whose influence and tutelage he has grown up" (p. 148). Blos has termed adolescence as the second individuation phase, the first having been completed in early childhood, usually before age four. What occurs in the first stage is the emergence of a clearly individuated toddler, a toddler who has developed a sense of his or her own separateness from mother and who, though very dependent upon parental figures for the growth of most aspects of personality functioning, is also emerging as an individual in his or her own right. What emerges by the end of a healthy adolescence is an individuated young adult whose ties to the parents of early childhood have loosened to the point of being able to shed family dependencies, move on to new love objects, and become a member of society at large. Old patterns of relatedness to parents (developed in early childhood) must be relinquished, and new patterns based on emerging cognitive, social, and physiological competencies must evolve. By the end of the adolescent period a young adult should have a clearly delineated inner experience or representation of self and a more or less realistic inner representation of significant others. There should have been a reappraisal and reworking of old parent–child relationships as experienced in thought, fantasy, and action, utilizing the more mature cognitive capacities of the adolescent. There should have been a relinquishment of old (primitive) wishes and fears in relation to parent figures. These achievements are only more or less attainable by most individuals. Where there have been significant difficulties getting needs met, where there has been excessive infantilization or trauma, and where more mature resources (ego capacities) have been insufficiently developed, it may be particularly difficult for the adolescent to accomplish these tasks. In particular, the sense of identity, a component of the self, may be impaired, and the relationship of the self to the parents may remain dominated by more childlike images and patterns of interaction.

There are many components to the experience of self. As described earlier, we reflect upon ourselves and decide if we like what we see. We evaluate our self in relation to an ego ideal, a structure formed as an outgrowth of identification with the idealized parents of earlier childhood and their derivative or substitute idealized (hero) figures of adolescence. The idealized figures are those we initially envy and decide we would like to emulate; we admire them. The contents of the ego ideal also become modified with time and by the end of the phase of early adolescence the ego ideal should have been consolidated as a substructure of the personality. It has been emphasized by psychoanalysts that youngsters who have experienced trauma such as loss through divorce or death may exhibit significant difficulty in the development or consolidation of the ego ideal (Tessman, 1978). Blos states "The ego ideal constitutes a prerequisite for the choice and pursuit of a vocational goal and ideational stability. Whenever the formation of the ego ideal is critically impaired, a sense of uncertainty, floundering, indecisiveness, restlessness, and lowered self-esteem occurs" (1979, p. 199).

A highly significant component of the self relates to sexual identity. While it is now believed that gender identity (a sense of being a boy or a girl) is developed in earliest childhood, Blos suggests that sexual identity, as well as clarity with regard to choice of a sexual object, is consolidated in adolescence. The preadolescent boy's concern with being one of the guys and the preoccupation with the development of male competencies (physical strength and bodily prowess, etc.) are some of the behaviors that are stimulated by the emergence of puberty. Whether one is or is not a Freudian, one cannot help but be aware of the enormous importance physiological changes have for the functioning of the adolescent.

The experience of one's self as having mastery over one's body is an aspect of self that, while begun in early childhood with mastery over bodily functions such as feeding and toileting, is further developed in adolescence. The sense that I am in charge of me, I can cope with my physical urges, is challenged anew at this stage.

Related to issues of bodily mastery are issues of autonomy from parental figures. Old battles for control and dominance (who is in charge of whom) emerge with renewed vigor. In preadolescence the primary battles are with mother or figures who are stand-ins for mother. School authorities often stand in place of parental figures and their demands are dealt with as displaced parental demands. Youngsters with unresolved dependency needs may also enact these needs in school. Often adolescents are struggling with conflicts between desires to be taken care of and desires for autonomy. The symptoms they present may reflect aspects of both sides of a conflict. The resolution of this conflict with mother is affected in significant ways by the quality of the boy's relationship to his father. The boy at this stage needs a positive relationship with his father both as a figure with whom to identify and as an alternate source of nurturance and support during the process of severing the dependence upon mother. If the father is absent or unavailable during this period of development, the boy will be forced to cling to an idealized and/or fantasized version of him.

The Impact of Divorce and Remarriage on Development

Because of its widespread prevalence in contemporary American culture, we have to be careful not to underestimate the impact of divorce on the lives of developing children. Interestingly, Vince's family has tended to do so. Vince's mother has denied any ill effects of the "amicable" divorce and remarriage on Vince's life, nor does she understand their relationship to his current symptomatology. Before proceeding with the case analysis, I will describe some of the findings regarding the impact of these life events on the course of development.

According to Chethik (1989, p. 196), children have to deal with four major affects in relation to parental divorce: "anger/rage; loss/grief; guilt/self-blame; fears." The age of the child and level of psychological development are important factors in determining the child's management of these inner experiences.

Chethik notes that children are typically enraged by the disruption of their family life. They often feel cheated and their sense of security is undermined. Depending upon prior development the child's tendency may be to act out this rage directly toward parents or in school, or the child may repress or suppress it, becoming symptomatic (e.g., becoming neurotic or phobic). The rage becomes incorporated into the inner fantasy life of the child, and object relations (the inner representations of self and others) may be significantly shaped by the intensity of the feelings involved. Intense anger may be extremely frightening and may shape the experiences of self as extremely dangerous and/or powerfully bad. Rage may be denied and projected onto others (e.g., "my father's gonna kill me") causing the object to be perceived as unduly fearsome.

Children whose parents have been divorced frequently blame themselves for the marital breakup. Their egocentric belief is that aspects of their thoughts, feelings, fantasies, and behaviors have been the cause of the divorce. In their competitive strivings, some children fantasize themselves as the winner of the love of the remaining parent and fear that their "victory" was the causative factor in the divorce. Anger toward the noncustodial parent for experiences that occurred before and during the divorce (e.g., prior absences or failures) may be perceived by the child as the cause of the departure. Loyalty conflicts regarding continued love for both parents when they are at odds with each other may further exacerbate guilt.

Coping with the experience of loss means dealing with the loss of the family structure as well as the loss, through diminished involvement, of the noncustodial parent. Children and adolescents have particular difficulties managing strong grief reactions. The literature on bereavement in children is replete with examples of the variety of reactions children have that may be substantially different from those of adults. Among the defenses children use to tolerate painful emotions are denial, detachment, heightened activity level, and regression to previous means of coping. In assessing children who have experienced loss or partial loss of a parent through divorce, it is important to determine the ways in which they have managed this extremely painful feeling.

Tessman (1978) has described many of the coping mechanisms that children use, some of which promote healthy development and some of which may interfere with healthy development. One of the most significant ways of coping with loss is through identification with the person who has departed. By becoming like that person we forever keep him or her with us. Identificatory processes often occur outside our awareness and may reflect positive or negative characteristics of the absent person, as well as attributes that may not be genuine, but based rather on the child's fantasies of the parent. Because the child needs the parent for so many reasons, an idealized image of the parent may be developed to substitute for the parent who has been partially or completely lost. Any threat to the image of the parent may be perceived as a threat of total loss—thus the need for maintenance of idealization. In early childhood we all tend to have larger-than-life pictures of our parents. They are seen either as extraordinarily powerful and wonderful, or at times awesomely bad, but throughout development children's images of their parents usually become increasingly realistic. Gradually and necessarily, children become disillusioned, a sometimes painful process. If there is a defensive need to maintain an idealized image of the parent, and/or if the parent is insufficiently available for reality testing, children may persist in maintaining unrealistic images. The defensive maintenance of an idealized parent image may have a significant impact on the experience of the self and its relation to the object. A child may feel small in relation to a larger-than-life parent with whom the youngster can never compete, or whose expectations can never hope to be fulfilled. The child may be unable to accept any substitute parent because that person will always be inadequate in comparison to the idealized absent individual. A child may search for years for the absent parent (in fantasy as well as in fact) attempting to be reunited or to reinstitute things the way they used to be, or the way the child wished them to be. The desire to recapture the past might interfere with the process of moving on developmentally and may also interfere with the child's capacity to accept a stepparent.

Tessman (1978, p. 108) notes that children who have experienced parental loss through separation or divorce may exhibit significant symptoms that upon exploration are found to relate to the quest for the absent parent. Unconscious searching, in a variety of forms, is frequently evident in the behavior of older children, adolescents, and adults. A common symptom is motor restlessness, as well as cutting classes.

CASE ANALYSIS

Earlier, some aspects of normal adolescence were described so that the reader might think about the psychological tasks with which Vince must be wrestling. It is also necessary to assess Vince in relation to others of his age. Additionally, the impact of divorce and remarriage upon some aspects of development was highlighted. From the preceding discussion it should be evident that family relationships prior to and subsequent to the traumatic experiences of his parents' divorce and remarriages are considered to play an important role in Vince's adjustment difficulties. These issues will have major significance for the treatment recommendations; however, it should be emphasized that a psychoanalytic approach would consider most of the data provided to be relevant to a formation of an understanding of the case. Included as useful information would be the data regarding Vince's physical development, the concerns raised regarding neuro-psychological functioning, and academic weakness, as well as the impact of such environmental factors as school experiences and the disruptive effect of family moves. Vince's behaviors are thought to be multidetermined and thus all these factors will affect treatment recommendations.

General Assessment

Vince is described in the case material as a youngster of average intelligence who, despite high average verbal intelligence, doesn't seem to be functioning well in academic areas. He is also apparently not utilizing his good intelligence sufficiently in the service of containment of anxiety or frustration. His general style of coping with stressful situations is impulsive and low frustration tolerance has been noted to be a problem of long duration. However, these symptoms seem to have been of greater or lesser concern depending upon the degree of stress in Vince's life. While there is some suggestion in the case material of a heightened constitutional vulnerability, and some possible neurophysiological dysfunction, there is no clear-cut medical data to substantiate these hypotheses. In psychodynamic terms, Vince's low frustration tolerance and impulsive, at times explosive, behaviors are suggestive of relative weaknesses in one area of ego functioning. These factors will have to be taken into account in the development of any intervention plan. It was noted that Vince's relatively delayed capacity to express himself verbally (because of articulation rather than language difficulties) could indeed have contributed to the development of an impulsive style of response to stressful situations. Vince became a youngster who was predisposed to displays of affect and to an action orientation when stressed, rather than to the use of verbal communication for the expression of needs.

Previous attempts at aiding Vince in the containment of his impulses have been aimed at the physiological level with the administration of medication (Ritalin and antihistamines). No attempts have been made up to this time to explore psychological factors contributing to the heightened impulsivity and lessened frustration tolerance, or to use psychological interventions. Without totally discounting the possibility of physiological vulnerability, those unexplored psychological areas leading to the recommendation of additional forms of intervention will be investigated.

As a psychoanalyst the author finds it particularly important to review the case history to look for interpersonal and environmental triggers of symptomatic behavior. In assessing Vince's history, the relationship of increased impulsivity and aggressiveness, as well as decreased frustration tolerance to family events, separation, divorce, remarriage and so forth is of interest. It is important to note that the decision to place Vince on Ritalin at age eight, seems to coincide with the period of time just preceding and congruent with his parents' divorce. The practitioner would certainly want more information about what was happening in Vince's relationships with each of his parents at those times. It seems reasonable, however, to speculate that the impact of the loss of his ''family'' and the final departure of his father, could stimulate heightened anger, irritability, and restlessness in Vince, all factors that contribute to the symptom of school failure. The psychoanalyst would also inquire as to whether Vince's expulsion from school in fourth grade corresponded in any way with his mother's involvement with and subsequent marriage to Mr. Kirk. Now at the age of thirteen years nine months, in addition to struggling with the tasks of adolescence, Vince faces the further concretization of his father's departure from the family due to his impending remarriage. Further proof of loss and inability to fulfill any fantasy of reunion is occurring. Could these events in any way be related to Vince's current school failure? This practitioner's hypothesis is yes.

Vince can be described as a youngster who is having difficulty dealing with some of the important psychological tasks of early adolescence. While he seems to be appropriately concerned with the development of his physical strengths and seems to be enjoying his burgeoning masculinity, his exclusive emphasis on this aspect of his identity suggests the presence of some degree of anxiety regarding his adequacy. Without more extensive projective testing and/or exploration of his fantasy life, further analysis cannot be undertaken. It does seem on the surface, at least, that the only aspect of himself that Vince feels invested in is his developing male identity.

Despite his attempts at denial, Vince probably experiences himself as abandoned by his parents. Defensively denying any need, in actuality, he is a rather dependent youngster who has yearnings to be taken care of by parental figures or in magical ways. Though he describes in a TAT story a guy who makes it in life without his parents, he also talks about being provided for by his stepfather, being taken into his business, or perhaps winning a million dollars. These statements, which were made during the clinical interviews and on projective tests (Sentence Completion and Three Wishes), can be seen as wishes. Though he aspires to a good job, and marriage, there is very little in the case material to suggest that Vince experiences himself as agent of his future success. One senses he has no idea of how, using his own skills, he will attain autonomy and mastery. His primary asset seems to be his physical attractiveness. Thus one could be seriously concerned about Vince's ability to resolve the normal dependency conflicts of the adolescent.

Various factors in his life have contributed to this dependent and aimless state. One hypothesis is that Vince's development has been significantly affected by the relative absence of his father since early childhood and the subsequent loss of a significant degree of real relatedness with him since the parental divorce. With his father not available, Vince's dependency upon his mother was heightened, perhaps predisposing him to greater difficulty with issues of identity formation, individuation, and separation and thus making her subsequent remarriage quite a traumatic loss. Throughout the case material there are numerous statements that support the belief that family difficulties, concerns about divorce, loss and remarriage are of major importance to Vince.

Like many children of divorce, Vince fantasizes that his mother will remarry his father, and he expresses negative feelings regarding his current family that show a lack of acceptance of the situation and an inability to derive appropriate support from the parental figures who are available (his stepfather in particular).

The insufficiency of available male figures with whom to relate and identify has contributed to difficulties in the development of greater real autonomy in several ways. While wishing to make his father proud of him, Vince does not seem able to mobilize himself to do that which his father would probably want, that is, achieve in school. Perhaps Vince does not anticipate that gaining further autonomy will meet his needs for more contact and nurturance from his father. Perhaps unconsciously he is resisting moving forward in his life (taking charge or truly individuating) because that would mean relinquishing his wish for the father of early childhood, the one who takes care of and nurtures a little boy. Perhaps in his school failure, he also expresses his fury over his losses, in particular, the sense of abandonment that he probably experiences but cannot acknowledge. Lacking the loving presence of a man with whom it "pays" to identify and emulate, Vince is somewhat hampered in his efforts to begin defining himself with respect to personal goals and career aspirations. He seems to be playing with the idea of forming that sort of relationship with his stepfather but has conflicts about doing so. To do so would require relinquishing the fantasy of his father's return, would require the acceptance of his father as a less than ideal parent, and would necessitate the taking of a risk, the risk of investing hopes and feelings in another man who might disappoint him in painful ways. Finally, as previously noted, the absence of a man as an alternative person in the family to love and be supported by, exacerbates Vince's dependency upon his mother.

Diagnostically, the author would describe Vince as a depressed adolescent, whose symptoms include unexpressed rage, restlessness, irritability, and aimlessness. Vince and his family have utilized the defense of denial in dealing with painful feelings connected with unmet needs, disappointment, abandonment, and loss. Vince's air of independence and bravado serve a defensive function and are not reflective of an appropriately developing sense of autonomy. These issues will all need to be addressed as part of an intervention plan.

RECOMMENDATIONS
AND SUGGESTED INTERVENTIONS

This section is divided into two subsections. In the first section recommendations are made that relate to the development of a more facilitating environment. The focus is on interventions with the family and recommendations for the school. The second subsection describes interventions with Vince in individual psychotherapy. The goals of the interventions with family and school will enable them to provide appropriate support for Vince's emotional development. The goals in individual psychotherapy will also relate to the facilitation of personality growth, but emphasis will be on the resolution of inner conflicts, the development of a greater individuated sense of self, including the reduction of the use of maladaptive defenses, and the expansion of the capacity to cope with painful affects.

Work with the Family

The practitioner's first concern is with aiding the family in coming to an understanding of the full range of Vince's psychological and learning needs. Therefore, any intervention plans will begin with feedback to Vince and his family regarding the results of the analyses of issues involved. In providing feedback, the psychoanalyst must be fully aware of the tendency of everyone in the family to utilize denial as a means of coping with painful affects. They also may have a tendency to avoid issues until forced to confront them. Thus Vince's mother denies that the divorce was traumatic and she denies that his father's absence is experienced as a rejection of Vince. Withdrawals from involvement are rationalized as being caused by life circumstances. His stepfather is too busy, his father cares but is otherwise occupied. Everyone in the family has trouble coping with anger and hurt. Vince denies that his father has hurt him and displaces his anger with his father onto his stepfather. He prefers to believe that his stepfather is the cause of his father's not seeing him more, and in so doing protects his father and mother from the intensity of his anger about the situation, thus preserving his relationships with them. Vince utilizes this pattern of denial in other areas as well, denying any problems at school and saying things would be different if he wanted them to be.

This defensive denial needs to be understood by the clinician as a way of warding off feelings that are believed to be intolerable and dangerous. Among other things, Vince utilizes his anger in the service of maintaining a tie to his father, as well as preserving the fantasy of parental reunion. Having experienced strong feelings of abandonment, Vince does not dare address his fury to his parents directly, fearing further abandonment and sensing their inability to tolerate strong feelings. One way of beginning to approach the family and Vince would be to present their issues as rather typical of those found in families in which there has been divorce and remarriage. This is a family that needs education about the impact of divorce and remarriage on child development. They need assistance in understanding the feelings with which Vince is grappling as well as the feelings that other family members have about being in this reconstituted family. Normalizing the behaviors and problems they are all experiencing, presenting them as not unusual under the circumstances, might give Vince and the family permission to begin the process of acknowledging feelings and connecting them to external behavioral outcomes. This will be a continuing aspect of any intervention plan. The family pattern of not acknowledging feelings has impeded Vince's capacity to come to terms with them, to bear them. He is left alone and unsupported, further exacerbating his anger. Vince needs permission to feel anger, grief, guilt, and fears connected with his life experiences so that he can stop experiencing himself as just a problem kid who will never do well in school.

Work with Vince's mother and stepfather should have as one goal the development of their capacities to understand and to empathize with him. Particular interventions should include an exploration of their beliefs about the reasons for his behaviors, and an exploration of their personal feelings and anxieties that interfere with their capacity for empathy. Mrs. Kirk's anxieties about dealing with anger as well as with feelings regarding Vince's emerging sexuality should be explored. Mr. Kirk's feelings about his role as a stepparent, and his experience with Vince should be discussed. Another goal should be to enable both mother and stepfather to feel less helpless in relating to Vince and in coping with his aggressiveness toward his stepfather, to withdraw less, and to develop concrete plans for engaging Vince in an empathic but firm manner. It is hoped that with a greater degree of understanding within the family, some of Vince's anger and restlessness would dissipate.

An important outcome goal of work with the family and with Vince would be an improved relationship with his stepfather. It is hoped that with increased understanding of Vince, his stepfather would have the capacity to reach out to him in ways that are nondisciplinary, perhaps even offering him some after-school work in his business.

Work with the School

The case material presents no data to suggest that Vince's teachers are familiar with him as an individual, other than as a troublesome kid. This is not unusual in a middle or junior high school in which there is increased departmentalization, a greater degree of orientation to subject material, and a less personalized relationship with students. Vince is emotionally unprepared to deal with the demands of his current school placement. For a youngster as angry and alienated as Vince, it is essential that work go on in school to engage him more actively in an interpersonal way. With Vince's knowledge and permission, a meeting or meetings should be held with Vince's teachers to familiarize them with Vince's individual educational and emotional needs. The educational recommendations will not be elaborated on here as they will be dealt with in other chapters in this book. This is in no way intended as a diminishment of the importance of providing appropriate educational intervention, including individual tutoring where necessary. What a psycho-analytic perspective should offer the educator, is increased sensitivity to the subjectively experienced needs of the youngster so that consultation can proceed with these needs in mind. His teachers should be apprised of Vince's long-standing discomfort about being called upon to recite in class, his extreme sensitivity to peer opinion, his low self-esteem, and the defensive nature of his bravado. Members of the school staff who might be available to develop a personal relationship with Vince should be involved (e.g., school psychologist, counselor, coach, gym teacher) and teachers should be aided in developing concrete ways of responding to Vince that do not include retaliatory humiliation, and that involve consistent follow-through. If a group is available for adolescents whose parents have divorced, Vince should be referred to it. Having the coach or gym teacher reach out to Vince (even if he is not eligible for the team) to engage him in activities or discussion that could motivate him could be of importance. The goal in each of these cases is to decrease Vince's alienation from important facets of school life and to enhance his involvement with people with whom he might identify in positive ways.

Individual Interventions with Vince: Psychotherapy

Some of the case material will now be used to illustrate the way in which the clinician could approach a youngster such as Vince in individual psychoanalytically oriented therapy. Describing the unfolding of the therapeutic process is not easy, because it does not evolve in a stepwise fashion and there are no readily applied formulas from which to develop interventions. In general, the therapist attempts to utilize interventions that support adaptation, including those that are educative. The therapist also intervenes in ways that should help the youngster relinquish problematic defenses and facilitate the development of awareness of a full range of feelings and beliefs that may be contributing to maladaptive styles of coping. The kind of interventions the therapist uses depends on his or her assessment of the pertinent issues in the case. Because Vince's difficulties are related in part to current life circumstances, and because he is an adolescent who is not particularly predisposed to communicate feelings verbally, the therapist will need to be very active in facilitating the process of talking.

The difficulty of engaging an angry adolescent in individual psychotherapy should not be underestimated, and it must be emphasized that the process of engagement begins at the time of referral. Vince must be convinced that those who speak with him are truly able to empathize with his position, and are not trying to force compliance with other people's goals and rules. The person who makes the referral, and the potential therapist as well, must be seen as strong, knowledgeable, and concerned, as well as undaunted by Vince's testing of him or her. This is particularly important because Vince currently is not experiencing any parental figures as being able to hold their own with him.

Throughout the evaluation process Vince has revealed his feelings regarding his family and school difficulties. Though overtly denying any difficulty, Vince does acknowledge his dislike for school, and his feelings that his family is not a real family. These statements can be utilized to engage him in a process of talking about himself, his feelings, desires, and ambitions. The therapist might empathize with the plight of having to sit all day in a place one feels is bad, and suggest that this process of talking might help him figure out how to make things more bearable. The therapist might comment on the degree to which Vince feels he has to go it alone, and might note that that's a tough spot to be in for even the most independent of people. Thus the therapist does not directly challenge Vince's pseudoindependent stance, but notes it, and lets the patient know that who he is and what he is about, has been heard and is open to discussion and understanding. The efficacy of psychoanalytic psychotherapy is significantly affected by the therapist's capacity to understand the concerns, conflicts, and styles of adaptation of the youngster, to hear the manifestations of these in the material provided by the client, and to provide feedback to him as to what is noted by the therapist. The therapist thus guides the process by using an understanding of the case to inform his or her listening and by using the material provided by the client to raise and confirm or disconfirm hypotheses.

In individual psychotherapy Vince should be afforded the opportunity to begin to discuss his beliefs about, and feelings toward, family members as well as toward friends. He should be encouraged to talk about all the people in his life who are important to him, including "chicks," guys he hangs out with, and heroes. Work should center on current life circumstances, with historical material brought in only as relevant. The therapist's initial task should be to get to know Vince's point of view and to convey to Vince his or her sincere desire to see the world as Vince sees it. The therapist should pay particular attention to emotions expressed, such as anger toward his stepfather for standing in the way of his seeing his own father more. The therapist might question Vince as to why he thinks his stepfather does this, and why he thinks his father permits it. His fantasies would be explored. "Tell me what you imagine; how you see it," should be frequent requests of the therapist. The therapist should encourage a full expression of feelings through the use of words.

Understanding that Vince needs to maintain his anger at his stepfather for a variety of reasons, the practitioner should keep in mind the multiple functions that the anger serves. No attempts should be made to talk Vince out of his belief or anger, because this most likely would be of no use. The therapist should continue to provide feedback to Vince about how he or she heard him, organizing the data provided according to the themes that emerged. Work could proceed around the defensive aspects of his anger toward his stepfather in the following way. The clinician would note the absence of anger expressed toward his parents, being somewhat curious about this. The clinician would thus call attention to what is and what is not expressed, and any incongruities would be noted. Thus the way would be paved for an exploration of feelings toward his parents around this issue. The therapist might attempt to give permission for the experience of anger under these circumstances, noting that most kids whose parents are divorced would feel some anger toward not only their stepparent but toward their natural parents as well. Depending upon Vince's response to this statement, the therapist might or might not have to proceed further with support for the experience of some anger. If Vince persisted in denying anger, the therapist might begin to ask Vince whether he is able to feel anger toward his parents about other issues, and wonder what Vince thinks would happen if he got angry with his father in the way he gets angry with his stepfather. Thus the psychoanalyst would gently begin to approach the issue of the difficulty of being angry with a parent, and would begin to help Vince understand the perceived dangers related to the experience and expression of the feeling. The therapist might make an interpretation of a motive for the defense of "denial," suggesting that perhaps Vince could be afraid that his father might see him even less often if he showed him how hurt and angry he was. An exploration would then be made of Vince's reactions. The practitioner might also interpret the defense of "displacement" by commenting that for Vince it might be easier to be angry with his stepfather than with either of his parents, because it's really hard to be angry with people you love and need so much. It must be noted that the therapist explores only those issues that are either within awareness or close enough to awareness to be acknowledged by the patient without overwhelming distress. Interpretation should only be made in the context of knowing that adequate inner resources and external support will be available for dealing with the feelings unleashed.

REFERENCES

Arlow, J., & Brenner, C. (1979). *Psychoanalytic concepts and the structural theory.* New York: International Universities Press. (Original work published in 1964.)

Blos, P. (1979). *The adolescent passage.* New York: International Universities Press.

Bowlby, J. (1969). *Attachment.* Volume 1 of *Attachment and loss.* New York: Basic Books.

Chethik, M. (1989). *Techniques of child therapy.* New York: Guilford.

Fairbairn, W. R. D. (1952). *An object relations theory of the personality.* New York: Basic Books.

Freud, A. (1965). *Normality and pathology in childhood.* New York: International Universities Press.

Freud, A. (1966). *The ego and the mechanisms of defense.* New York: International Universities Press. (Original work published in 1936.)

Freud, S. (1905). *Three essays on sexuality.* In *The standard edition of the complete psychological works of Sigmund Freud* (Vol. 7). London: Hogarth.

Freud, S. (1920). *Beyond the pleasure principle.* In *The standard edition* (Vol. 18). London: Hogarth.

Freud, S. (1923). *The ego and the id.* In *The standard edition* (Vol. 19). London: Hogarth.

Greenberg, J., & Mitchell, S. (1983). *Object relations in psychoanalytic theory.* Cambridge: Harvard University Press.

Mahler, M. S., Pine, F., & Bergman, A. (1975). *The psychological birth of the human infant.* New York: Basic Books.

Mitchell, S. A. (1988). *Relational concepts in psychoanalysis.* Cambridge: Harvard University Press.

Pine, F. (1985). *Developmental theory and clinical process.* New Haven and London: Yale University Press.

Stern, D. (1985). *The interpersonal world of the infant.* New York: Basic Books.

Sullivan, H. (1953). *The interpersonal theory of psychiatry.* New York: Norton.

Tessman, L. H. (1978). *Children of parting parents.* New York: Jason Aronson.

CHAPTER 5

A Psychoeducational Approach to Intervention

Barbara A. Rothlisberg
Ball State University

Agnes E. Shine
Mississippi State University

The psychoeducational perspective offers a method for objectively evaluating individuals for the purpose of educational diagnosis and classification. This perspective is not derived from a unified set of theoretical principles; actual implementation of testing techniques and interpretive strategies is dependent upon the theoretical orientation of the psychoeducational examiner. Prescriptive interventions for modifying behavior and remediating educational difficulties are then drawn from the range of techniques provided by other educational or psychological theories.

STRATEGY ORIENTATION

Calling the "psychoeducational approach" a theoretical orientation is somewhat misleading. It assumes that this method of psychological data analysis arose from a specific, unified, theoretical framework which determines the way in which information is interpreted. Instead, the psychoeducational perspective is not a theory per se, but a decision-making strategy associated with the particular kinds of data collected in school settings when a child is experiencing educational difficulties. Therefore, it can be thought of as a data-driven approach rather than a theory-driven approach. Because of the approach's association with the educational setting, its application can be ascribed to the psychological specialty of school psychology. Grounded in early attempts to apply psychological research findings to the real-world educational needs of children, the psychoeducational perspective has a heritage that draws heavily from several disciplines—psychometrics (i.e., the testing movement), academic and research psychology, and education (Reynolds, Gutkin, Elliot, & Witt, 1984; Trachtman, 1981; Wisland, 1974). As such, its implementation by practitioners is highly individualistic. Consequently, the way in which data sources are combined and interpreted depends upon the theoretical predisposition and training of the psychological examiner involved. At its best, however, the approach attempts to objectively measure interindividual and intraindividual differences in the hope of explaining and assisting educational performance.

In practice, the psychoeducational approach also may shift in orientation with the prevailing psychological/educational attitudes of the time or fall prey to the fads of either discipline (Bardon, 1989; Reynolds et al., 1984; Tindall, 1979; Trachtman, 1981). For example, current psychoeducational evaluations are molded by the practical and/or legal requirements of educational institutions to diagnose conditions that interfere with an individual's ability to function academically. Federal legislation (e.g., P.L. 94–142 and P.L. 99–457) stipulates that diagnosis and intervention in cases of exceptional educational need must be conducted to insure both ethical and equal treatment (Abramowitz, 1981; Sattler, 1988). To this end, specific categories of exceptionality (e.g., mental retardation, emotional disturbance, learning disability) have been created and defined in psychometric terms to offer guidance to the identification process. Information derived from psychoeducational testing is used within a multidisciplinary team setting to support or discount diagnoses of exceptionality using the procedural framework set down by law. Therefore, a major function in the psychoeducational decision-making process involves the diagnosis and classification of educational disabilities so that alternative placement options can be considered.

HISTORICAL DEVELOPMENT

While the traditional psychoeducational approach is heavily laced with norm-referenced assessment procedures, the "birth" of the perspective appears to have preceded the introduction of testing instruments as they are currently known (French, 1984). For example, much of the credit for the present existence of school psychology can be traced to Lightner Witmer at the end of the nineteenth century (Baker, 1988; French, 1984). Witmer's training in the experimental methods of Wundt, and his tutelage under James McKeen Cattell, may have created the impetus for Witmer's passion for applied psychology and for psychoeducational evaluation.

Early Antecedents

During the nineteenth century, forces were at work that fostered increased interest in individual differences. Perceptions of the mentally retarded were coming under scrutiny along with a growing interest in new training techniques. The measurement of sensory and motor behaviors intrigued such early researchers as Galton and Wundt, and led to the development of both the experimental strategies and statistical methods necessary to access information on the parameters of human performance (Anastasi, 1988; Gould, 1981; Wisland, 1974). Thus, the desire to understand the range of abilities in populations and the mechanisms to measure them furthered the perception of psychology as a science and suggested the practical applicability of psychological principles to concrete problems.

J. M. Cattell brought to the United States the orientation that mental testing may be useful in predicting academic success. Cattell helped to meld the experimental approach advocated by Wundt and the anthropometric assessment of Galton into a plan to investigate the individual differences present in educational achievement (French, 1984). As Cattell's student, Witmer believed that psychology could be advanced by the application of its tenets to practical issues and, in addition, saw the handicapped child as a natural client for such applied psychology. To formalize the study of individual differences, he opened the first psychological clinic in Philadelphia in 1896 and treated children thought to be suffering from "mental and moral" retardation (Baker, 1988; French, 1990). Children's skills were evaluated and treatment plans suggested. In his work, Witmer anticipated the use of the team concept for treatment and coined the term, "diagnostic teaching" (Baker, 1988). He believed that effective interventions were possible and that academic competency could be assessed through performance measures. Consequent educational treatment could then remediate learning deficits. Witmer's perspective on educational evaluation and treatment foretold the remedial perspectives to come.

The Early Twentieth Century

While the philosophy of a psychoeducational approach espoused by Witmer held appeal and provided a mechanism for service delivery based on the evaluation of individual differences, the early decades of the twentieth century saw no integrated implementation of such a strategy to educational issues (French, 1984, 1990; French & Hale, 1990). Trends such as the child study movement, the mental health movement, and the expansion of "child guidance clinics," as well as interest in the origins of intelligence encouraged the use of applied procedures but without clear professional guidelines for practice (Bardon,1981; French & Hale, 1990). For instance, the release of the first Binet scale (of intelligence) in the United States provided practitioners of the time with a tool with which to evaluate cognitive ability, but also served to highlight the varied way in which examiners were trained. Generally, anyone from teacher to physician might call themselves psychoeducational examiners and claim that they could assess a handicapped child's potential. In response, Wallin (as cited in Fagan, 1986) lamented the diversity of background among psychoeducational practitioners and the uneven training obtained by testers using the Binet test. However, while a professional training curricula was proposed in the 1920s that involved mental testing, the study of retardation, and clinical experience, training programs were unavailable that integrated the testing component with psychological and educational foundations (Fagan, 1986).

Although there was no general agreement about the range of skills a psychoeducational examiner should possess, expectations for practice were high. Walter (1925) devised a list of professional functions that could be attributed to school psychologists, psychoeducational examiners, or psychometrists (the labels attached to the practitioner were varied). These functions included research, the establishment of mental health programs in schools, and the direction of testing, both group and individual (Tindall, 1979). Therefore, it was implied by early commentators that practitioners of the psychoeducational approach should not only assess individuals but offer a unique perspective that related the best of psychological principles to the solution of academic dilemmas.

The approach's natural link with special education also afforded early practitioners an available and needy client population. As schools began to identify students for special class placement, school psychological practice became linked to the assessment process (Tindall, 1979). In fact, the principal task for psychoeducational examiners in metropolitan areas during the 1920s and 1930s was the testing of children for special education placement (French, 1984). Because of the connection between psychoeducational assessment and special education, state education agencies began to establish regulations for certification and employment to help insure competent practice. By the 1930s, attempts to recognize the status of and need for psychoeducational practitioners, and thereby assure training standards, were well under way (Trachtman, 1981). "The 'psychologist in the schools' concept began to fade and 'school psychology' was born" (French, 1984, p. 982).

Formative Development of the Profession

Identity diffusion for school psychologists persisted until the 1950s and the Thayer Conference. The conference, conducted under the auspices of the American Psychological Association, considered issues of qualifications, training, and functions for the professional specialty. School psychologists were defined as professional personnel who could provide an array of services to the schools including therapy, consultation, assessment, and program evaluation (Fagan, 1981; White & Harris, 1961). Unfortunately, the limited number of trained school psychologists and the accelerating demand for assessment services in special education strained the availability of service and led to a public perception of professional function confined to the testing role. The assessment context of practice was further reinforced in the 1970s by the passage of federal laws addressing the rights of special populations. Public Law 94–142—Education for all Handicapped Children Act of 1975—seemed to codify the school psychologist's function as primary diagnostician and tester within the educational context, at least as far as special education was concerned (Abramowitz, 1981; Reynolds et al., 1984; Trachtman, 1981). Regrettably, the designation of the school psychologist as tester or assessment expert tended to overshadow other aspects of training and practice. Thus, while breadth of training was (and is) required, actual school-based practice may be more restricted to assessment related contexts than psychologists prefer (Tindall, 1979).

Balancing Psychology and Education

A contrast between psychological and educational agendas in the profession of school psychology also has created dissonance in the implementation of the psychoeducational approach. The "rivalry" between these two philosophically distinct disciplines for supremacy within the profession (i.e., is school psychology more closely affiliated with psychology or education) has occurred in assessment as well as in other aspects of practice. For example, current discussions of future goals for the field have addressed the function of "classic" norm-referenced assessment procedures relative to curriculum-based methods in the planning and implementation of educational intervention. One faction of the profession is urging school psychology to be more educationally oriented (Fuchs & Fuchs, 1986; Lloyd & Loper, 1986) while another seems to support a stronger association with psychology (D'Amato & Dean, 1989).

It would appear then, that the development of the psychoeducational approach took place not only to further the applied study of psychology but to address the real educational requirements of children who were not able to function adequately in school. The "scientific" underpinnings of the perspective (i.e., experimental psychology and psychometrics) and its perceived ability to classify individuals according to skill level suggested that the psychoeducational method could clearly identify those for whom alternative educational techniques would be necessary.

CRITICAL ASPECTS

As mentioned earlier, the psychoeducational perspective is a problem-solving strategy rather than a theoretical paradigm. As such, it responds to the theoretical orientation of the practitioner using it. If the psychologist has a behavioral, developmental, dynamic, or other orientation, that perspective will make its way into the assessment strategy but there are certain presuppositions that are involved with the psychoeducational view (e.g., see Reynolds et al., 1984).

Evaluative Assumptions

First of all, the process undertaken can be equated with the scientific method of problem solving (Flavell, 1977). When there is a concern about a student's academic progress, he or she can be referred for evaluation to see if the student is exhibiting an exceptional educational need. The referral statement identifies the educational and/or behavioral areas of interest. Based on the referral information, a question or series of questions is formulated. For instance, if reading is the stated problem area, the psychologist and other professionals involved in the case would try to determine the kinds of data required to best describe the reading behaviors observed and review what interventions or modifications of instruction had already been explored. Alternative hypotheses are framed to try to explain how the student approaches the reading task. Certain explanations may seem more plausible than others, yet the psychologist will try to structure the evaluation in a way that provides information on the critical aspects of the referral and allow the strongest hypotheses to be addressed (Kaufman, 1979; Levine, 1987).

Second, to accomplish the hypothesis testing, the psychoeducational approach depends upon the appropriate use and interpretation of norm-referenced instruments. Since the perspective is so closely identified with psychometrics, it is likely that the observer will see a greater number of standardized testing instruments incorporated with this perspective than with others. Measures chosen for administration should relate to the issues involving the student as outlined by the referral question, yet also be as technically sound as possible (American Psychological Association, 1985). The psychologist should choose to use evaluation techniques that provide the most reliable and valid measurement available. Of course, such considerations must be weighed against the choice of tests or procedures that the professional thinks will provide the most clinically useful information (Dwyer, 1987).

Third, formal standardized assessment is complemented by other types of information (Dwyer, 1987; Stewart, Reynolds, & Lorys-Vernon, 1990). Consistencies and inconsistencies in the data are explored; supporting evidence is sought for hypotheses (Levine, 1987). Although the psychoeducational approach may focus efforts on the individual's qualities, his or her interaction with the environment cannot be denied. However, ecological or system variables are presently assessed with less rigor than the intrapersonal variables associated with traditional testing (Trachtman, 1981). Therefore, the psychoeducational approach may be seen to treat norm-referenced findings as the cornerstone of its assessment process.

It should be noted at this point that assessment, classification, and programming decisions are not undertaken solely by the school psychologist although he or she may play a critical role (Arasim & Frankenberger, 1989). Instead, multidisciplinary teams have been mandated by law to be responsible for the evaluation process (Bardon, 1983). The makeup of the multidisciplinary team will vary depending on the needs of the individual child (Davies, 1987). However, school-based personnel (i.e., school psychologist, administrator, counselor, special, and regular education teachers) and parents are most often involved. The use of the multidisciplinary team format was designed to improve service through the provision of a broader range of opinions and treatment options than would be available from a single professional. Group decision making represents a means to reduce bias and afford a better understanding of the conclusions reached (Abelson & Woodman, 1983; Pryzwansky & Rzepski, 1983). Each team member contributes to the data collection process. Therefore, while the psychologist typically completes the ability testing, others on the team may take charge of observations, interviews, or other kinds of assessment. The combined efforts of the team should provide a rich and complete view of the student so that appropriate decisions about student status are a result.

Relation of Evaluation to Intervention

Testing in and of itself serves no purpose unless it results in a clearer understanding of the child and the way the child relates to the academic enterprise (Stewart et al., 1990). Assessment becomes useful if it promotes positive change for the child involved. Thus, synthesis and evaluation of test data should lead to effective interventions (Kaufman, 1979; Levine, 1987; Reynolds et al., 1984). The psychologist might be the responsible party for establishing a diagnosis, but the psychoeducational intervention planned will depend upon the active professional participation of other multidisciplinary team members. The goal of the psychoeducational approach is to provide the individual with an opportunity to succeed in school; thus, any component of the child–school interaction can come under scrutiny and be considered for change.

Since the psychoeducational approach is atheoretical and functions as a problem-solving method to answer diagnostic/prescriptive questions, it provides no predetermined direction for prescriptive change. The practitioner is therefore challenged by the flexibility such an open-ended process offers to pull from his or her understanding of other theoretical positions a set of workable recommendations. While such flexibility can allow a great range of potential treatment options, it has been rebuked as ineffective because no integrated treatment stance follows directly from test data. Psychologists have tried to counter complaints regarding the applicability of test results by searching for commonalities in student performance using case typing or profile analysis to structure their educational interventions (Rosner & Selznik, 1987).

Generally, educational programming is effective when it is geared to the level of the learner and offers a means to motivate effort (Rosner & Selznik, 1987). It has been widely acknowledged that learners exhibit unique patterns of strengths and weaknesses and that some understanding of common patterns might assist in structuring programs for learning difficulties (Kaufman, 1979; Lyon, 1988). However, the range of learner profiles makes matching prescriptive suggestions to specific students an inexact process at best.

A good illustration of early efforts to remediate academic deficits through analysis of student characteristics can be seen in the implementation of the diagnostic-remedial teaching model in special education. The model reached prominence in the decades of the 1960s and 1970s and was based on the assumption that failure to perform academically was the result of a dysfunction in one or more of the basic underlying psychological processes. The processes involved included perceptual, integrative, and expressive functions and were related to either auditory, visual, motor, or psycholinguistic domains (Arter & Jenkins, 1979; Bateman, 1967). The belief that one needed only to identify the area(s) of information-processing difficulty before applying the appropriate prescriptive instructional treatment spoke to the perceived power of and faith in diagnostic instruments to accurately define component processing skills as well as the educator's ability to intervene (Arter & Jenkins, 1979; Mann, 1971). The diagnostic-remedial perspective oriented attention not only on what to teach but how to teach; curriculum was less critical than the child's purported learning profile (Bateman, 1967; Sabatino, 1971). This treatment model created a number of coordinated remedial programs specifically focused on helping the child attain processing competence (Arter & Jenkins, 1979).

Lerner (1981) presented a comprehensive overview of the variations in remedial systems available to educators devoted to treating processing difficulties. The options included Kephart's Perceptual-Motor Approach, Getman's Visuomotor Theory, and the Frostig System of Visual Perception. Suffice it to say that each method advocated the training of basic perceptual or motor abilities as a means of correcting underlying processing weaknesses that interfered with the attainment of academic skills. Unfortunately, although the training programs seemed to improve student responses to the perceptual, motor, or linguistic tasks employed, little evidence of academic gain accumulated in favor of such processing approaches to remediation (Arter & Jenkins, 1979; Glass, 1988). Current intervention tactics drawn from instructional, cognitive, and behavioral psychology recognize the interaction between learner, teacher, and task and direct prescriptive efforts beyond the internal characteristics of the child.

In Summary: Overview of the Approach

Within the past century, the belief that educational decision making could be improved by consideration of individual differences in academic performance spurred the development of a psychoeducational perspective. This position is psychometrically based and has as its main outcome the ability to diagnose categories of exceptional educational need. Once diagnosis is accomplished the problem-solving strategies used to formulate hypotheses about learner characteristics are turned to a consideration of treatment options but these options must be borrowed from other theoretical approaches since the psychoeducational method subscribes to no one theoretical base. Therefore, the treatment recommendations will vary depending on the psychologist's ingenuity and philosophy toward educational change.

In order to get a clearer view of the functional orientation of the psychoeducational approach it seems that exploration of the actual case material is now warranted.

CASE ANALYSIS: TYPES OF INFORMATION CONSIDERED

As with other instances when clinical judgment is employed, it is difficult to explain the way in which different sources of information are combined by psychologists using the psychoeducational approach with case material. As mentioned previously, the problem-solving model is used to develop a set of hypotheses that can be compared and weighed against one another to determine which best explains the observed educational situation and answers the referral question. Essentially, the practitioner uses assessment procedures and interview material to reconstruct and understand the individual and the situation (Rosner & Selznick, 1987). Clues are investigated and sources checked to try to "solve the mystery" behind the individual's behavior. The outcome may be a specific diagnostic label and associated special education services or simply a more complete explanation of the student with suggestions on how the student's relation to the learning situation can be improved.

Historical and Observational Information

The Referral.   The referral statement is typically the first definition of the student's problem that the practitioner reads. It raises questions about the types of behaviors that must be investigated. In Vince's case, the referral indicated that Vince has experienced a progressive decline in school performance with a concurrent increase in problem behaviors. These statements help to frame and provide a context for data collection. First, the practitioner determines what the referral sources meant by "progressive decline" and "problem behavior." Clinical interviews with Vince, his parents, and/or his teachers establish how the statements were operationalized (i.e., exact descriptions of behaviors/actions that are problematic). After the areas of investigation have been delineated, each piece of information collected (e.g., formal assessment, interview, observation) is reviewed for clues that explain the referral questions.

Medical History.   Vince's medical background might be reviewed first since such information could suggest hypotheses as well as offer etiological information on current conditions. It seemed that Vince's birth as well as early physical development was normal with the exception of the reported ear infections and febrile convulsions. While no additional indicators of long-term hearing impairment were provided, reference to delayed language development was made. An inability to accurately discriminate sounds could have accounted for the slowing of Vince's speech (Gulick, Gesheider, & Frisina, 1989; Vess, Gregory, & Moore, 1987). Likewise, the presence of medication, in this case phenobarbital, can cause drowsiness or behavioral difficulties (Gadow, 1986a) and influence development of language or motor behaviors.

A psychologist would also be alert to the potential effects, both immediate and residual, of the Ritalin prescribed when Vince was 8 years old (Gadow, 1986b; Mattes &

Gittleman, 1983). Since such drug therapy is designed to help improve attention in educational settings, evidence to this effect would be sought. In addition, the psychologist would be interested in the behavior changes Vince experienced once the medication was withdrawn. Given that no direct reference was made to Ritalin therapy in Vince's academic records and that he was expelled during the period when he reportedly was medicated, the prescribed treatment did not appear to alleviate concerns about Vince's behavior.

Possible Hypothesis: A residual language difficulty.

Family Interactions. Although the psychoeducational approach would be intimately concerned about the educational experiences of the referred individual, there would also be interest in the interpersonal/social events to which the person was exposed. In Vince's case, his parents' divorce apparently constituted a critical event in his family background. The divorce occurred in the period when Vince's activity level increased and medication was prescribed. Research in the area of divorce and its impact on children indicates that the event may have a greater negative impact on boys than girls and that subsequent behavioral and academic difficulties may ensue (Hetherington, 1989; Kaye, 1988–1989; Knoff, 1987). In addition, Vince's response to his reconstituted family was mixed; he seemed to respond well to the support and needs of his stepsister but reserves judgment on or blames his stepfather for the rift with his biological father. Coupled with changes in the family constellation, there was evidence of inconsistent discipline and a lack of attention by both father and stepfather. Vince's reaction to his lack of control over family events and the inattention by male role models might be related to the acting out behavior commented upon in the referral. Vince has learned he can receive needed attention by behaving inappropriately.

Possible Hypothesis: Behavioral problems are a method of receiving attention or venting frustration when control is lost.

Educational History. Given Vince's current academic decline, his educational background should be scrutinized closely to see if behavioral patterns are evident.

Since preschool development indicated hearing difficulties and language delays, school behaviors associated with language function would be of particular interest. Indeed, Vince's early grades in reading and spelling were lower than those in applied areas like science and math while recitation and memory work were described as the least satisfactory areas. The language-related difficulties were again highlighted in sixth grade when writing, grammar, and sentence diagramming were recorded as particularly difficult. Present performance continues to indicate problems with written language whether it be in the completion of assigned work or in the organization of any written product.

Aside from concerns over language, Vince's behavioral responses to academic and social situations must be reviewed. Even early elementary reports commented upon his difficulty controlling frustration when tasks became difficult. Perhaps when school frustrations were compounded by family upheaval, Vince was particularly prone to "acting up" in class.

Vince had to deal with several academic transitions during his school career. For example, Vince moved from a private parochial to a public school setting after fourth grade. This required him to adjust to a new peer group as well as new teachers. Adjustment to such a new routine and new expectations may have an influence on subsequent academic progress (Goldsmith & Clark, 1987). Surprisingly, Vince's performance in fifth grade demonstrated the ability to achieve at grade level and work cooperatively in team sports. This indicated that Vince had the capability not only to achieve but to relate well to peers when teamwork was required. Since behavioral concerns were not an issue during this grade, the school psychologist may entertain the notion that Vince's problematic actions are related to situations when Vince's self-perceived educational competence is at risk and/or when interactions with teachers are strained. In essence, then, learning or behavior problems are not a constant, global phenomena but specific to particular contexts. Vince's fifth-grade teacher had a relaxed attitude to discipline and may have been a valued model for Vince. Thus, the practitioner might investigate how Vince currently views different teachers and subject areas to determine if identifiable patterns of reaction exist.

In sixth grade when written language issues strongly surfaced, Vince was faced with a complex school context. Previously, Vince appeared to have one teacher for all content classes. Teacher-directed work assignments may have been the norm and provided Vince with a necessary structure. In sixth grade, he had to adapt to multiple teachers and probably take more responsibility for his own work. Vince may not have the organizational skills or sense of maturity necessary to make this transition. His ability to adapt to varied classrooms or teachers and his problem-solving flexibility need to be considered when attempting to understand his responses to educational situations.

Interview data as well as direct observation proposed that Vince is defensive about his educational performance and may not have the most efficient coping strategies for dealing with failure. For example, Vince downplayed the need for academic success and reported that he "could get a job in his stepfather's business" yet displayed frustration with the results of his math quiz (e.g., sitting and staring straight ahead without responding to teacher inquiries). Such behavioral responses strengthen the need to evaluate academic skill level, and Vince's view of his academic experience.

Possible Hypotheses: 1. Vince has a written language deficit that makes it difficult for him to complete written assignments.

2. Vince's behavioral problems result from frustration over classwork and an inability to cope with academic and personal inadequacies.

3. Vince may not have flexible problem-solving strategies or organizational skills to effectively work at grade level.

In Summary.   Information obtained from the review of Vince's background and supplemental data from interviews affords a picture of Vince in context. The associations between historical and present status will help structure the more formal aspects of the assessment and suggest several avenues of investigation to the psychoeducational evaluator. Possible explanations for Vince's behavior are kept in mind as data collection continues. Corroborating evidence could strengthen some hypotheses while conflicting evidence could weaken others.

Formal Testing

Formal testing involves the use of standardized, norm-referenced instruments. Use of such tests allows the psychologist to gather an objective sample of behavior yet provides a reference group from which to evaluate performance (Anastasi, 1988). In the formal testing of a child, the cognitive domain has particular relevance for the psychoeducational approach. Since the institution of the Binet test in the early 1900s, intellectual testing has taken the pivotal position in assessment armamentaria (Sattler, 1988). Faith in the utility of cognitive measurement can also be estimated by its integration into the legal mandates that help define exceptional educational status. For instance, the academic designation of learning disability is operationalized to include reliance on cognitive information; a significant discrepancy between ability and achievement scores is to be obtained before this classification is assigned (Rothlisberg, 1987). In addition, the broad spectrum of abilities measured in a typical intelligence test may help to generate a range of hypotheses. Because the items on an ability test require the synthesis of multiple elements, the psychologist can look for patterns in performance and observe whether particular combinations of capabilities appear to be strengths or weaknesses. Hence, apart from the total score or product, the intelligence test can offer indications of the process in which the examinee engaged to solve the items or tasks presented (Kaufman, 1979).

Cognitive Assessment.   In Vince's case, the Wechsler Intelligence Scale for Children– Revised (WISC–R) was chosen as the primary cognitive measure. Numerous studies attest to the WISC–R's validity and reliability in assessing ability (Eastabrook, 1984; Hutton & Davenport, 1985; Keith & Novack, 1987; Lawson & Inglis, 1988; Nichols, Inglis, Lawson, & MacKay, 1988; Sattler & Ryan, 1981; Schuerger & Witt, 1989; Tingstrom & Pfeiffer, 1988), as well as its popularity as an ability test (Chattin & Bracken, 1989). Computed WISC–R subtest scores can be used as an initial "yardstick" to test the relevance of inferred hypotheses. Kaufman (1979) provided a systematic method for evaluating the meaning of WISC–R performance in the context of this hypothesis testing. The interpretive procedure systematically moves from consideration of the most global combination of scores through qualitative analysis of items within a subtest to aid in hypothesis generation. As a consequence, performance is seen as a totality, with each item or subtest relevant to the understanding of the others and to other data sets in the evaluation. Just as Verbal and Performance Scale scores can be compared with one another, the psychologist can look at factor scores or combinations of subtests to generate, support, or dismiss hypotheses.

Vince's obtained scores placed him within the upper limits of the average range. His Verbal Scale score was significantly higher than his Performance score, implying a preference for verbally oriented tasks. Within each scale, Vince's subtest performance showed little fluctuation or inconsistency. Vince's fund of knowledge may be relatively weak; however, given his history of marginal academic performance, it may not be surprising that his recall of factual information is not as extensive as that of his peers.

The strength of Vince's verbal score is somewhat unexpected given his delayed language development and his purported written language difficulties. Yet, verbal subtests demand more than just verbal skill. Performance also may require crystallized ability or a well-ingrained method of problem solution. For instance, ability with sequential, step-by-step procedures of problem solving should work well with the language-related subtests. The items are structured in such a way that ambiguity of response expectations may be avoided; items are similar to what the child experiences in a typical educational setting. In contrast, the Performance Scale of the WISC–R necessitates a greater flexibility of problem solution. The individual must organize and analyze relatively unique tasks to receive a high score. This unusual task demand is also present on the Test of Nonverbal Intelligence (TONI) where the examinee must discern the relation between displayed figures. If a hypothesis of organizational difficulty or inflexibility to problem solving is entertained for Vince, the pattern of WISC–R and TONI performance supports this notion.

Elements of the Halstead–Reitan Neuropsychological Battery (HRNB) also appeared to integrate well with the WISC–R and TONI to bolster understanding of Vince's cognitive functioning. Typically, the HRNB information would not be available to the practitioner of the psychoeducational approach because of the demands it makes in terms of specialized training, equipment, and administration time. Nevertheless, when the HRNB has been administered, it allows for the estimation of cortical integrity. Vince reportedly displayed some impairment on several of the subtests of the battery. He had some difficulty with the Category Test, which measures concept formation and the ability to learn from feedback, as well as with Speech-Sounds Perception, which can be influenced by concentration skills. Other areas of suggested deficit included mental flexibility (Trails B) and tactile perception of spatial relations (TPT-dominant) (Rattan, Rattan, Dean, & Gray, 1989). The results of Vince's performance on the HRNB, in the context of other cognitive measures, lend further support to the idea that he may not be at his best when dealing with novelty or when he must adjust his problem-solving method.

Possible Hypotheses: 1. Inflexibility in problem-solving situations.

2. Difficulties in organizing material.

Language and Achievement.   Once cognitive ability data have been evaluated, practitioners can use them as a foundation for comparison with more circumscribed data sources. For example, since Vince scored in the average range cognitively, he would be expected to maintain a similar performance on achievement measures. Frankly, if consistency between achievement and ability is supported by test data, the presence of a learning difficulty is often discounted and other avenues examined to explain the lack of successful adjustment to school. If an inconsistency is established between tested ability and achievement, the operationalization of learning disability may allow for a formal diagnosis. In Vince's case, the significant discrepancy between his ability as measured by the WISC–R and academic achievement as measured by the Woodcock–Johnson Tests of Achievement (WJTA) in the area of written language supports the multiple references to learning difficulties in written expression found in the supplemental case information (i.e., parent reports, teacher reports, writing samples).

The presence of a written language deficiency tantalizes the practitioner with the challenge of explaining such a finding against the backdrop of solid WISC–R performance in the verbal area. With questions about language function as a constant thread through different aspects of the case material, the psychologist would consider whether the WISC–R provides an adequate sample of language capabilities. Unfortunately, the WJTA provides only an "atomistic assessment" of written expression (Bain, 1988). Written language can encompass everything from handwriting and spelling to organization, writing style, and audience awareness. The WJTA evaluates only spelling, punctuation, and word usage. Thus, it cannot reflect the higher-order writing skills expected. Additional testing or writing samples would need to be requested to help pinpoint the exact state of Vince's writing skills. Samples of written work as well as discussion with Vince could shed light on the way in which he attacks written assignments (i.e., his method for organizing his thoughts, his editing process, etc.). However, anecdotal references to writing as well as observations of his behavior strongly suggested that Vince resists written work. This most complex of language skills appears to be the area in which Vince shows real and persistent difficulties. Vince may not be able to transfer the syntax and semantics of his speech to a written format. Accordingly, Vince's ability to apply grammatical rules, organize his thoughts, and write for an audience could be scrutinized for additional insights on his writing capacity (Levine, 1987).

Possible Hypothesis: Vince has a written language disability.

Once the cognitive and achievement areas have been assessed, the psychoeducational practitioner will select other domains to investigate (i.e., perceptual-motor, memory), depending on the additional data required. The test data provided in the present case far exceeds that which is normally available. Given that the information is present, the school psychologist could use it to build a composite picture of Vince.

Affective Assessment.   Despite its penchant for norm-referenced testing and a focus on ability and achievement, the psychoeducational perspective makes use of data from other psychological domains. Information about the student's reactions to and interactions with the classroom environment can provide depth to the survey information available from the academic testing. Aside from the scores obtained on the affective measures, the psychologist looks for recurring themes in client responses. For example, Vince's answers were evaluated to see if he is generally negative toward school or only specific aspects of it. The number of times a topic is addressed by a student may also be significant; repetition of ideas in different contexts gives the psychologist an indication of the student's level of concern or emotional intensity. For instance, the tone and frequency of Vince's comments about his father may offer evidence regarding the father's importance, or it could reflect the direction of the questioning undertaken by the psychologist.

Vince's responses offered documentation on a number of issues. For instance, it was reported that Vince had difficulty getting his ideas down on paper. Observations of Vince's behavior during the sentence-completion task and review of his final product might offer support for any written language hypotheses being made (i.e., long response time, erasures, etc.). Complexity of written response as well as meaning value could be appraised. To the sentence stem "School is . . . ", Vince added the term "bad." The examiner would need to determine whether "bad" was being used in the traditional sense or in the popular sense (i.e., cool, awesome, great). Additionally, sentence completions provided indications of the value Vince places on particular aspects of his life. Taken literally, Vince's responses seemed to indicate that he is impulsive, that school is not a rewarding place, and that physical appearance is an integral part of his self-esteem (i.e., "Girls often enjoy looking at my body."). The responses could be taken as accurate reflections of his reality. Vince is doing poorly in school and attaining less and less success academically. He also holds physical characteristics as important aspects of who he is, like others of his age (Siegel, 1982).

The recurrent themes of school and physical status were supported in other measures as well. For instance, Vince's responses to the Piers–Harris denoted difficulties in school-related areas and a strength in the physical domain. Hence, Vince seemed to consistently acknowledge academic concerns while making the most of his physical attributes. Physical status may be important to Vince not only for the usual reasons but because it affords him greater status with his peers, status not available through academic success. Paradoxically, social concerns displayed themselves in the Children's Manifest Anxiety Scale. Consequently, Vince may not feel as certain of his social status as his overt remarks or behaviors convey.

Evaluation of affective status can include the use of traditional personality measures like the TAT. Such instruments are used to help the psychologist gain insight into the motives of the student and how he or she may cope with various situations. Vince's stories suggested realistic themes and plots appropriate for teenagers. His characters experienced consequences implying that Vince is aware of the consequences of his actions. Interestingly, Vince's stories included plots involving couple relationships. He portrayed parents who are divorced as unhappy and parents who stay together as happy and contented. The psychologist could discuss such stories within the context of Vince's own experience to further expand on Vince's perceptions of his home life. Again, Vince did not appear to be accepting of his stepfather yet expressed care for his stepsister. The ambivalence toward elements of his family was not pursued in the case materials but could have helped to explain how Vince copes with changes in his life.

Possible Hypothesis: Vince has not yet resolved his feelings toward his parents' divorce. These emotions have "spilled over" to affect the concentration he needs for school.

Behavioral Adaptation. Up to this point, assessment instruments have focused upon the responses of the student. Another component of assessment can include the perceptions of others toward Vince. In this case study, the Behavior Evaluation Scale was used, with four teachers providing ratings. Difficulties can be associated with such respondent ratings. First, naive teachers may either gloss over a student's problems or exaggerate behavioral differences once they are asked to comment on their perceptions of student behavior. Second, a teacher may not know the student well enough to make informed ratings. When a number of teachers respond, a more accurate picture of the student emerges. Unfortunately, one cannot know if all teachers rated Vince using the same criteria of average performance.

It appeared that Vince's family living teacher demonstrated the greatest concern over Vince's behavior. Mathematics and physical education instructors reported no evidence of inappropriate behaviors. It seems, then, that academic or behavioral difficulties could be perceived as being curriculum or instructor specific. Since no information was available as to the course requirements (i.e., papers, tests, class presentations) for family living, the authors can only speculate as to the causes for Vince's inappropriate actions in this class.

However, Vince's average ratings in mathematics and physical education implied that Vince does have acceptable behaviors within his behavioral repertoire. His capacity to behave situationally may suggest a better outlook for positive change since the responses sought by the educational setting seem available but underutilized.

CASE SYNTHESIS: THE COMPOSITE PICTURE

Once data sources have been reviewed, the school psychologist selects those case elements that he or she thinks are most critical to the student's perception of or reaction to the educational experience. The psychoeducational perspective is concerned first with the issues of diagnosis and then with improving the child's interaction with the school setting. The practitioner needs to effectively communicate what he or she thinks are the key hypotheses in the case to the other members of the team so that problem solving relative to intervention options can proceed (Shellenberger, 1982). Since the perspective wants to initiate positive educational change, the authors selected the following hypotheses as those most relevant to Vince's present educational experiences.

Hypotheses Selected as Relevant to Intervention:

1. Vince appears to have a written language deficit that makes it difficult for him to complete written assignments successfully.
   In addition,
2. organizational difficulties and
3. inflexibility in problem solving seem to be confounding factors in Vince's school responses.

As the members of the multidisciplinary team review the findings and opinions related to Vince's case, they would try first to agree to the presence or absence of a specific category of exceptional educational need. The major categories include mental retardation, emotional disturbance, and learning disability. The school psychologist's data on ability and achievement are critical to the selection of learning disabilities. This educational classification requires that a significant discrepancy be found between the student's intellectual performance and his capability to apply that ability to educational tasks. The discrepancy cannot be due to other handicapping conditions or because of cultural or instructional differences. Each state has adopted its own guidelines on learning disability diagnosis. In Vince's case, the school psychologist could propose a written language disability since a significant discrepancy is present between performance on the WISC–R and WJTA Written Language areas. Given this information, members of the committee would consider the strength of the evidence and propose action. If the multidisciplinary team agreed that there was sufficient evidence to suggest the presence of a learning disability, they would then determine the type of assistance to be offered. Programming options could range from placement within a regular education setting with resource assistance to placement in classes designed specifically for learning disabled students. The degree (i.e., the amount of time provided per day or week) of special education programming could also vary.

Although the committee structure may expand problem-solving options, it also can complicate service delivery. It is likely that interventions would be monitored by a special education teacher through the use of an individual educational plan (I.E.P.) if the committee rules that compelling evidence exists for a disability. However, responsibility for monitoring Vince's progress is less clear if Vince's difficulties are deemed too mild to warrant a specific diagnosis (Davies, 1987). Typically, the psychologist does not directly implement his or her recommendations so follow-through with suggested interventions is not assured. It would therefore be appropriate for the multidisciplinary team to select one of its members to monitor and account for change in student functioning.

Vince and his family should be invited to participate in the multidisciplinary review of Vince's case. Family involvement is not only sought but can aid in clarifying information presented. It also can serve the purpose of investing the student and his family in academic change and clear up any concerns relative to Vince's performance. For example, if Vince were operating under the misconception that he is less able intellectually than his peers, his performance on the ability test should correct that. Vince could be enlisted to change and be presented with options that suit his personal style and expectations. Based on the case data, the authors hypothesize that Vince's behavioral difficulties are a result of his underlying deficits in the written language area and general aspects of organizational habits and problem-solving flexibility and are further exacerbated by issues of family and self-acceptance. Vince seems to be fighting a battle to preserve his sense of self and perceived importance despite shifts in his school and home life. Since his youth, Vince has had to adjust to changes in schools and to a family life in which his needs may not have been judged as a consideration (Pollack, 1985). His father's lack of time, his teachers' sensitivity (or lack thereof) to his speech difficulties, and the impression he may have gained from Ritalin treatment or from his school expulsion could have implied that there was something intrinsically "wrong" with him. Such self-perception may have culminated in his current attitude of maintaining an image and refusing to admit to the need for assistance. Yet, an encouraging component to Vince's performance is that he can behave appropriately when written self-expression is not expected and/or when the instructor is perceived positively. Thus, teachers in Mathematics and Physical Education did not express behavioral concern while instructors in Family Living and English did. Vince may then respond appropriately when he perceives himself as valued and competent and perhaps when guidelines for performance are consistent and clear. It seems that a sense of competence and control is essential if Vince is to change his attitude toward school.

It was decided by the authors that recommendations for changing Vince's behavior would center on academic issues. General attitude change could occur as an associated benefit. Although family factors played an important role in Vince's interaction with school, intervention in the family unit could be beyond the scope of the educational resources available (other psychologists may disagree; see for example, O'Hara & Levy, 1988). It was perceived that family intervention could not provide the potential for immediate change that other procedures might secure. In other words, Vince's school behaviors cannot wait for additional months or years for his relationships with his family members to be resolved. The psychoeducational approach as applied here considers intervention options that encourage immediate modifications in the academic situation.

INTERVENTION OPTIONS

As outlined earlier, intervention may be the most difficult component of an evaluation because no standard approach is available that guarantees educational change. However, prescriptions for change must consider the here-and-now needs of the client. Intervention strategies should be designed to improve Vince's academic skills as well as his ability to learn from past experiences and cope with disappointment.

Vince's hypothesized difficulties involve written language, organization, and flexibility in problem solving. It is believed that these problems engender negative behavioral and emotional reactions that exacerbate Vince's ineffective approach to his class work. Although all parties in the case may recognize the validity of the hypotheses, they will also need to be made aware that Vince's problem areas defy simple solution. After all, he has had years to establish his method of dealing with academic requirements. In addition, the areas selected for intervention are not independent of one another; therefore, one cannot address organization outside a particular context. Written products depend upon the organization of ideas in a logical sequence; likewise, different forms of writing require flexibility in writing approach and an awareness of the potential audience. True change in academic behavior will need a concerted effort on several fronts.

One of the first issues the school psychologist will need to consider is the range of treatment options. Often a given set of recommendations is less aligned with one specific orientation than it is to approaches with which the psychologist has experienced some success. In essence, then, the practitioner can make suggestions based upon several theoretical orientations.

After consideration of the hypotheses, the authors selected potential interventions that could encourage positive educational change. These suggestions seemed to encompass several schools of thought (perhaps as eclectic as the psychoeducational approach itself) with the majority apparently associated with behavioral, cognitive, or instructional psychology.

Behaviorally Oriented Recommendations

Behavioral psychology, through its modification procedures and task analysis, has established itself as a premier approach for educational change. It identifies the degree of task or situational manipulation necessary to facilitate learning. Within its scope of analysis, the psychologist could suggest sequencing of subskills, consideration of the pacing of instruction, the amount and type of instruction and feedback administered, as well as teacher and self-monitoring procedures (Bergan, 1990; Wong, 1988).

> The behavioral approach to remediation of academic-related behaviors is defined by the characteristics: (1) individualization and mastery learning, (2) direct teaching, and (3) emphasis on measurement. (Neeper & Lahey, 1988, p. 5)

In Vince's case, his written language difficulty could involve many levels of performance and increase the chances that he will resist completing written assignments. His problems with written expression may make him argumentative when he is asked to perform. A first step to increasing performance may simply involve increasing the amount of work Vince completes and decreasing the negative response made to individual teachers. Teachers could also provide guidelines or frameworks for Vince to follow when he is presented with an actual writing task. Recommendations reflecting a behavioral method could include the following:

1. Vince and his parents and teachers should be asked to cooperate on the development of a behavioral contract. The contract needs to specify the level at which completed assignments are necessary in his classes. This will accommodate Vince's need for structure and direction. The contract will stipulate a specific behavior change (for example, number of completed written assignments) and outline the consequences for success or failure. All involved parties would be enlisted in behavioral change; the participants would recognize that improvements in Vince's assignment-completing behavior do not occur in isolation. The contracting procedure offers guidelines for all parties, allows for measurement of change, and can be renegotiated as behaviors evolve. Thus, such shaping of behavior allows reinforcement of interim steps while encouraging further improvement in completed work.

   Once rate of work completion increases, attention is directed to the quality of work produced. Resource materials are available that provide a broad array of intervention suggestions (see, for example, Cummins, 1988; Maher & Zins, 1987; McCarney & Cummins, 1988). Specific interventions are based on the results of ongoing performance analyses.
2. Vince showed poor performance on the Written Language Cluster of the Woodcock–Johnson. The behaviors involved in answering the questions on this cluster consist of spelling and comprehension of basic rules of punctuation and word usage. Therefore, component writing skills could be addressed.
   a. Vince could be instructed in dictionary use to help correct his spelling errors. A teacher or peer could model an appropriate method of attack when spelling is questioned. Vince would have opportunities to practice this skill and monitor his performance.
   b. If a computer is available, Vince could be encouraged to learn a word processing package complete with a spell check. If handwriting is a problem, the word processing component also could eliminate issues of legibility in writing.
   c. Vince could be given exercises in English class that support practice in grammatical rules. His English teacher could explain the utility of grammatical relations and offer Vince a chance to exercise his understanding of rule usage. Specific exercises could reinforce Vince's ability to identify word tenses, noun–verb agreement, and punctuation.
   d. Vince might be asked to edit the work of his peers to get him to employ the rules covered in class. Feedback given could reinforce his successful application of the modeled skills.
3. To improve the organization of Vince's written work, the teacher could model organizational strategies for Vince and provide him with an outline that details

the important elements in developing a paragraph or story. He would practice constructing paragraphs following the model provided. In addition,

a. Vince's teachers could provide him with isolated sentences and ask him to order them to make a sensible story.

b. Vince could edit written samples and be asked to strike sentences that do not belong or are out of context.

Performance could be monitored in terms of the percentage of material accurately edited. Increases in level of accuracy should offer Vince an impetus for continued improvement.

Since organizational skills can impinge on a student's effective studying, intervention recommendations could be made here as well.

4. Vince could be asked to keep track of the amount of time he studies each day with the intent of increasing the length of time he spends on such activity.

5. Teachers could be asked to provide Vince with objective sheets helping him to define the key elements in the class work and structure the use of his time. Instead of leaving him to his own devices to determine the major conceptual points in a class, the objective sheets would provide him with the conceptual framework he may find necessary to organize the material.

The behavioral approach appears particularly useful in highlighting the areas for change and for specifying exactly the skills needed for academic progress. Unfortunately, this method of intervention may not adequately define how the skills can be taught in a way that modifies the student's thinking process (Neeper & Lahey, 1988). In other words, behaviorally based recommendations may "fix" the outward trappings of educational performance through imposing solutions to problem situations on the learner; they may be less effective in restructuring and expanding the learner's self-initiated method of problem attack.

Cognitive/Instructional Recommendations

Although many behavioral methods of intervention include aspects of cognitive modification as part of their agenda for change (see for example, Meichenbaum, 1977), interventions based on a cognitive or instructional psychology orientation tend to emphasize the information-processing components of learning and view the educational experience as student directed rather than teacher directed.

> A cognitive approach to educating learning disabled students advocates the following. First, learning disabled students must actively participate in their learning and must assume control of the learning situation. . . . Second, it is important for teachers to inculcate in learning disabled students self-monitoring, planning, and self-evaluation skills. (Wong, 1988, p. 20)

Instead of reacting to the learning situation as it has been structured by the teacher, the student must actively participate in the learning exchange. It is hoped that this student empowerment will create actual changes in student thought and in active responsibility for the learning process.

The proactive stance of cognitive psychology to make inefficient learners efficient is based on research investigating models of information processing. Findings on the roles of attention and perception in task situations have begun to define the parameters of learning and point out where learning strategies may be implemented or improved (Glover & Corkill, 1990; Wiig, 1984). For example, students' perception of new material seems to hinge on the availability of prior knowledge. Consequently, providing a context for learning so that new learning is meaningful can aid in acquisition. Tactics such as advanced organizers, mnemonics, imagery, and questioning techniques seem to facilitate efficient learning by pointing out the key aspects of the task (Wiig, 1984). Likewise, making students aware of their own thinking processes can personalize the learning experience; students "own" learning and thus may think of it as an integral part of development (Glover & Corkill, 1990; Wong, 1988).

Instructional psychology subsumes cognitive psychology under an umbrella involving the interaction of the student with the educational environment. Not only do student behaviors and cognitions come under scrutiny, but the task requirements and teacher behaviors do as well (Kamphaus, Yarbrough, & Johanson, 1990; Simmons & Kameenui, 1990). Under this system, the focus for change expands beyond the learner and can be placed on instructional methods/teacher behaviors and/or the tasks themselves. Instruction is driven by the learner's needs; the learner is not shaped to fit the standards demanded by instruction (McKee & Witt, 1990). In addition, academic skills are not as easily separated into compartments but may be viewed in a more wholistic fashion. For instance, written expression is not really separate from other aspects of the curriculum and cannot be confined to an English class. Students must see its relevance for other classes and for learning in general (Chiang & Ford, 1990; Dagenais & Beadle, 1984).

As with the recommendations for changes listed as representing the behavioral approach to intervention, those following will try to address the needs Vince expressed regarding written language, organization, and problem-solving flexibility. Although they may superficially resemble behaviorally oriented prescriptions, their intended purpose is to affect either Vince's strategies for problem solving or adjust teacher behaviors and task requirements to maximize understanding and application of content. (Additional suggestions for instruction/intervention can be found in Englert & Raphael, 1988; Graham & Harris, 1988; Levy & Rosenberg, 1990.)

6. Vince's written expression has been designated as a problem area for him. He may not have the strategies in his behavioral repertoire to successfully cope with writing demands. Therefore, instructors need to focus on providing Vince with the tactics he needs to tackle written assignments.
   a. Writing subskills should not be addressed in isolation but be integrated into the total writing process. For example, spelling skills, punctuation, and word usage would not be seen as isolated writing exercises but as part of the greater whole of writing for meaning. The communication of his ideas would be the focus for Vince.
   b. Vince would be introduced to the various forms writing can take (narrative, expository, etc.). The teacher could provide Vince with a set of questions that would help him to identify the intent of the assignment (i.e., what is the purpose of the writing assignment, what is the topic, who is going to read it,

etc.), and the aspects that differentiate one form of writing from another. The questioning sequence would be modeled for him to show him how the procedure can work. Guided practice is then used to give Vince support in following through with the process. This could consist of teacher-guided practice, verbal rehearsal, or even peer interactions to aid him in establishing a clear understanding of the writing process.

c. In line with the suggestions above, the organizational aspects of writing could be addressed through the introduction of charting or mapping techniques. The instructor could model and explain the various organizational structures one could employ to sequence ideas. Group writing could also cement the ideas behind idea generation and organization (Levy & Rosenberg, 1990). Peer editing and review could also be introduced to reduce the amount of ''special attention'' given to Vince's difficulties. That is, the entire class might be given instruction in the kinds of organizational strategies available to them to accomplish written expression.

d. Independent writing could be encouraged through the use of journals or independent reaction sheets. Interested more in encouraging the act of writing, these assignments would not be evaluated for syntactic or spelling errors. Instead, personal practice in employing student-selected strategies could occur.

e. Once the writing process becomes more comfortable for Vince, he could be introduced to the ideas of revising and editing (Bos, 1988). Again, strategy options could be introduced and modeled by teacher or peers. Mnemonic devices or mapping techniques should be available to help Vince remember such tactics when he is asked to practice them independently.

7. Vince may need more time to complete his assignments than other students. Since he is having to learn methods of attacking a written assignment that his peers may have developed somewhat spontaneously, he will probably require additional time and direction in making the leap from his current level of writing to one more acceptable to teachers.

8. Vince's teachers may also need to consider lowering the number of assignments or decreasing their length so that Vince will be able to experience some positive writing experiences.

It should be noted that one of the strengths of the strategy, or cognitive/instructional approach, is that issues such as organization and problem-solving flexibility are ordinarily nested within recommendations for addressing academic skills. Because this process technique does not presuppose that the student has available to him or her a range of methods of problem attack, it sets out to define for the student his or her options for completing the task. This provides the student with greater personal control and ownership (Bos, 1988).

9. Vince could be aided in his study skills by introducing him to the various tactics available to improve understanding and recall. Different types of note-taking methods, approaches for reading, and organization of study time could be discussed and modeled for him. It is likely that, after trying out various methods

for the studying process, he could choose those most suited to his style of learning.

The suggestions for intervention have thus far have focused upon Vince as the central character in any proposal for change. It must also be acknowledged that the instructional environment and teacher behaviors may require adjustment. As the psychologist communicates to the members of the multidisciplinary team his or her information about Vince, he or she must be cognizant that the change process might very well also center on the teachers' interaction with Vince and other students. Consultation with teachers about their methods of organizing the classroom may be necessary here, particularly since only a subset of Vince's teachers expressed real concerns about his behaviors or academic performance. For example, one of the behavioral observations conducted observed that the English teacher did not follow through on the stated consequences for Vince's misbehavior. The lack of consistency in discipline could be influencing not only Vince's behavior but that of the entire class, setting the teacher up for a less effective teaching environment. Similarly, it would be necessary for the psychologist to offer to assist the Family Living instructor if he or she is having problems with class management. Teacher planning of classroom procedures, management of student behaviors, and aspects of instruction (i.e., review, presentation, practice, and evaluation) all will influence the quality and ease with which instruction occurs (McKee & Witt, 1990). Therefore the interventions resulting from consultation with teaching staff may have more far-reaching impact on future learning problems than those emphasizing the individual student. Improve instruction in general and all the students may benefit.

CONCLUDING REMARKS

The psychoeducational approach gained its reputation because it offered a means of diagnosing and classifying children who were unable to benefit from a regular educational environment. Since it is atheoretical in orientation and based upon analysis of individual performance relative to some normative group, it has been viewed by some as too generic to provide workable interventions promoting educational change. However, the authors submit that the core aspects of the process (i.e., a problem-solving strategy, use of norm-referenced instrumentation, flexibility in data collected) can provide an anchor from which the practitioner can investigate multiple hypotheses. Since the psychologist can integrate any number of theoretical viewpoints in his or her review of case material, the range of intervention options is limited only by the level of expertise available.

REFERENCES

Abelson, M. A., & Woodman, R. W. (1983). Review of research on team effectiveness: Implications for teams in schools. *School Psychology Review, 12*, 125–135.

Abramowitz, E. A. (1981). School psychology: A historical perspective. *School Psychology Review, 10*, 121–126.

American Psychological Association. (1985). *Standards for educational and psychological testing.* Washington, DC: Author.

Anastasi, A. (1988). *Psychological testing* (6th Ed.). New York: Macmillan.

Arasim, B., & Frankenberger, W. (1989). Assessment procedures used by multidisciplinary team members in the assessment of learning disabilities. *Mental Retardation and Learning Disability Bulletin, 17,* 38–50.

Arter, J. A., & Jenkins, J. R. (1979). Differential diagnosis-prescriptive teaching: A critical appraisal. *Journal of Educational Research, 49,* 517–555.

Bain, A. M. (1988). Written expression. In K. A. Kavale, S. R. Forness, & M. Bender (Eds.), *Handbook of learning disabilities (Vol. 2): Methods and interventions* (pp. 73–88). Boston: College-Hill.

Baker, D. B. (1988). The psychology of Lightner Witmer. *Professional School Psychology, 3,* 109–121.

Bardon, J. I. (1981). A personalized account of the development and status of school psychology. *Journal of School Psychology, 19,* 199–210.

Bardon, J. I. (1983). Viewpoints on multidisciplinary teams in schools. *School Psychology Review, 12,* 186–189.

Bardon, J. I. (1989). The school psychologist as an applied educational psychologist. In R. C. D'Amato & R. S. Dean (Eds.), *The school psychologist in nontraditional settings* (pp. 1–32). Hillsdale, NJ: Erlbaum.

Bateman, B. (1967). Three approaches to diagnosis and educational planning for children with learning disabilities. *Academic Therapy Quarterly, 2,* 215–222.

Bergan, J. R. (1990). Contributions of behavioral psychology to school psychology. In T. B. Gutkin and C. R. Reynolds (Eds.), *The handbook of school psychology* (2nd ed.) (pp. 126–142). New York: Wiley.

Bos, C. S. (1988). Process-oriented writing: Instructional implications for mildly handicapped students. *Exceptional Children, 54,* 521–527.

Chattin, S. H., & Bracken, B. A. (1989). School psychologists' evaluation of the K–ABC, McCarthy Scales, Stanford–Binet IV, and WISC–R. *Journal of Psychoeducational Assessment, 7,* 112–130.

Chiang, B., & Ford, M. (1990). Whole language alternatives for students with learning disabilities. *LD Forum, 16,* 31–34.

Cummins, K. K. (1988). *The teacher's guide to behavioral interventions.* Columbia, MO: Hawthorne Educational Services.

Dagenais, D. J., & Beadle, K. R. (1984). Written language: When and where to begin. *Topics in Language Disorders, 4,* 59–85.

D'Amato, R. C., & Dean, R. S. (Eds.). (1989). *The school psychologist in nontraditional settings. Integrating clients, services, and settings.* Hillsdale, NJ: Erlbaum.

Davies, D. G. (1987). Multidisciplinary team assessment. In K.A. Kavale, S. R. Forness, & M. Bender (Eds.), *Handbook of learning disabilities: Vol. 1: Dimensions and diagnosis* (pp. 363–377). Boston: College-Hill.

Dwyer, K. P. (1987). School psychology assessment. In K. A. Kavale, S. R. Forness, & M. Bender (Eds.), *Handbook of learning disabilities (Vol. 1): Dimensions and diagnosis* (pp. 325–347). Boston: College-Hill.

Eastabrook, G. E. (1984). A canonical correlation analysis of the Wechsler Intelligence Scale for Children–Revised and the Woodcock–Johnson Tests of Cognitive Ability in a sample referred for suspected learning disabilities. *Journal of Educational Psychology, 76,* 1170–1177.

Englert, C. S., & Raphael, T. E. (1988). Constructing well-formed prose: Process, structure, and metacognitive knowledge. *Exceptional Children, 54,* 513–520.

Fagan, T. K. (1981). Special educational services and the school psychologist. *Journal of Learning Disabilities, 14,* 383–384.

Fagan, T. K. (1986). The historical origins and growth of programs to prepare school psychologists in the United States. *Journal of School Psychology, 24,* 9–22.

Flavell, J. H. (1977). *Cognitive development*. Englewood Cliffs, NJ: Prentice Hall.

French, J. L. (1984). On the conception, birth, and early development of school psychology: With special reference to Pennsylvania. *American Psychologist, 39*, 976–987.

French, J. L. (1990). History of school psychology. In T. B. Gutkin and C. R. Reynolds (Eds.), *The handbook of school psychology* (2nd ed.) (pp. 3–20). NY: Wiley.

French, J. L., & Hale, R. L. (1990). A history of the development of psychological and educational testing. In C. R. Reynolds & R.W. Kamphaus (Eds.), *Handbook of psychological and educational assessment of children: Intelligence and achievement* (pp. 3–28). New York: Guilford.

Fuchs, L. S., & Fuchs, D. (1986). Linking assessment to instructional intervention: An overview. *School Psychology Review, 15*, 318–323.

Gadow, K. D. (1986a). *Children on medication* (Vol. 1). San Diego: College-Hill.

Gadow, K. D. (1986b). *Children on medication* (Vol. 2). San Diego: College-Hill.

Glass, G. V (1988). Controversial practices. In K. A. Kavale, S. R. Forness, & M. Bender (Eds.), *Handbook of learning disabilities (Vol. 2): Methods and interventions* (pp. 157–193). Boston: College-Hill.

Glover, J. A., & Corkill, A. J. (1990). The implications of cognitive psychology for school psychology. In T. B. Gutkin and C. R. Reynolds (Eds.). *The handbook of school psychology* (2nd ed.) (pp. 104–125). New York: Wiley.

Goldsmith, D. F., & Clark, E. (1987). Children and moving. In A. Thomas and J. Grimes (Eds.), *Children's needs: Psychological perspectives* (pp. 372–378). Washington, DC: NASP.

Gould, S. J. (1981). *The mismeasure of man*. New York: Norton.

Graham, S., & Harris, K. R. (1988). Instructional recommendations for teaching writing to exceptional students. *Exceptional Children, 54*, 506–512.

Gulick, W. L., Gescheider, G. A., & Frisina, R. D. (1989). *Hearing, physiological acoustics, neural coding and psychoacoustics*. New York: Oxford University Press.

Hetherington, E. M. (1989). Coping with family transition: Winners, losers, and survivors. *Child Development, 60*, 1–14.

Hutton, J. B., & Davenport, M. A. (1985). The WISC–R as a predictor of Woodcock–Johnson achievement cluster scores for learning disabled students. *Journal of Clinical Psychology, 41*, 410–413.

Kamphaus, R. W., Yarbrough, N.D., & Johanson, R. P. (1990). Contributions of instructional psychology to school psychology. In T. B. Gutkin and C.R. Reynolds (Eds.), *The handbook of school psychology* (2nd ed.) (pp. 143–174). New York: Wiley.

Kaufman, A. (1979). *Intelligent testing with the WISC–R*. New York: Wiley.

Kaye, S. H. (1988–1989). The impact of divorce of children's academic performance. Special issue: Children of divorce: Developmental and clinical issues. *Journal of Divorce, 12*, 283–298.

Keith, T. Z., & Novack, C. G. (1987). Joint factor structure of the WISC–R and K–ABC for referred school children. *Journal of Psychoeducational Assessment, 5*, 370–386.

Knoff, H. M. (1987). Children and divorce. In A. Thomas and J. Grimes (Eds.), *Children's needs: Psychological perspectives* (pp. 173–182). Washington, DC: NASP.

Lawson, J. S., & Inglis, J. (1988). Factorial verbal and performance IQ's derived from the WISC–R: Their psychometric properties. *Journal of Clinical Psychology, 44*, 252–258.

Lerner, J. W. (1981). *Learning disabilities: Theories, diagnosis, and teaching strategies* (3rd ed.). Boston: Houghton Mifflin.

Levine, M. D. (1987). *Developmental variation and learning disorders*. Cambridge, MA: Educators Publishing Service.

Levy, N. R., & Rosenberg, M. S. (1990). Strategies for improving the written expression of students with learning disabilities. *LD Forum, 16*, 23–30.

Lloyd, J. W., & Loper, A. B. (1986). Measurement and evaluation of task-related learning behaviors: Attention to task and metacognition. *School Psychology Review, 15*, 336–345.

Lyon, G. R. (1988). Subtype remediation. In K. A. Kavale, S. R. Forness, & M. Bender (Eds.), *Handbook of learning disabilities (Vol. 2): Methods and interventions* (pp. 33–58). Boston: College-Hill.

McCarney, S. B., & Cummins, K. K. (1988). *The prereferral intervention manual*. Columbia, MO: Hawthorne Educational Services.

McKee, W. T., & Witt, J.C. (1990). Effective teaching: A review of instructional, and environmental variables. In T. B. Gutkin and C. R. Reynolds (Eds.). *The handbook of school psychology* (2nd ed.) (pp. 821–846). New York: Wiley.

Maher, C. A., & Zins, J. E. (Eds.). (1987). *Psychoeducational interventions in the schools*. New York: Pergamon.

Mann, L. (1971). Psychometric phrenology and the new faculty psychology: The case against ability assessment and training. *Journal of Special Education, 5*, 3–14.

Mattes, J. A., & Gittleman, R. (1983). Growth of hyperactive children on maintenance regimen of methylphenidate. *Archives of General Psychiatry, 40*, 317–321.

Meichenbaum, D. (1977). *Cognitive behavior modification: An integrative approach*. New York: Plenum.

Neeper, R., & Lahey, B. B. (1988). Behavioral approaches. In K. A. Kavale, S. R. Forness, & M. Bender (Eds.). *Handbook of learning disabilities (Vol. 2): Methods and interventions* (pp. 3–18). Boston: College-Hill.

Nichols, E. G., Inglis, J., Lawson, J. S., & MacKay, I. (1988). A cross-validation study of patterns of cognitive ability in children with learning difficulties, as described by factorially defined WISC–R verbal and performance IQs. *Journal of Learning Disabilities, 21*, 504–508.

O'Hara, D. M., & Levy, J. M. (1988). Family intervention. In K. A. Kavale, S. R. Forness, & M. Bender (Eds.), *Handbook of learning disabilities (Vol. 2): Methods and interventions* (pp. 215–235). Boston: College-Hill.

Pollack, J. M. (1985). Pitfalls in the psychoeducational assessment of adolescents with learning and school adjustment problems. *Adolescence, 20*, 479–492.

Pryzwansky, W. B., & Rzepski, B. (1983). School-based teams: An untapped resource for consultation and technical assistance. *School Psychology Review, 12*, 174–179.

Public Law 94–142. (1975). *Federal Register.*

Public Law 99–457. (1986). *Federal Register.*

Rattan, A. I., Rattan, G., Dean, R. S., & Gray, J. W. (1989). Assessing the commonality of the WISC–R and the Halstead–Reitan Neuropsychological Test Battery with learning-disordered children. *Journal of Psychoeducational Assessment, 7*, 296–303.

Reynolds, C. R., Gutkin, T. B., Elliott, S. N., & Witt, J. C. (1984). *School psychology: Essentials of theory and practice*. New York: Wiley.

Rosner, S. L., & Selznick, R. (1987). Case-typing assessment. In K. A. Kavale, S. R. Forness, & M. Bender (Eds.), *Handbook of learning disabilities (Vol. 1): Dimensions and diagnosis* (pp. 379–398). Boston: College-Hill.

Rothlisberg, B. A. (1987). Assessing learning problems: How to proceed once you know the score. In R. S. Dean (Ed.), *Assessing human intelligence* (pp. 207–228). Springfield, IL: Thomas.

Sabatino, D. A. (1971). A scientific approach toward a discipline of special education. *Journal of Special Education, 5*, 15–21.

Sattler, J. M. (1988). *Assessment of children* (3rd ed.). San Diego, CA: J. M. Sattler.

Sattler, J. M., & Ryan, J. J. (1981). Relationship between WISC–R and WRAT in children referred for learning difficulties. *Psychology in the Schools, 18*, 290–292.

Schuerger, J. M., & Witt, A. C. (1989). The temporal stability of individually tested intelligence. *Journal of Clinical Psychology, 45*, 294–302.

Shellenberger, S. (1982). Presentation and interpretation of psychological data in educational settings. In C. R. Reynolds & T. B. Gutkin (Eds.), *The handbook of school psychology* (pp. 51–81). New York: Wiley.

Siegel, O. (1982). Personality development in adolescence. In B. B. Wolman (Ed.), *Handbook of developmental psychology* (pp. 537–548). Englewood Cliffs, NJ: Prentice Hall.

Simmons, D. C., & Kameenui, E. J. (1990). Academic learning problems and instructional design: Translating research into practice. *LD Forum, 16*, 2–5.

Stewart, K. J., Reynolds, C. R., & Lorys-Vernon, A. (1990). Professional standards and practice in child assessment. In C. R. Reynolds & R. W. Kamphaus (Eds.), *Handbook of psychological and educational assessment of children: Intelligence and achievement* (pp. 105–126). New York: Guilford.

Trachtman, G. M. (1981). On such a full sea. *School Psychology Review, 10*, 138–181.

Tindall, R. H. (1979). School psychology: The development of a profession. In G. D. Phye and D. J. Reschly (Eds.), *School psychology: Perspectives and issues* (pp. 3–24). New York: Academic Press.

Tingstrom, D. H., & Pfeiffer, S. I. (1988). WISC–R factor structure in a referred pediatric population. *Journal of Clinical Psychology, 44*, 799–802.

Vess, S. M., Gregory, L. S., & Moore, S. L. (1987). Children and hearing. In A. Thomas and J. Grimes (Eds.), *Children's needs: Psychological perspectives* (pp. 268–275). Washington, DC: NASP.

Walter, R. (1925). The functions of the school psychologist. *American Psychologist, 29*, 167–170.

White, M. A., & Harris, M. W. (1961). *The school psychologist.* New York: Harper.

Wiig, E. H. (1984). Language disabilities in adolescents: A question of cognitive strategies. *Topics in Language Disorders, 4*, 41–57.

Wisland, M. V. (1974). *Psychoeducational diagnosis of exceptional children.* Springfield, IL: Thomas.

Wong, B. Y. L. (1988). Cognitive methods. In K.A. Kavale, S. R. Forness, & M. Bender (Eds.), *Handbook of learning disabilities (Vol. 2): Methods and interventions* (pp. 19–32). Boston: College-Hill.

CHAPTER 6

A Person-centered/Humanistic Approach to Intervention

Avis J. Ruthven
Mississippi State University

The person-centered/humanistic approach to intervention presented is based upon the therapeutic approach developed by Carl Rogers. The primary goal of this approach is to provide a climate that will promote the actualizing tendency of the individual. With positive regard, acceptance, and trust being the core of the relationship between the helper and the individual, this climate of acceptance allows the individual to experience greater self-regard, a more realistic view of self, and greater effectiveness in coping with problem situations.

HISTORICAL ANTECEDENTS

The person-centered/humanistic approach to psychoeducational intervention is based upon the therapeutic approach developed by Carl R. Rogers (1902–1987). Rogerian therapy was originally described as *nondirective*, then later it was referred to as *client-centered*. Since the 1970s, it has been referred to as *person-centered* therapy (Moore, 1983).

Since Rogers's person-centered approach is based upon "a basic trust in human beings" (Tosi, Leclair, Peters, & Murphy (1987), it is closely associated with the humanistic school of psychology. "Humanistic psychologists view people as being rational and basically trustworthy and as having dignity and worth, striving to grow and enhance their potentialities and become socialized and in harmony with others in their environment" (Moore, 1983, pp. 228–229). Rogers' person-centered approach has influenced the work of many others in the helping professions; for example, Gerard Egan, the author of *The Skilled Helper* (1975); Canfield and Wells, the authors of *100 Ways to*

Enhance Self-Concept in the Classroom (1976); Thomas Gordon, author of *T.E.T.: Teacher Effectiveness Training* (1974) and *P.E.T.: Parent Effectiveness Training* (1970); Simon, Howe, and Kirschenbaum, authors of *Values Clarification* (1978); and William W. Purkey, author of *Self-Concept and School Achievement* (1970).

By the time of Rogers's death in 1987, "the person-centered approach had moved from the counselor's office into the mainstream of society. . . . Every theory or system of helping that we know has benefited from the thoughts and works of Carl R. Rogers" (Gilliland, James, & Bowman, 1989, p. 68).

CRITICAL ASPECTS

To understand the person-centered therapeutic perspective of Carl Rogers, one first needs to understand his theory of behavior. Two concepts are central to his theory: the *phenomenal/perceptual field* and the *self/self-concept*.

Rogers's Theory of Behavior

The *phenomenal* or *perceptual field* "includes all that is experienced by the organism, whether or not these experiences are consciously perceived" (Rogers, 1951, p. 483). The phenomenal field is constantly changing; it is the individual's reality. Reality is the private world of individual perceptions. Anything that is experienced by the organism whether it is real or not is part of the individual's perceptual field. If a woman walking down a street at night believes that a "suspicious character" is following her, but in fact no one is following her, the "suspicious character" she thinks is following her is part of her perceptual field.

One of the basic postulates of the humanistic/person-centered approach is that "all behavior, without exception, is completely determined by, and pertinent to, the perceptual field of the behaving organism" (Combs & Snygg, 1959, p. 20). The quickened pace of walking, the tightening of the grasp on her purse, the rush of adrenaline to the bloodstream of the woman who thinks she is being followed is completely determined by her perception of the situation—her perceptual field.

The *self*, as explained by Rogers (1951), is that portion of the total perceptual field that as the individual develops gradually becomes recognized as "me," "I," or "myself." The self is far more than the individual's physical self; it is everything one "experiences as 'me' at that instant" (Combs & Snygg, 1959, p. 44). One's concept of self develops through interaction with the environment and particularly through evaluational interaction with others. When others behave toward a person in ways that indicate to the person that one is valued, worthwhile, and capable, one tends to see oneself as valued, worthwhile, and capable; that is, one tends to have a positive concept of self. When others behave toward a person in ways that indicate to the person that one is unimportant, unworthy, and not capable, one tends to see oneself as unimportant, unworthy, and not capable; that is, one tends to have a negative concept of self.

Rogers's theory of behavior rests upon one all-important motivational construct, which Rogers (1951) expressed as follows: "The organism has one basic tendency and striving—to actualize, maintain, and enhance the experiencing organism" (p. 487). Our behavior is motivated "by this unitary active force of energy that aims to the future and strives for the fulfillment of self-directed goals and purposes to facilitate our growth and development" (Wallace, 1986, p. 89). Combs and Snygg (1959) refer to this basic need as the need for adequacy and describe it as follows:

> Thus, man seeks not merely the maintenance of *a* self but the development of an *adequate* self—a self capable of dealing effectively and efficiently with the exigencies of life, both now and in the future. To achieve this self-adequacy requires of man that he seek, not only to maintain his existing organization, but also that he build up and make more adequate the self of which he is aware. Man seeks both to maintain and enhance his perceived self. (p. 45)

To understand Rogers's view of psychological adjustment, it is necessary to consider the following proposition:

> As experiences occur in the life of the individual, they are either (a) symbolized, perceived, and organized into some relationship to the self, (b) ignored because there is no perceived relationship to the self-structure, (c) denied symbolization or given a distorted symbolization because the experience is inconsistent with the structure of the self. (Rogers, 1951, p. 503)

In a sense, an individual's self-concept "provides a screen through which everything else is seen, heard, evaluated, and understood" (Combs, Avila, & Purkey, 1971, p. 43). Experiences that meet no need related to the self, that neither reinforce nor contradict one's self-concept are ignored or "never raised to the level of conscious symbolization . . . " (Rogers, 1951, p. 504). Experiences that meet a need or are consistent with one's concept of self and thus reinforce it "are accepted into consciousness and organized into some relationship with the self-structure . . . " (Rogers, 1951, p. 504). Experiences that are inconsistent or incongruent with one's concept of self

> are regarded as a threat in that, if such experiences were accurately symbolized in awareness, they would disturb the organization of the self-concept. . . . Thus, such experiences create anxiety in the person and arouse defense mechanisms which either distort or deny such experiences, thereby maintaining the individual's consistent perception of self. (Holdstock & Rogers, 1977, pp. 135–136)

Combs et al. (1971) provide the following example of how the preceding proposition might operate with a child who believes that he cannot read:

> For one reason or another he has developed an idea that he is unable to read. Thereafter, he is caught in a vicious circle which goes something like this: Because he believes that he can't read, he avoids it. In this way he avoids the very thing that would be helpful for him. Because he avoids reading, he doesn't get any practice and so he doesn't read very well. Then, when his teacher asks him to read, he reads very poorly and she says, "My goodness, Jimmy, you don't read very well!" This, of course, is what he already believed in the first place! Then, to make matters worse, a report card is often sent home telling his parents how badly he reads and so they, too, join the act confirming the child's belief that he is indeed a very poor reader. In this way a poor reader is frequently

surrounded by a veritable conspiracy in which all of his experience points out his deficiency to him. This conspiracy, moreover, is produced for the most part by persons whose intentions were excellent. They *wanted* the child to be a good reader, even though the net effect of their pressures was to prove to him he was not. (pp. 44–45)

In essence, psychological adjustment exists when the concept of self is such that all the individual's experiences are, or may be, assimilated into a consistent relationship with the concept of self. "Under certain conditions, involving primarily complete absence of any threat to the self-structure, experiences which are inconsistent with it may be perceived, and examined, and the structure of self revised to assimilate and include such experiences" (Rogers, 1951, p. 517). One of the principal conditions for facilitating psychological adjustment or congruence between self and experiencing is an interpersonal relationship in which the person experiences unconditional positive regard and respect (Holdstock & Rogers, 1977).

The Therapeutic Process

The heart of the therapeutic process is the counselor–client relationship (Rogers, 1961). Three conditions must be present and communicated in the relationship to create a climate for the client that is growth enhancing. The three conditions are: (a) genuineness (or congruence), (b) acceptance (or unconditional positive regard), and (c) empathic under-standing. These conditions provided by the counselor are considered to be the "necessary and sufficient" conditions of the therapeutic process (Rogers, 1957).

Genuineness or Congruence.   Genuineness on the part of the counselor involves being oneself, being real, not putting up a front or "playing a part," being aware of and honestly communicating one's own feelings and attitudes. Egan (1986) states that you are genuine in relationships with clients when you:

Do not overemphasize your professional role and avoid stereotyped role behaviors

Are spontaneous but not uncontrolled or haphazard in your relationships

Remain open and nondefensive even when you feel threatened

Are consistent and avoid discrepancies—between your values and your behavior, and between your thoughts and your words in interactions with clients—while remaining respectful and reasonably tactful

Are willing to share yourself and your experience with clients if it seems helpful. (p. 67)

Acceptance or Unconditional Positive Regard.   Person-centered therapists sometimes refer to this second condition as respect. Acceptance, unconditional positive regard, or respect involves

a deep and genuine caring for the client as a person; a positive regard or prizing without reservations, conditions, judgments, or evaluations; a respect for the client's individu-ality, complexity, freedom, and potential; and a firm belief or faith in the client's innate goodness as a human being, regardless of his or her present situation, values, feelings or behaviors. (Wallace, 1986, p. 99)

Possessing unconditional positive regard for the client means that the client may be talkative or not, may address any issue of interest, and may come to whatever resolutions that are personally meaningful without the client's particular choices or characteristics affecting the therapist's regard for the client (Raskin & Rogers, 1989).

Empathic Understanding.   The third condition, empathic understanding, means that the therapist understands what the client is experiencing, thinking, and feeling from moment to moment and communicates that understanding to the client. Empathic understanding involves understanding what the client is experiencing from the client's own internal frame of reference. Tosi et al. (1987) describe accurately empathy as "a process wherein a counselor attempts to fully comprehend the innermost thoughts and feelings of a person within that person's phenomenal field of experience" (p. 108). Counselor–client relationships in which the counselor feels and communicates empathic understanding, acceptance, genuineness, and a nonjudgmental attitude result in a therapeutic climate in which clients feel safe, can be open, are free to be themselves, and "to become what they would like to be" (Moore, 1983, p. 235).

For the conditions of genuineness, acceptance, and empathic understanding to be an integral part of the counselor–client relationship, they must be communicated to the client. That is, it is not enough for the counselor to *feel* genuine, accepting, and empathic toward the client, the counselor also must *communicate* these feelings to the client. Egan (1986, 1990) has identified four communication skills that he feels are basic to the helping process: attending, listening, empathy, and probing.

> Attending refers to the ways in which helpers can effectively orient themselves toward and be with their clients, both physically and psychologically. (Egan, 1986, p. 71)

Attending involves such behaviors as facing the client, maintaining an open posture, leaning toward the client, maintaining eye contact, and being relaxed (Egan, 1986).

> Listening refers to the ability of helpers to capture and understand the messages clients communicate, whether these messages are transmitted verbally or nonverbally, clearly or vaguely (Egan, 1990, p. 108). Listening involves understanding the core messages being conveyed, noting recurring themes, and understanding the client's point of view without judging or evaluating what is being said. (Egan, 1990)

> Empathy refers to the helper's ability to communicate to clients that he or she understands what they are saying. Central to empathy is letting clients know their viewpoints have been listened to and understood. (Egan, 1986, p. 71)

Empathic understanding may be communicated to the client in many different ways; e.g., a nod of the head, saying *uh-huh*, making reflective, nondirective statements, or summarizing the client's comments.

> Probing refers to the counselor's ability to help clients identify and explore experiences, behavior(s) and feelings that will help them engage more constructively in the helping process. (Egan, 1986, p. 71)

Probing is necessary when the client does not spontaneously discuss a relevant aspect of a problem situation. Probing by person-centered clinicians usually takes the form of an open-ended, invitational statement. With clients who do not present themselves voluntarily for counseling, probing is frequently necessary to get the client to talk about problem situations.

INTENDED GOALS

The primary goal of the person-centered approach (Rogers, 1951, 1961, 1980) is to provide a climate that will promote the actualizing tendency of the individual. With positive regard, acceptance, and trust being the core of the relationship between the helper and the individual, this climate of acceptance allows the individual to explore and discover his or her "perceptions, feelings, attitudes, beliefs, values, hopes, fears, and aspirations" (Wallace, 1986, p. 97).

Through this process of exploration, the individual brings into focus specific objectives or goals, developing an awareness and trust in his or her own inner direction. Thus the individual experiences greater self-regard, more responsibility for his or her value systems (that is, the individual tends to shift from an external locus of evaluation to an internal locus of evaluation), greater effectiveness in coping with problem situations, and a more realistic view of self because of decreases in defensiveness. In other words, the individual's real and ideal self move closer together and incongruities in experiences are minimized (Raskin & Rogers, 1989; Rogers, 1942, 1951, 1961; Tosi et al., 1987; Wallace, 1986).

Holdstock and Rogers (1977) describe the outcome of the therapeutic process as follows:

> In the process of growth, the self-concept the person has keeps changing, as previously denied experiences are assimilated. The individual also comes to realize personal responsibility for the meanings given to these experiences. Thus, the concept of self becomes more internally based, more congruent with immediate experiencing. And since experiencing is ever changing, the self-concept also becomes more fluid and changing. The increasing congruence between self and experience reflects the improved psychological adjustment. (p. 140)

ANALYSIS OF CASE DATA

Relevant Aspects of Case Data

Before analyzing the case of Vince Chandler, it is imperative that the reader realize that the person-centered psychologist would administer few, if any, of the instruments included in the battery provided in Chapter 2. Instead, the person-centered psychologist would rely almost exclusively upon counseling sessions with Vince for insight into how he perceives himself, significant others in his life, and the situations in which he finds himself. As noted by Knoff (1986), observation during counseling is the predominant "assessment" technique used by clinicians with a humanistic perspective. The person-centered approach places emphasis upon the client's disclosure of feelings, perceptions, and attitudes, rather than information obtained from standardized assessments of cognitive or neuropsychological functioning and academic achievement. Therefore, the author has selected for discussion in this section those data sources that pertain to Vince's feelings, perceptions, and attitudes.

Referral Information.   Vince is not a self-referral. He was referred by his parents and teachers after a progressive decline in school performance. Moreover, his parents and teachers report that there has been an increase in problem behavior associated with the drop in academic performance. Vince has displayed low frustration tolerance, excitability, and an inability to relate appropriately to adults and peers.

Family/Social History.   The most important part of the family/social history for the person-centered psychologist is the section on Vince's perspective. To understand Vince's behavior, one must understand his perceptual field—how things seem to him. The best way to understand Vince's perceptual field is to look at things from Vince's point of view, from his internal frame of reference or perspective.

Educational History.   Vince's earlier articulation problems combined with the private school's practice of class recitations seem to have created a negative attitude toward school and most teachers. Vince singled out his fourth-grade teacher, Mr. Millberger, as a teacher that he disliked. Vince indicated that Mr. Millberger belittled him and called him lazy and stupid. However, Vince did respond well to social reinforcement and performed at an above average level in Mr. Angelo's class at Jefferson School. Mr. Angelo's more relaxed attitude and positive concern about his students' progress combined with Vince's success in athletics created a positive school experience for Vince. Brookline Middle School, with different teachers for each subject and the expectation of more self-direction (as well as an increase in work requiring writing skills), seems to be the beginning of the current decline in grades and increase in acting out in class.

School Observations.   Vince's difficulties in writing are a frequent source of frustration for him. When confronted with tasks that are difficult for him, Vince typically withdraws from the task, sometimes by acting out in class. Vince seems to defend himself against failure by not completing his writing assignments.

Evaluation Observations.   Vince suggested that he was doing just fine and that he could "do a good job in school if he wanted." Vince displayed an impulsive approach to problem-solving situations. If a question or task seemed too difficult, Vince gave up and did not persist with the problem.

Evaluation Results

Sentence Completion Test.   Vince seemed to have difficulty responding to the incomplete sentences, which may be indicative of his unwillingness to reveal his innermost thoughts and feelings. In fact, he did not respond at all to the incomplete sentence, "If I feel I am not good at something. . . ." Responses of particular interest are: "When I feel like mouthing off in class I let it rip," "If someone plays a practical joke on me I get even," "School is bad," and "When people pressure me it pisses me off," "Girls often enjoy looking at my body," and "My family is not a real family."

Revised Children's Manifest Anxiety Scale.   Vince's score on the Social Concerns/Concentration scale suggests that he experiences anxiety regarding his inattentiveness and difficulty in remaining task-oriented in class.

Piers–Harris Children's Self-Concept Scale.   Vince's scores in the areas of Popularity, Anxiety, and Happiness & Satisfaction are in the average range. His score in the Physical Appearance & Attributes area indicates that his physical self-concept is quite positive; however, his scores in the areas of Behavior and Intellectual & School Status indicate these are areas in which he has a negative self-perception.

Thematic Apperception Test.   Vince's stories about Card 4 and Card 20 reveal the tension caused by the divorce of his parents. Stories about other cards suggest a desire to be successful in school and in relationships with others.

Three Wishes Interview.   Vince's three wishes were: for his father to remarry his mother, to be out of school, and to win a million dollars.

Behavior Evaluation Scale.   The teacher's evaluation of Vince's behavior in his Family Living class indicates that Vince has an inability to learn, which cannot be explained by intellectual, sensory, or health factors; an inability to build or maintain satisfactory interpersonal relationships with peers and teachers; and a general pervasive mood of unhappiness or depression.

Vineland Adaptive Behavior Scales.   Vince's mother reported his adaptive behavior in the Communication, Daily Living Skills, and Socialization Domains to be in the average range.

Process Undertaken to Analyze Data

As mentioned previously, one of the basic postulates of the person-centered/humanistic approach is that all behavior is determined by and is pertinent to the individual's perceptual field. Therefore, the process used by a person-centered psychologist to analyze available data about a client is primarily one of attempting to understand the client's perceptual field. The psychologist examines the information, striving to look at the circumstances or situations involving the client from the client's point of view or from the client's unique internal frame of reference, which is the best vantage point for understanding the client's behavior (Rogers, 1951).

First, the person-centered practitioner strives to understand the client's self-perceptions. For example:

1. Is Vince's view of himself generally positive or negative? Does he see himself as generally good or bad?

2. Does he feel positive about himself and his interactions with others?
3. Does he think that there is a problem? If he thinks there is a problem, does he see himself or others as the cause of the problem?
4. Is he satisfied or dissatisfied with the way things are in his life?
5. Does he see himself as strong in some areas? If so, what are his strengths?
6. Does he see himself as weak in some areas? If so, what are his weaknesses?

Second, the person-centered practitioner attempts to understand how the client perceives significant others in his or her life at home and at school. For instance:

1. How does Vince feel about his mother, his father, his stepfather, and his stepsister?
2. Does Vince like his teachers? Is there a particular teacher that he really likes or dislikes?
3. How does he perceive his peers? Does he have a particularly good friend?

Third, the person-centered clinician studies the data for clues to the perceptions that significant others in the client's life have of the client. For example:

1. How do Vince's mother, father, stepfather, stepsister, and teachers feel about Vince?
2. Do they seem to like him, dislike him, see him as a worthwhile individual?
3. Are they supportive of his endeavors? Do they want to help him?
4. Have they given up on him?

Fourth, the clinician using a person-centered approach examines the data for discrepancies between the client's perceptions and the perceptions of significant others in the client's life and for discrepancies between the client's actions and verbalizations. For instance:

1. Is Vince's perception of situations, experiences, or events consistent with the perceptions of his family members?
2. Is Vince's perception of "the problem" congruent with the perceptions of those who referred him for evaluation?
3. Are there discrepancies between what Vince says and what others say about him?
4. Is Vince's body language consistent with his verbalizations?
5. Do Vince's actions coincide with his expressed feelings?

The person-centered therapist is more interested in establishing a growth-enhancing relationship with the client than in examining a data file consisting largely of results from various standardized assessments for clues to understanding the client's "problem." Moreover, the practitioner regards the feelings, perceptions, and attitudes disclosed by the client in face-to-face sessions as the most important data about the client, since this information is most likely to provide insight into the client's perceptual field.

Discussion of Findings

In keeping with the person-centered approach, the interpretation of findings will focus primarily upon the "findings" or "insights" gained from review of the sections of the Psychological Evaluation in Chapter 2, which include Vince's views and perspectives. The interpretation will be organized around the four questions presented in the Process Undertaken To Analyze Data section. The questions are: (a) How does Vince perceive himself? (b) How does Vince see significant others in his life? (c) How do significant others perceive Vince? and (d) Are there discrepancies between Vince's perceptions and the perceptions of significant others or between Vince's actions and his verbalizations?

How Does Vince Perceive Himself?   Vince's physical self-concept appears to be quite positive; Vince indicates that he enjoys and is good in sports. While his scores on the Piers–Harris in the areas of Behavior and Intellectual & School Status indicate that these are areas in which he has a negative self-perception, he denies this when questioned. However, his reaction to making a "C" on the surprise mathematics quiz confirms his concern about his school performance.

Vince sees writing as something that is difficult for him, as indicated by his low frustration tolerance and tendency to withdraw from the task when presented with writing assignments. Other clues to Vince's poor opinion of himself in terms of school achievement are: He seems to feel comfortable only with other peers who are also performing poorly in school; his response that "School is bad" to the incomplete sentence, School is . . . ; he remembered the fifth grade (when he performed above average) as his best year in school and commented that he had really liked the school and had fit in; and his comment that academic achievement was not important for him because he could get a job in his stepfather's business.

Like all people, Vince needs to see himself as a worthwhile individual. Based upon his comments about his stepsister and his mother, it is important to Vince to feel needed. Until his mother remarried, he appeared to see himself in more positive ways. He felt that his mother depended upon him and needed him. With the remarriage of his mother and the pending remarriage of his father, he sees himself as being less important to both of his parents.

In light of the information gained in interviews and observations, the practitioner might interpret Vince's three wishes in the following manner. His first wish, that his father remarry his mother, would solve his problems with his stepfather and allow him to be physically closer to his father. His second wish, being out of school, would remove him from a situation that constantly reinforces his negative perception of himself. The third wish, to win a million dollars, would bring him instant recognition and importance in the eyes of others.

How Does Vince See Significant Others in His Life?   Vince thinks highly of his mother. He reported, "Mom has been there for me. . . . She is pretty easy on me too. If I want anything, I know she'll be easier to convince than my stepfather or real Dad."

Vince respects and looks up to his father. He sees his father as a hard-working individual with an important job. Vince wants to make his father proud of him. However, he does not understand why his Dad has broken away as much as he has since the divorce.

Vince seems to be ambivalent about his stepfather. He states, "He's O.K. when he's not telling me what to do. . . . He's not my Dad and he isn't around much, so it's not a big deal. He is for Mom, not for me." Since Vince's mother and not the father assumed responsibility for practically all aspects of Vince's life (including discipline), Vince resents his stepfather's setting behavioral guidelines for him. In the past Vince only had one adult that he had to please; now he has two, his mother and his stepfather.

As stated earlier, Vince really likes and gets along well with his stepsister, Beatrice. He characterizes her "as the best part of my mom remarrying." Vince feels that Beatrice depends on him and stands by him.

When asked about his teachers, Vince indicated that his first and second grade teachers were "O.K." and they seemed to do a good job. He mentioned that both of these teachers would sometimes allow him to say his passages to them without having to stand in front of the entire class. This was an important factor to Vince, and provides an indication of the embarrassment that his articulation problems caused him. Vince was less positive toward his third-grade teacher, and openly disliked Mr. Millberger, his fourth-grade teacher. He indicated that Mr. Millberger made fun of him and called him lazy and stupid for not doing his work well. The last teacher mentioned by Vince was his fifth-grade teacher, Mr. Angelo. Vince appeared to really like Mr. Angelo, apparently because he had a more relaxed attitude toward discipline and displayed an interest in Vince's progress.

How Do Significant Others Perceive Vince?   Vince's mother, Mrs. Kirk, obviously cares about and is concerned about Vince. She tried to make up for his father's absence by stressing the importance of the father's contribution to the family and downplaying his absence from family outings. She stated that she tried to ignore or punish Vince when he disobeyed, but often ending up comforting him instead of punishing him. She feels that Vince's early articulation problems and lack of companionship caused much of Vince's frustration and his outbursts. Mrs. Kirk expressed concern that Vince does not appear to see his parents' viewpoint regarding his behavior.

Vince's father, who lives in another state, reports that he is interested in his son, but that he will soon be remarrying and will be unable to provide additional support for Vince. When his father and mother were married, Vince's father was seldom present. Since the divorce and remarriage of Vince's mother, his father seems to make less and less effort to spend time with Vince.

Vince's stepfather, Mr. Kirk, states that he and Vince "get along" but that Vince increasingly questions his authority in setting behavioral guidelines. Mr. Kirk relates that these confrontations make him very angry and that he typically withdraws until he calms down. Mr. Kirk seems concerned about Vince and his performance in school.

Vince's current teachers tend to see Vince as a poor student. That is, they report that he lacks writing skills, frequently does not hand in written work, does his reading assignments only sporadically, tends to become defensive and argumentative when questioned about his lack of performance, acts disrespectful, acts out in class, and hangs out with a clique of students who do not seem interested in academic achievement. None of the comments by his teachers were positive in nature. When Vince failed to bring his essay to the English Composition class, his teacher told Vince that he could finish it after school; however, when Vince did not report for the after-school session, the teacher did not follow up. It seems that this teacher has "given up" on Vince.

Are There Discrepancies between Vince's Perceptions and the Perceptions of Significant Others or between Vince's Actions and His Verbalizations?   Vince appears to lack insight into how his behavior is perceived by others; there is definitely a discrepancy between the way he describes himself and the way others describe him. According to Vince there is no problem relative to his relationships with peers and school personnel; he relates that it is all exaggerated, whereas he was referred by his parents and teachers partially because of low frustration tolerance, excitability, and an inability to relate appropriately to adults and peers. His teacher for Family Living indicated on the Behavior Evaluation Scale that he has an inability to build or maintain satisfactory interpersonal relationships with peers and teachers.

Vince apparently has difficulty admitting that his father is becoming increasingly uninvolved in his life. Rather than placing the blame for this on his father, whom he appears to admire and respect, he blames his stepfather for his not being able to spend time with his father. Based upon information provided by Vince's father and by his mother, the stepfather may have little to do with Vince's not spending time with his father. Vince's mother reported that even during the marriage Vince's father seldom spent time with him. His mother almost always attended school functions without his father. The mother justified Mr. Chandler's absence or unavailability on the basis of the importance and time-consuming nature of Mr. Chandler's job.

Some of Vince's comments during the interview contradict his responses/scores on the Piers–Harris Children's Self-Concept Scale and the Revised Children's Manifest Anxiety Scale (CMAS). Vince's statements indicate that he is not concerned about his performance in school; however, his reaction to receiving a "C" on the mathematics quiz contradicts his statements.

RECOMMENDATIONS
AND SUGGESTED INTERVENTIONS

Areas of Emphasis

The person-centered approach to intervention, as the term "person-centered" suggests, focuses upon the whole person. No particular area of emphasis, other than developing the counselor–client relationship and providing a climate that will be growth-enhancing, would be determined prior to working with Vince. Vince himself would determine the area or areas to be emphasized or not to be emphasized in the counseling sessions with him. Since genuineness on the part of the counselor is an essential part of the person-centered approach, the reason(s) for referral would be shared with Vince during the first counseling session. However, the person-centered psychologist would not have "a hidden agenda for the child . . . " (Moore, 1983, p. 237). The person-centered helper believes in the client's ability to become self-directing and "respects the right of the child to choose to change or not to change attitudes and behaviors which bother other people or appear to be self-defeating for the child" (Moore, 1983, p. 238). The underlying purpose of the intervention would be to help Vince to identify and solve his own unique problems, to help him see himself as capable of dealing with problem situations, and thereby enhance his concept of self. Egan (1986) describes the goal of helpers as helping "their clients to *manage* the problem situations of their lives" (p. 33).

Program of Change

The essence of any person-centered/humanistic intervention program is the counselor–client relationship. Vince's problem situations can be revealed only if Vince feels free to openly express and explore his innermost thoughts and feelings with the clinician. Therefore, the first and most critical thing the practitioner must do is to establish such a climate. This is done by providing and communicating to Vince, the three growth-enhancing conditions of acceptance or respect, empathic understanding, and genuineness. These three conditions must permeate the relationship throughout the helping process. Vince must feel that the practitioner really cares about and values him, that the practitioner wants to help him, that the practitioner is "on his side," that he can trust the practitioner not to discuss with others what he says unless he gives his permission, that the practitioner isn't judging thoughts or actions, and that the practitioner sees him as being capable of dealing effectively with problem situations.

By using the four communication skills discussed in the section The Therapeutic Process—attending, listening, empathy, and probing—the person-centered clinician encourages Vince to "tell his story" (Egan, 1986). The clinician attends to Vince by facing him, leaning toward him, maintaining eye contact with him, and being relaxed. The practitioner actively listens to Vince's story and communicates empathic understanding as illustrated below:

VINCE: I get mad sometimes, but I don't know why people can't take a joke.

PRACTITIONER: You feel angry because others don't understand that you are just joking with them.

. . .

VINCE: We used to help each other a lot [talking about his mom], but I guess things change.

PRACTITIONER: You seem to be saying that you liked having your Mom depend on you and that you don't think she needs you as much now.

. . .

VINCE: I got really pissed off when that teacher gave me a "C" on the math test.

PRACTITIONER: You were angry at her because you thought you had done well?

When Vince fails to spontaneously discuss something that appears to the clinician to be a relevant aspect of his problem situation, the clinician may use probing. For example:

VINCE: As long as he [his stepfather] stays off my back about things [like school] we'll get along.

PRACTITIONER: It bothers you when he gets on you about not doing well in school. Tell me more about his getting on you about school.

. . .

PRACTITIONER: It must have been really difficult for you when your parents got a divorce?

Other behaviors and feelings that might be explored are: How does Vince feel when confronted with a task that is difficult for him? Is his acting out a way of avoiding failure? Is he afraid that people will make fun of him, think he's a dummy, as Mr. Millberger and others did when he had to recite in front of the class?

In addition to exploring problem situations, the person-centered clinician should help Vince to realize his strengths and explore unrealized potential. In Vince's case, sports is an area in which he excels, but he is not eligible for the junior varsity teams because of his poor grades. Vince also appears to be an excellent baby-sitter for his stepsister, Beatrice.

Throughout the sessions with Vince, the practitioner encourages him to verbalize his thoughts and feelings. The practitioner strives to understand the feelings, perceptions, and attitudes expressed in his verbalizations so that those feelings, perceptions, and attitudes can be accurately reflected and clarified to Vince. Through this process of disclosure and reflection in an accepting and nonthreatening relationship, Vince will come to develop greater self-awareness and self-understanding. According to Patterson (1985), ''with increasing self-awareness, clients' self-concepts become clearer'' (p. 130). With clearer self-concepts, they begin to see specific ways in which they are failing to actualize themselves. Patterson (1985) continues:

> self-concept becomes more congruent with experiences and thus more realistic. . . . clients become more accepting of themselves and feel more confident and self-directing. . . . They experience more acceptance from others, both because they perceive more realistically and accurately and because their changed selves elicit more positive reactions from others. . . . Their feelings of adequacy and of self-esteem increase. (p. 130)

If Vince comes to realize that there are ways in which he would like for himself and his life to change, the person-centered therapist would help him conceptualize what his home and school life would be like if improvements were made. Vince has indicated that he wants his stepfather to ''get off his back.'' The therapist might explore with Vince what it would take for his stepfather ''to get off his back.'' Since Vince has indicated that their conflict seems to center on his school problems, Vince may decide that improvement in his grades would be a way of ''getting him off his back.''

Once desired outcomes are generated by Vince, the practitioner would help Vince evaluate or critique the goals he has established. According to Egan (1986), the goals ''need to be clear, specific, realistic, adequately related to the problem situation, in keeping with the client's values, and capable of being accomplished within a reasonable time frame'' (pp. 44–45). A clear, specific, and realistic goal that is related to the problem situation and capable of being accomplished within a reasonable time frame in Vince's case would be ''to make a passing grade in English Composition at the end of the next grading period.'' It is important that the goal(s) be realistic—be within reach of the client. Locke and Latham (cited in Egan, 1986, pp. 262–263) reiterate this point:

> Nothing breeds success like success. Conversely, nothing causes feelings of despair like perpetual failure. A primary purpose of goal setting is to increase the motivation level of the individual. But goal setting can have precisely the opposite effect if it produces a yardstick that constantly makes the individual feel inadequate. (Locke & Latham, 1984, p. 39)

To allow Vince to set a goal of making an "A" in English Composition would probably not be a realistic goal for Vince. It also may not be in keeping with Vince's values. Making "A's" does not appear to be something that Vince values. Whereas, "getting his stepfather off his back" is something that Vince *does* value. Chances are that his stepfather doesn't expect Vince to make "A's" anyway. He probably just wants him to perform at the level at which he is capable of performing.

Clients are more likely to commit themselves to meeting new goals if they are helped to see the attractiveness of the outcomes (Egan, 1986). "Clients need *incentives* for choice and commitment" (Egan, 1986, p. 272). In Vince's case, the clinician could help him picture what his relationship with his stepfather might be like if he were to improve his grades. In addition to more harmonious relations with his stepfather, the possibility of becoming eligible for the junior varsity basketball team (assuming that this is something that he values) might serve as an additional incentive for Vince.

If Vince does identify a goal that he wants to reach, the counselor might help him identify and evaluate a variety of strategies by which the goal(s) can be reached, help him develop a plan or plans of action, and help him implement the plan(s) (Egan, 1986). Assuming that Vince decides upon the goal of making a passing grade in English Composition, the therapist would encourage Vince to think of ways of accomplishing the goal. What does he need to do in order to pass English Composition? The therapist would encourage him to think of and discuss as many strategies as possible. Some strategies that might evolve for reaching the goal of "passing English Composition" are: to do his homework assignments and turn them in on time, to study English Composition every day, to ask his mother or stepfather to assist him when he has difficulty with a homework assignment, to seek assistance from his English Composition teacher when he has difficulty with an assignment in class, to select topics (when given the freedom) to write about that interest him (e.g., sports), to hire a tutor to help him improve his writing skills. It is anticipated that in a case like Vince's, the client will realize that improvement in writing skills is going to be necessary to make a passing grade in English Composition. Therefore, much of the discussion would be about possible strategies for improving his writing skills.

In Vince's case, it is possible that substantive improvement of his writing skills may ultimately lead to: less conflict with his stepfather over school and less conflict with his teachers and peers. Improvement in his writing skills would make doing his homework assignments less frustrating for him so he would be more likely to do them and turn them in. He would be less frustrated doing classroom writing assignments which should increase his on-task behavior and decrease the number of acting-out episodes. His grades in English and several other subjects would probably improve, which in turn would improve his teachers' and stepfather's attitudes toward him. The more positive evaluational feedback from significant others would result in Vince's seeing himself as more worthwhile and so gain an improved concept of self.

Once a number of possible strategies have been derived, the person-centered practitioner could help Vince (assuming that Vince sought such assistance) choose which strategy or strategies will work best for him. The criteria for selecting among strategies are the same as those for choosing among a number of goals. The strategies selected must be specific, measurable, realistic, adequate, owned by the client, in keeping with the values of the client, and can be accomplished within a reasonable time frame (Egan, 1986).

Once Vince begins implementing his plan of action, the clinician continues to see Vince periodically (if Vince so desires) to discuss his progress toward accomplishing his goal(s) and to assist him in identifying ways of overcoming unforeseen obstacles that may arise. The counseling sessions would end whenever Vince chose to terminate them.

Expected Outcome

Success of the intervention could be documented in a number of ways. The primary source of feedback on the effectiveness of the intervention would be the self-report of the client, Vince. If Vince reports that he has succeeded in passing English Composition (and hopefully his other courses) and that he is experiencing less conflict with his stepfather and teachers, the intervention would certainly be judged as successful. Even if Vince does not improve his grades, but gains greater self-regard and sees himself as being more capable of managing problem situations as they arise, the person-centered/humanistic helper would feel that the intervention had been successful.

Other sources of feedback on the outcome of the intervention could be Vince's parents and/or his teachers. For example, if his teachers report that his on-task behavior and motivation to achieve have increased and that distracting his peers and acting out in class have decreased, these changes could be evidence of successful intervention. From the person-centered/humanistic approach, improvement in Vince's relationships with others could be explained as follows: Through the relationship established between the practitioner and Vince, Vince moves from experiencing himself as an unworthy, unacceptable, and unlovable person to the realization that he is worthy, accepted, and cared about in this relationship with the person-centered psychologist. With these changes in his self-concept, he becomes more accepting of others and, in turn, experiences more acceptance from others. Through the therapist's unconditional acceptance of Vince and trust in his ability to grow in self-adequacy, he becomes able to manage problem situations more effectively and to utilize his unrealized potential.

REFERENCES

Canfield, J., & Wells, H. C. (1976). *100 ways to enhance self-concept in the classroom: A handbook for teachers and parents.* Englewood Cliffs, NJ: Prentice Hall.

Combs, A. W. Avila, D. L., & Purkey, W. W. (1971). *Helping relationships: Basic concepts for the helping professions.* Boston: Allyn & Bacon.

Combs, A. W., & Snygg, D. (1959). *Individual behavior: A perceptual approach to behavior* (rev. ed.). New York: Harper & Row.

Egan, G. (1975). *The skilled helper: A model for systematic helping and interpersonal relating.* Monterey, CA: Brooks/Cole.

Egan, G. (1986). *The skilled helper: A systematic approach to effective helping* (3rd ed.). Monterey, CA: Brooks/Cole.

Egan, G. (1990). *The skilled helper: A systematic approach to effective helping* (4th ed.). Pacific Grove, CA: Brooks/Cole.

Gilliland, B. E., James, R. K., & Bowman, J. T. (1989). *Theories and strategies in counseling and psychotherapy* (2nd ed.). Englewood Cliffs, NJ: Prentice Hall.

Gordon, T. (1970). *P.E.T.: Parent effectiveness training.* New York: Wyden.

Gordon, T. (1974). *T.E.T.: Teacher effectiveness training*. New York: McKay.

Holdstock, T. L., & Rogers, C. R. (1977). Person-centered theory. In R. J. Corsini (Ed.), *Current personality theories* (pp. 105–151). Itasca, IL: Peacock.

Knoff, H. M. (1986). Identifying and classifying children and adolescents referred for personality assessment: Theories, systems, and issues. In H. M. Knoff (Ed.), *The assessment of child and adolescent personality* (pp. 3–33). New York: Guilford.

Locke, E.A., & Latham, G. P. (1984). *Goal setting: A motivational technique that works*. Englewood Cliffs, NJ: Prentice Hall.

Moore, H. B. (1983). Person-centered approaches. In H. T. Prout & D. T. Brown (Eds.), *Counseling and psychotherapy with children and adolescents: Theory and practice for school and clinic settings* (pp. 225–286). Tampa, FL: Mariner.

Patterson, C. H. (1985). *The therapeutic relationship: Foundations for an eclectic psychotherapy*. Monterey, CA: Brooks/Cole.

Purkey, W. W. (1970). *Self-concept and school achievement*. Englewood Cliffs, NJ: Prentice Hall.

Raskin, N. J., & Rogers, C. R. (1989). Person-centered therapy. In R. J. Corsini & D. Wedding (Eds.), *Current psychotherapies* (4th ed.) (pp. 155–194). Itasca, IL: Peacock.

Rogers, C. R. (1942). *Counseling and psychotherapy: Newer concepts in practice*. Boston: Houghton Mifflin.

Rogers, C.R. (1951). *Client-centered therapy*. Boston: Houghton Mifflin.

Rogers, C. R. (1957). The necessary and sufficient conditions of therapeutic personality change. *Journal of Consulting Psychology, 21*, 95–103.

Rogers, C. R. (1961). *On becoming a person: A therapist's view of psychotherapy*. Boston: Houghton Mifflin.

Rogers, C.R. (1980). *A way of being*. Boston: Houghton Mifflin.

Simon, S. B., Howe, L. W., & Kirschenbaum, H. (1978). *Values clarification: A handbook of practical strategies for teachers and students* (rev. ed.). New York: A & W Visual Library.

Tosi, D. J., Leclair, S. W., Peters, H. J., & Murphy, M. A. (1987). *Theories and applications of counseling: Systems and techniques of counseling and psychotherapy*. Springfield, IL: Thomas.

Wallace, W. A. (1986). *Theories of counseling and psychotherapy: A basic issues approach*. Boston: Allyn & Bacon.

CHAPTER 7

A Neuropsychological Approach to Intervention

Janice Campbell Whitten
Mississippi State University

Rik Carl D'Amato
University of Northern Colorado

Mary Mathai Chittooran
University of Mississippi Medical Center

Neuropsychology is an approach that combines the distinctive disciplines of medicine and psychology to study brain–behavior relationships. This perspective stems from the assumption that the brain is the origin of all nonreflexive behavior. It bridges the gap between the psychoanalytic and the behavioral perspectives by looking both inward, at the brain, and outward, at behavior; the goal is to integrate both aspects of functioning. In rehabilitation, neuropsychologists emphasize compensatory strategies and basic remediation with the premise that—both in education and in psychotherapy—some individuals need to learn new skills whereas others must learn ways to circumvent previously established weaknesses.

Neuropsychology may be conceptualized as an integrative approach that brings the combined influences of the disciplines of neurology, psychometry, and psychology, to bear upon the study of brain–behavior relationships. The science of clinical neuropsychology is predicated upon the assumption that the brain is the origin of all nonreflexive behavior (Lezak, 1983). Given this assumption, proponents of the neuropsychological approach consider it the function of psychology to directly study behavior, and from that basis, to draw logical, empirically defensible inferences about brain functioning (Reitan, 1955, 1989).

Although biomedical evidence continues to mount in support of the relationship between brain functions and behavior, there has been less than an implicit acceptance of the neuropsychological approach (D'Amato, 1990). Some of this resistance has, inevitably, resulted from its novelty. Another contributory factor may be that the history of psychological thought has been plagued by a continuing struggle for precedence between diametrically opposed theories. For example, early explanations of behavior were mainly psychoanalytical, with its proponents looking for causes of behavior within the individual, the so-called "within-child model" (Gaddes, 1985). The behavioral perspective, introduced in the 1920s by Watson, focused almost exclusively on the outward, observable aspects of human functioning. Subsequent theories intended, for the most part, to align themselves with one or other of these basic perspectives and by the 1940s, most psychologists had ensconced themselves either in the psychoanalytic or the behavioral camp (Gaddes, 1985). Without denying the legitimacy of such traditional approaches to human behavior, it is becoming increasingly clear that neither one of these approaches, nor indeed, any approach that looks exclusively at external or internal factors, can adequately explain many common behaviors. Clearly, there is an urgent need in psychology for the introduction of a perspective that can adequately fill the gaps in knowledge.

The neuropsychological perspective represents a viable solution to the current controversy that surrounds the psychoanalytic and behavioral approaches. Serving as a conscious and continuing attempt to look not only inward, at the brain, but outward, at behavior, it is the goal of neuropsychology to integrate both these aspects of functioning (Reitan, 1989). As some authors (e.g., Dean, 1986a; Gaddes, 1985) have suggested, behavioral and educational data cannot be interpreted and evaluated outside the context of the basic social and physiological functioning of the individual. Such an approach, of necessity, provides the neuropsychologist with a greater volume of data, as well as more comprehensive information about the individual (D'Amato & Dean, 1988). This information may provide an understanding of etiology, which in turn, may result in the rehabilitation of existing problems, or the prevention of future difficulties. It is clear that as an explanation for human behavior, neuropsychology offers a breadth and comprehensiveness that is lacking with many other psychological perspectives.

HISTORICAL ANTECEDENTS

The interest in brain–behavior relationships can be traced back about 2,500 years (Gibson, 1962). As early as 400 B.C., the physician Hippocrates speculated about the relationship between individuals' behavior and regions of the anatomy. Other precursors of thought in this area were Galen, who thought the mind was in the brain; Aristotle, who believed that the mind was situated in the heart; and Descartes, who with his emphasis on mind–body dualism, suggested that the soul was located in the brain (Puente, 1989). Early discussions of brain functioning were offered in the seventeenth century, in cases that described the behavioral effects of traumatic brain injury (Gibson, 1962).

In keeping with the *zeitgeist* of the eighteenth century, observational analyses and conjecture gave way to an emphasis on the experimental study of brain functions and localization. Fritsch and Hitzig's important work in 1790, on the electrical stimulation of rat brains and resulting behavior, served as a catalyst for concerted attempts to seek answers to the relationship between biological factors and behavior (Puente, 1989). In 1810, Gall introduced the study of phrenology to an awed and receptive audience, and in so doing, encouraged others, although erroneously, to describe the cortical localization of function.

The nineteenth century saw a growing emphasis on the experimental study of the physiological aspects of behavior. Much of the research on brain–behavior relationships during this time revolved around resolution of the issue of localization. The work of Flourens and Broca with its attention to accuracy and systematic procedures heavily influenced other physiologists of the time, both in the focus of research and in the methods they employed (Puente, 1989). The continuing work of Lashley, Goldstein, Sperry, Gazzaniga, Orton, and others in the twentieth century further advanced the experimental study of brain–behavior relationships (Puente, 1989).

The establishment, in 1935, of the first laboratory devoted to the study of brain–behavior relationships, is credited to Ward Halstead who is often identified as the "pioneer of modern-day clinical neuropsychology" (Reitan, 1989, p. 388). Although much of the early work in neuropsychology dealt with the detection of organicity and the "three Ls" (Localization, Lateralization, and Lesion Detection), it has been argued that despite conceptions to the contrary, the emphasis in the field was not limited to such endeavors (Reitan, 1989). In fact, Reitan (1989) claimed that the field of clinical neuropsychology would have developed very differently, if the detection of brain impairment or dysfunction had been its only concern. Clinical neuropsychology began to flourish after the search for tests of brain damage was abandoned in favor of a more overarching, comprehensive involvement in studying brain–behavior relationships (Lezak, 1983; Reitan, 1989). The relationship between brain functioning and behavior was studied through research in areas as varied as head injuries, learning disabilities, neuropsychological correlates of hypertension and aging, the relationship between affective disorders and brain damage, and the neuropsychological effects of medications (Hynd & Willis, 1988; Reitan, 1989; Wedding, Horton, & Webster, 1986).

The methods used in neuropsychology have been significantly influenced by Luria (1966), whose emphasis on a clinical, individual, qualitative case-study approach, with extensive long-term client involvement, is responsible for many of the methods used today in the application of neuropsychological principles to the understanding of behavior. The British tradition in neuropsychology has traditionally taken a more psychometric approach, seen mainly in the work of Head and Jackson who preferred to focus on short-term client contact and utilized more structured assessment procedures (Puente, 1989). The North American tradition in neuropsychology, which can be traced to Goldstein's work with brain injured patients, began with a clinical approach similar to Luria's, but has, since the 1950s, adopted a more psychometric orientation. This may be partially attributed to the influence of seminal works by Reitan (1955), who argued that a major purpose of the neuropsychological evaluation was to measure deficits accurately, in a standardized, psychometric manner.

Despite the long history of neuropsychology it is only within the past 25 years or so that the field has begun to attract significant attention. Its growing popularity is evident in the concomitant increase in the number of university training programs that offer courses in neuropsychological theory and practice and in the realization that almost 10 percent of the employment opportunities in psychology call for neuropsychological skills (D'Amato, Dean, & Holloway, 1987; D'Amato, Hammons, Terminie, & Dean, 1990; Hynd, Quackenbush, & Obrzut, 1980; Leavell & Lewandowski, 1988).

An increasing sophistication in neuropsychological practice coupled with almost daily progress on the medical forefront, has resulted in a dramatic improvement in our ability to understand the complex relationship between cortical functioning and its behavioral correlates (Hynd & Willis, 1988). The development of radiological and noninvasive techniques like computerized axial tomography (CAT), positron emission tomography (PET), magnetic resonance imaging (MRI), and single photon emission computerized tomography (SPECT) have allowed us to study in vivo brain–behavior relationships and thus to expand our conception of cerebral functioning (Hynd & Willis, 1988). For example, Parks, Crockett, and McGeer (1989) describe PET as allowing us to see neuropsychological test performance from a "systems" perspective, that is, as a function of the workings of a complex and interrelated neuronal network, rather than as a result of a narrow focus on localization of specific functions.

Early neuropsychological conceptualizations of individuals tended to view them either as brain-damaged (i.e., with organic impairment) or not brain-damaged. However, many authors in the field have called for a less arbitrary differentiation between individuals. It has been suggested (e.g., D'Amato, 1990; Gaddes, 1985; Lezak, 1983) that cortical functioning can more accurately be perceived as a continuum ranging from neurologically intact functioning at one end of the spectrum to brain impairment or dysfunction at the other end. Such a conceptualization allows us to view individuals not dichotomously, but as possessing varying degrees of cerebral impairment. Similarly, the archaic notion that all disorders were either of organic or functional (arising from environmental stress) origin has given way to a reconceptualization that allows us to see causation on a continuum ranging from purely organic at one end of the spectrum to functional at the other end (D'Amato, 1990; Dean, 1986a). For example, many psychiatric disorders such as depression and schizophrenia that were previously thought to be environmentally induced have been found to have varying levels of organic involvement (Dean, 1986a). Research findings such as these expand our understanding of the relationships between cortical impairment and behavior to include human emotions and psychopathology.

NEUROPSYCHOLOGICAL ASSESSMENT

Although the roots of neuropsychology can be traced back some years, interest in the area of neuropsychological assessment is relatively recent. The neuropsychological assessment of children is of even more recent origin, having grown out of successful attempts to define brain-behavior relationships in adults (Boll, 1974; Dean, 1986a; Hartlage & Telzrow, 1985).

Neuropsychological assessment is a noninvasive method of examining brain function by studying its behavioral product (Lezak, 1983). In some respects, neuropsychological assessment does not differ greatly from traditional psychoeducational assessment in that it relies on some of the same theories and techniques used by the latter. Where it does differ, however, is in its assumption that all behavior is mediated by cerebral function, if not its direct result. Neuropsychological assessment differs also in that it uses instruments that are designed to assess deficits in specific neuropsychological functional systems (Hartlage & Telzrow, 1985; Hynd & Willis, 1988; Lezak, 1983, Luria, 1966). Further, neuropsychological assessment emphasizes the identification and measurement of cognitive, emotional, and control deficits, because it is primarily in these deficits that brain impairment is behaviorally manifested (Lezak, 1983). A number of specialized assessment procedures have been developed that aid in the diagnosis and localization of cerebral dysfunction, and allow valid, empirically based conclusions about the integrity of cerebral functioning in both cognitive and affective dimensions of behavior. Two of the most frequently used neuropsychological measures are the Halstead–Reitan Neuropsychological Battery (HRNB) (Reitan & Wolfson, 1985) and the Luria–Nebraska Neuropsychological Battery (LNNB) (Golden, Hammeke, & Purisch, 1980).

A growing number of authors (e.g., Chittooran, D'Amato, & Dean, 1990; D'Amato, Gray, & Dean, 1988; Hynd & Obrzut, 1981a, 1981b) have advocated the inclusion of neuropsychological measures as a valuable adjunct to traditional psychoeducational assessment since these measures provide additional unique information. Although proponents of the neuropsychological approach do not deny the validity of other perspectives, they realize the limitations of competing approaches in the ability to offer explanatory statements about an individual's behavior. For example, many children with learning problems (Gaddes, 1985), as well as behavior problems (Selz & Wilson, 1989), have been shown to have some degree of neurological impairment. Many important neuropsychological functions upon which learning is predicated (i.e., sensory perception, motor functions) cannot be adequately addressed using only a traditional psychoeducational approach. Therefore, neuropsychological assessment generally allows for the examination of a wider spectrum of functions than the traditional assessment batteries and has been shown to improve differential diagnosis of learning problems both between and within groups of students (e.g., D'Amato & Dean, 1988; Hynd & Obrzut, 1981b). Often this differential diagnosis allows better decisions for rehabilitation, because neuropsychological profiles help to plan strategies of compensation based on strengths and deficits; whereas, remediation is successful in learning problems that are not biologically based.

A typical neuropsychological examination begins with a developmental history. Marked deviations from normal development often suggest potential problems that may need to be investigated more thoroughly. Information gathered on prenatal, perinatal, and postnatal development can highlight neurodevelopmental factors that may have impinged upon subsequent learning or behavior problems (D'Amato, Chittooran, & Whitten, in press; Volpe, 1987). Much of this information has traditionally been gathered informally; however, there have been some attempts to develop standardized measures in this area, for example, the Maternal Perinatal Scale (MPS) (Gray, Dean, & Rattan, 1987).

Once neurodevelopmental information has been gathered, the neuropsychologist examines current clinical indicators of neuropathology. The mental status examination (Lezak, 1983; Sattler, 1988) is used to examine clients' orientation to time, place, and persons, as well as to gain additional information about their appearance, speech, affect, and cognition. This examination, although brief, has been found to be invaluable as a screening measure for problems that might subsequently be studied more thoroughly (Sattler, 1988). Much of the information that the neuropsychologist gathers can be classified as addressing "soft neurological signs" (e.g., developmental difficulties, motor awkwardness, poor gait, inadequate reflexes, tremors, word-finding difficulties). Although the rehabilitation of "hard neurological signs" (e.g., seizures) is generally the domain of the neurologist rather than the neuropsychologist (Gaddes, 1985; Lezak, 1983), such signs add important information about the individual and are always considered in a complete neuropsychological assessment.

A typical neuropsychological evaluation includes a measure of neuropsychological functioning (e.g., Halstead–Reitan Neuropsychological Battery), general intellectual ability (e.g., the Wechsler scales), academic achievement (e.g., the WRAT–R), laterality (e.g., Lateral Preference Schedule), emotional functioning (e.g., the Minnesota Multiphasic Inventory), and a variety of supplemental measures selected to increase the accuracy of prediction of cerebral impairment. Ongoing clinical and situational observations are also a vital part of the evaluation. The generation of such a volume of developmental and clinical data is based upon the assumption that it will improve the ability of the practitioner to understand client functioning, aid in differential diagnosis, and facilitate the development of appropriate interventions (D'Amato, 1990; Dean 1981, 1982a, 1982b; Hynd & Obrzut, 1981b; Rourke, 1985).

NEUROPSYCHOLOGICAL CONTRIBUTIONS TO EDUCATIONAL REHABILITATION

Although the field of neuropsychology has made significant strides in recent years, much of the information gathered in the area of brain–behavior relationships is only slowly gaining acceptance in fields outside of neuropsychology. Education is one such area. Perhaps the greatest contribution that neuropsychology has made to education, relates to the notion of differential hemispheric functioning and how it affects learning (D'Amato, 1990). The human brain is divided into two structurally distinct but anatomically similar hemispheres, which are connected by the corpus callosum (Hynd & Willis, 1988). This physical configuration as well as early localization research suggests that the two hemispheres may serve some discrete functions. Each hemisphere has been shown to control the sensory input and motor output of the contralateral side of the body, as well as jointly mediating other functions. There are several ways of looking at differential hemispheric functioning that are potentially educationally significant. The right hemisphere is thought to control nonverbal functions, while the left is thought to be primarily verbal (Hynd & Willis, 1988). The right hemisphere appears to use a more visual, creative, spatial, holistic, and simultaneous processing approach, while the left hemisphere uses a more abstract, verbal, analytical, and sequential processing one (Table 7.1). According to various sources (e.g., Das, 1973; Dean, 1984, 1986c), the right hemisphere organizes information in terms of structural similarity, while the left hemisphere organizes it in terms of conceptual similarity.

Approaches to Rehabilitation

Since assessment is rarely, if ever, the end product of a practitioner's impact on individuals, it is imperative that the information gained during assessment be both significant and usable in terms of planning interventions. A vast amount of information is potentially available to the neuropsychologist concerning how brain impairment or dysfunction affects an individual's educational and psychological performance. A number of authors (Gray & Dean, 1989; Hartlage & Telzrow, 1983; Kaufman & Kaufman, 1983a, 1983b) have argued that superior outcomes were reported for educational intervention efforts that were based on strengths related to how the brain processes information. Although the science of neuropsychological rehabilitation is still in its infancy when compared with the diagnosis of such problems (D'Amato, 1990; Naglieri & Das, 1988; Telzrow, 1986), it is

TABLE 7.1 Lateralized Functions of the Right and Left Hemispheres

Right Hemisphere

Processing Modes	Reference
Simultaneous	Sperry (1974)
Holistic	Sperry (1969)
	Dimond & Beaumont (1974)
Visual/nonverbal	Sperry (1974)
Imagery	Seamon & Gazzaniga (1973)
Spatial reasoning	Sperry (1974)

Nonverbal Functions	Reference
Depth perception	Carmon & Bechtoldt (1969)
Melodic perception	Shankweiler (1966)
Tactile perception (integration)	Boll (1974)
Haptic perception	Witelson (1974)
Nonverbal sound recognition	Milner (1962)
Motor integration	Kimura (1967)
Visual constructive performance	Parsons, Vega, & Burn (1969)
Pattern recognition	Eccles (1973)

Memory/Learning	Reference
Nonverbal memory	Stark (1961)
Face recognition	Milner (1967)
	Hecaen & Angelergues (1962)

Left Hemisphere

Processing Modes	Reference
Sequential	Sperry, Gazzaniga, Bogen (1969)
	Mills (1977) Efron (1963)
Temporal	Morgan, McDonald, & McDonald (1971)
Analytic	Eccles (1973)

Verbal Functions	Reference
Speech	Wada (1949) Reitan (1955)
General language/verbal abilities	Gazzaniga (1970)
	Smith (1974)
Calculation/arithmetic	Reitan (1955)
	Gerstmann (1957)
	Eccles (1973)
Abstract verbal thought	Gazzaniga & Sperry (1962)
Writing (composition)	Sperry (1974)
	Hecaen & Marcie (1974)
Complex motor functions	Dimond & Beaumont (1974)
Body orientation	Gerstmann (1957)
Vigilance	Dimond & Beaumont (1974)

Learning Memory	Reference
Verbal paired-associates	Dimond & Beaumont (1974)
Short-term verbal recall	Kimura (1961)
Abstract and concrete words	McFarland, McFarland, Bain, & Ashton (1978)
	Seamon & Gazzaniga (1975)
Verbal mediation/rehearsal	Dean (1983)
	Seamon & Gazzaniga (1973)
Learning complex motor functions	Dimond & Beaumont (1974)

SOURCE: Reprinted with permission from "Lateralization of Cerebral Functions" by R. S. Dean, 1986, in D. Wedding, A. M. Horton, and J. S. Webster, Eds., *Handbook of Clinical and Behavioral Neuropsychology*, p. 83. New York: Springer. (Publishing information for the references listed can be found in Dean.)

expected that rehabilitation will eventually supersede diagnosis in terms of its contribution to the science of neuropsychology (Dean, 1985a, 1985b). This may be especially applicable to the kinds of neurologically related conditions that are most frequent in a pediatric population (i.e., learning disabilities, epilepsy, or specific head trauma; Telzrow, 1986). Although neuropsychological assessment batteries include many tests frequently used by the school psychologist, the interpretation of results obtained from identical measures may be quite different because of the neuropsychologist's emphasis on the biological factors involved in human behavior. Basing definitions of client strengths and weaknesses on a framework of empirically defined brain–behavior relationships allows the neuropsychologist to make decisions concerning the utility of compensatory or remedial rehabilitive therapy. Moreover, a variety of techniques and instruments that are not utilized by school psychologists are regularly used by neuropsychologists. The neuropsychological test battery includes tasks that measure sensory perception, spatial abilities, and motor tasks that allow the psychologist to compare functioning between the two hemispheres of the brain. These batteries are not set up like aptitude or scholastic ability scales; rather, they are deficit scales. Deficit scales pick tasks that are assumed to be easy for the majority of children for which the task is appropriate. Therefore, if a child cannot master a task a deficit is assumed. Neuropsychological assessment is not organized to reveal better-than-average performance. Either the child is adequate in his or her abilities or not.

Assessment results often point to specific strengths and weaknesses across a number of intellectual, reasoning, language, perceptual–motor, and memory tasks (Teeter, 1989). The neuropsychological approach to rehabilitation differs markedly from traditional approaches in that rather than attempting to remediate skill deficits by teaching, it builds upon identified strengths in order to compensate for weaknesses (Hartlage & Telzrow, 1983, 1985; Teeter, 1989; Telzrow, 1986). Neuropsychologists utilize a compensatory rather than merely a remedial approach to rehabilitation. Acknowledging and defining patterns of cerebral strengths and weaknesses allows the practitioner to teach compensatory skills that circumvent rather than accent idiosyncratic weaknesses. Neuropsychological rehabilitation is predicated not only upon the client's strengths and limitations, but also upon the use of sound educational theory and practice (Teeter, 1989).

Although compensation is often the preferred approach to rehabilitation, there are instances when remediation is appropriate. For example, children under five years of age have central nervous systems whose plasticity allows for the reorganization of neural pathways around dysfunctional zones (Rutter, 1983). Therefore a program of remediation could facilitate this rerouting of function, whereas a compensatory approach might actually hinder the child's rehabilitation. Another instance where rehabilitation might be most beneficial is with an older child, whose original learning problems have resulted in the child's not trying any longer. In this scenerio, the child may have tried to compensate for mild deficits by completely avoiding tasks that seemed beyond his or her capabilities, no longer trying. Thus, observed deficits may be more reflective of psychological or emotional variables than neuropsychological deficits. In cases such as these, as well as cases where there are reasons other than neuropsychological dysfunction for educational difficulties, attempts to remediate weaknesses would be considered an important and valid part of a rehabilitation program. In determining what type of interventions to attempt, the neuropsychologist must take into account such factors as age, known neurological damage, age when damage occurred, nature and severity of deficits, and premorbid performance, as well as all the environmental and motivational factors that are usually assessed (Rourke, Bakker, Fisk, & Strang, 1983).

Given recent medical advances, the numerous employment opportunities, and the growing number of professional organizations and journals that focus on this discipline, it seems very probable that neuropsychology will gain an increasingly firm foothold in the future. The basic premise of the science—that human behavior cannot be studied and understood outside the context of the brain that controls it—is simple. Yet its simplicity belies its utility and the implications that arise from it. Indeed, one of the basic premises that differentiates neuropsychology from other psychological disciplines is that the rehabilitation and hopefully ultimate prevention of problems must be preceded by an understanding of their etiologies. For those who are committed to serving the best interests of children and adults, neuropsychology would seem to hold promise for a more comprehensive understanding of human behavior.

ANALYSIS OF CASE DATA

When we consider assessment from a neuropsychological perspective, the main focus is the biological basis of the client's behavior. Information from all functional domains, although rendering the overall assessment more complex, is considered relevant and essential to provide precise descriptive information about current neuropsychological status. By accepting the premise that the central nervous system (CNS) controls behavior, it follows that all of Vince's behaviors, including his feelings and opinions, are relevant and must be considered. The evaluation is usually based upon information from the referral question, historical information, and the neuropsychological assessment.

Referral Question

As is the case with any type of assessment done by psychologists, the referral question is the first relevant issue. Vince was referred by his parents and teachers because of a decline in academic achievement and a perceived increase in antisocial behavior. Vince's grades fluctuated from high average to average until this year, when they dropped to D's and F's. His parents and teachers indicated that he seems to be having particular difficulty in organizing his writing as well as planning other aspects of his life. His study skills were also reported to be poor by his teachers; however, no specific skill deficiencies were noted. His behavior problems were described as a low frustration tolerance, a tendency to be easily excited, and an inability to relate to adults and peers. Although it is not specifically addressed in the case history, the assumption is that Vince's parents and teachers hope this assessment will provide information concerning the biological, educational, and socioemotional basis of Vince's behavior, as well as recommendations that will enable them to begin to help Vince solve, or at least learn to cope with some of his current problems.

After thoroughly exploring the referral concerns, the next step in the assessment process is to acquire a detailed history to determine as accurately as possible the course and etiology of Vince's difficulties (Lezak, 1983). A detailed history will enable the practitioner to understand how Vince's experiences have affected his neuropsychological development and his perceptions of himself and his world. The history integrates information from the areas of education, cognition, socialization, and family dynamics, as well as from neurological, medical, and developmental indicators. Since Vince's history has been detailed in Chapter 2, it will not be recounted here except as it specifically applies to a neuropsychological perspective, and indeed, there are several issues in Vince's background that are especially important.

Background Information

Neurodevelopment. Neuropsychological evaluations begin by assessing prenatal and perinatal as well as postnatal development because of the clear impact that neurodevelopment has been shown to have on later cognitive, social, and emotional development (Gray, Dean, & Rattan, 1987; Osofsky, 1979). When a child like Vince has sustained cerebral damage early in development, the damage may have a striking influence on the future development of brain–behavior relationships and therefore the resulting patterns of abilities are often quite different from those of a person who has displayed normal development (Reitan & Wolfson, 1985). Vince's mother reported no prenatal or perinatal abnormalities and Vince's postnatal medical history was unremarkable until he was 16 months old, at which time he contracted a series of severe ear infections. These ear infections were coupled with high fevers that resulted in three instances of febrile seizures.

Vince's mother indicated that the ear infections resulted in hearing problems and articulation difficulties that delayed Vince's language development. Of the many variables that can affect school performance, adequate oral language development, both receptive and productive, has been documented to be among the most critical (Rubin & Dworkin, 1985). By the time most children enter kindergarten, they are able to comprehend language effectively and are skilled conversationalists. Most are also able to use the rules of language correctly and consistently in speech, even though they don't formally learn grammar and syntax rules until several years later. The development of articulation and comprehension is usually complete by age eight, although the child continues to learn new words and new rules throughout his or her life (Rubin & Dworkin, 1985). Oral language impairments have been shown to hinder reading, writing, and comprehension of all subjects (Telzrow, 1990). Therefore, it is not surprising that during elementary school, language-intensive subjects such as recitation and memory work were reported to be especially problematic for Vince. In fact, these difficulties could well have been expected given Vince's hearing and articulation problems.

Psychopharmacology. A careful look at the drugs administered to clients throughout their lives are especially significant in a neuropsychological evaluation because transmission of information within the brain is electrochemical in nature. Any chemicals/drugs taken into the body have the potential of interfering with thought processes and altering feelings. Most drugs that can alter physical, mental, or psychological processes in adults have been shown to have profound or even permanent effects on developing children and young adults (Kalat, 1984). At 19 months, Vince was put on phenobarbital to control seizure activity associated with severe ear infection and high fever. The phenobarbital appeared to be effective in controlling the seizure activity. However, since there have been reported instances of intellectual deterioration resulting from the use of phenobarbital and other barbiturates (Kastrup & Olin, 1987), this drug regime may have had a bearing on some of the problems Vince is currently experiencing.

When Vince was eight years old, during his parents' divorce, he was placed on Ritalin because of his high activity level. Ritalin is a mild cortical stimulant whose exact mechanism of action is still not known (Kastrup & Olin, 1987). Sometimes insomnia is a side effect of Ritalin therapy and severe depression has been documented to result from abrupt cessation of the medication (Kastrup & Olin, 1987). Ritalin is used to control hyperactive behavior in children secondary to attention deficit disorder. It is not recommended for clients with marked anxiety, tension, or agitation because it has been shown to increase those symptoms (Kastrup & Olin, 1987). With this in mind, Ritalin could have exacerbated Vince's behavioral problems (e.g., increased his depression and anxiety relative to his parents' divorce).

Vince remained on Ritalin until he was 11 years old (fifth grade). It was discontinued because it seemed to be causing sleep difficulties and nightmares. Vince was then placed on the antihistamine diphenhydramine (Benadryl) once per day, two to three times per week as a sedative to help him sleep more peacefully. Diphenhydramine does not filter from the body into the brain at recommended dosages (i.e., cross the blood–brain barrier) and therefore would seem to have had no permanent effect on Vince's ability or desire to learn. Vince is not currently on any medications, and therefore the major psychopharmacologic concern at this time is the long-term effects of his previous medication history. No medical referral for psychopharmacologic therapy seems currently indicated.

Emotional Indicators.   Vince's early language problems appear further exacerbated by his attempts at compensation. He had what were portrayed as minor social problems (i.e., acting out behavior) during early elementary school. It was noted by parents and teachers that Vince's behavioral problems seemed to increase in proportion to his difficulties with academic tasks and that he used behavioral disruption as a tactic to direct attention away from his academic difficulties. This is important from a neuropsychological perspective because it suggests that Vince's efforts to avoid embarrassment may have led to even less academic success and further indicates that some remedial strategies as well as compensatory techniques may be needed in his rehabilitation program. It seems that as the pressure on Vince to perform academically increased, so did Vince's acting out, which eventually resulted in his dismissal from private school in fourth grade.

This background information coupled with the referral question suggests that a comprehensive neuropsychological assessment would be beneficial in understanding Vince's learning and emotional difficulties.

Neuropsychological Evaluation

A neuropsychological evaluation is undertaken to determine a child's strengths and weaknesses in an effort to effect optimal rehabilitation. A complete neuropsychological evaluation most often includes a test of intelligence, a measure of achievement, a neuropsychological instrument, an objective assessment of personality, and clinical information collected during the assessment process. Vince's mental status was stable; he was oriented to time, place, and person throughout the assessment.

Intelligence/Cognitive Abilities

Wechsler Intelligence Scale for Children—Revised.   Vince's overall Intelligence Quotient (IQ) on the WISC–R was 108 +/− 6 (see Table 7.2), which places his abilities in the Average range of intellectual functioning (Sattler, 1988). However, it is often more neuropsychologically advantageous to discuss individual scores and scores that cluster in areas of strengths and weaknesses than to just assess global cognitive functioning (Lezak, 1983). The first issue worthy of note in understanding Vince's cognitive ability is the difference in his verbal and performance scales, as defined by his verbal WISC–R score (118), and his performance score (96) (Sattler, 1988). Vince's 22 point difference suggests important differences in his ability to learn from different types of stimuli (Black, 1974; Kaufman, 1979). These two scales of the WISC–R have been shown to be indicative of differences in functional capacity of the two hemispheres.

Kaufman (1979) outlined several ways of grouping the WISC–R subtests based on current theories of the structure and nature of intelligence. These clusters have proved quite useful and are often used to elucidate specific idiosyncratic patterns of functional ability (Sattler, 1988). Overall, Vince showed no significant strengths or weaknesses when his scores were grouped within the areas of verbal abilities or performance. Vince displayed an overall and even ability in the average range of functioning.

Another educationally useful way to group scores from the WISC–R is in the overall areas of verbal comprehension—Information (IN), Similarities (SI), Vocabulary (VO), and Comprehension (CP)—perceptual organization—Picture Completion (PC), Picture Arrangement (PA), Block Design (BD), and Object Assembly (OA)—and attention/concentration—Arithmetic (AR), Digit Span (DS), and Coding (CO) (Kaufman, 1979). Within the area of verbal reasoning, Vince scored overall at the 84th percentile. His skills were not uniformly developed and ranged from the 95th percentile (verbal problem solving) to the 75th percentile (long-term memory, old learning). This latter score is most likely an indication of the extent of his earlier hearing disability rather than an inability to remember. Obviously, a student cannot remember that which was not heard. In the area of nonverbal reasoning Vince scored overall at the 50th percentile. Vince's abilities in this area appear to be uniformly developed. In the group of subtests that require sustained attention and concentration Vince scored overall at the 75th percentile.

Last, complete interpretation of the WISC–R requires that individual subtests be compared with each other to define specific strengths and weaknesses. Vince showed

TABLE 7.2   WISC–R Subtest Scaled Scores

Subtest	Scaled Score	Subtest	Scaled Score
Information (IN)	10	Picture Completion (PC)	9
Similarities (SI)	16	Picture Arrangement (PA)	11
Arithmetic (AR)	12	Block Design (BD)	10
Vocabulary (VO)	12	Object Assembly (OA)	8
Comprehension (CP)	15	Coding (CO)	9
Digit Span (DS)	14		

VIQ = 118 +/− 7; PIQ = 96 +/− 10; FSIQ = 108 +/− 6

Note: VIQ = Verbal Intelligence Quotient; PIQ = Performance Intelligence Quotient; FSIQ = Overall Intelligence Quotient.

significant strengths on both the subtests that required high verbal reasoning abilities (SI, CP). His ability to define similarities in objects usually defined by their differences fell in the very superior range. His ability to understand everyday situations was in the superior range (Sattler, 1988). Although Vince's math grades have remained the most stable his mathematical reasoning ability fell in the average range and was not considered an overall strength (Sattler, 1988). Vince displayed no weaknesses compared to his overall level of abilities as measured by the WISC–R.

Achievement

Woodcock–Johnson Tests of Achievement.   Intelligence as measured by an intelligence test is usually compared to a child's achievement as determined by his or her scores on a norm-referenced achievement test. This procedure is used to see if the child is actually performing at a level commensurate with his or her ability scores. If these levels are not similar (i.e., within 1 standard deviation of one another), this is considered an indication of a learning disability. While little research supports this notion, especially from a neuropsychological perspective, it remains common practice in psychoeducational assessment.

Vince's standardized scores on the WJTA, a nationally standardized test of academic achievement, were: Reading 94, Mathematics 100, Written Language 80, and Knowledge 87. With the exception of the Written Language component, which fell at the 9th percentile, Vince's scores all fell in the average range of achievement for his age. However, the discrepancy between his abilities as measured by the WISC–R (FSIQ = 108) and his achievement in Written Language and Knowledge, as measured by the WJTA, is large enough to qualify Vince for learning disability services in most school systems and suggests the need for an individualized educational program in the areas of reading, written language, and general knowledge. Therefore, an integrative look at the tests that were administered appears to be needed to further evaluate a possible learning disability and determine the best way to approach his special learning needs by defining the nature of any underlying learning problems that affect Vince's ability to achieve commensurate with his abilities.

Neuropsychological Functioning

Halstead–Reitan Neuropsychological Battery (HRNB).   The HRNB includes 13 tests that were chosen based on their ability to predict brain dysfunction. The entire battery, as proposed by Reitan and Wolfson (1985), consists of the 13 tests of the HRNB, the age appropriate Wechsler Scale, and an objective measure of personality, most often the Minnesota Multiphasic Personality Inventory. Vince's HRNB scores are shown in Table 7.3.

The *Category Test* has been shown to be useful in measuring nonverbal abstract reasoning and concept formation (Lezak, 1983; Reitan & Wolfson, 1985; Selz, 1981). The test requires students to select numbers corresponding to abstract problem-solving criteria, (i.e., using rules that are not explained to them). If the student's answer is correct a bell tone is sounded, if incorrect a buzzing sound indicates the error. This immediate feedback is important since the test assesses the ability to solve novel problems and learn

TABLE 7.3 HRNB Scores

Measure	Score	Range
Category	55	Mild impairment
Seashore Rhythm	5	Adequate
Speech–Sounds Perception	8	Moderate impairment
Tactile Performance Test (TPT)–Dominant	3.9	Mild impairment
Nondominant	1.8	Adequate
Both Hands	0.9	Adequate
Location	6	Excellent
Memory	6	Excellent
Trail Making A	17	Adequate
Trail Making B	60	Moderate impairment
Aphasia Errors	9	Mild impairment
Tapping Dominant	48	Adequate
Tapping Nondominant	44	Adequate

from feedback. This task has been shown to predict general neuropsychological impairment. Vince's score of 55 suggests a mild degree of impairment of general cognitive abilities.

The *Tactile Performance Test* (TPT) uses a form board and requires the student to place blocks in appropriate slots while blindfolded. This is done using the dominant hand alone, the nondominant hand alone, and then both hands together. The TPT offers five separate scores, three for time, one for location, and one for memory. This test provides information on tactual discrimination, sensory recognition, and spatial memory (Dean 1985a; Selz, 1981). With his dominant hand (right), Vince's score suggested a mild degree of impairment, implicating left hemispheric involvement. This could also be interpreted as a novelty issue, where his lowered score may have been more affected by the newness of the task than the hemisphere most likely to have mediated the behavior. In Vince's case the problem could also be one of integration of function (receptive and productive) between the two hemispheres. His nondominant hand score fell in the adequate range, as did his score using both hands. The localization and memory scores indicated an excellent range of functioning.

The *Speech–Sounds Perception Test* is a measure of verbal auditory discrimination, integration, and attention (Dean, 1985a; Lezak, 1983). A tape-recorded voice presents nonsense words, and the student selects the correct word from an array of four written possibilities. This test has been shown to be most sensitive to left hemispheric dysfunction. Vince's score on this test fell in the moderately impaired range, which again suggests left hemispheric impairment. However, given Vince's previous hearing problems it is possible that he may have sustained impairment in auditory discrimination because he has quit trying, or perhaps he never learned to discriminate between certain speech sounds. This differentiation is important in that the basis of the problem determines the type of rehabilitation that is most appropriate.

The *Seashore Rhythm Test* is a measure of nonverbally impacted auditory discrimination and perception (Lezak, 1983; Selz, 1981). On this test, the student identifies patterns of tones as being the same or different. Success depends upon concentration and attention as well as nonverbal auditory discrimination and is often considered indicative of the functioning of the right hemisphere. However, Reitan and Wolfson (1985) suggest that this test is also a test of overall impairment. Vince's score on this test fell in the adequate range, suggesting no concentration or nonverbal auditory discrimination problems.

The *Trail Making Test* is composed of two tracking tests, which conjointly measure symbolic recognition and visual tracking under time restraints (Reitan & Wolfson, 1985). Some authors suggest that Trails A is predominantly controlled by right hemispheric function, while Trails B is contingent upon left hemispheric function as well (Dean, 1985a; Selz, 1981). Therefore, it is often difficult to interpret Trails B if Trails A is impaired, because basic right hemispheric function is essential for success at both tasks. Reitan and Wolfson (1985) suggest that the Trail Making Tests measure overall functioning because symbolic recognition is a left hemisphere function, whereas the visual-scanning component is more clearly representative of right hemispheric functioning. Vince showed adequate skills on Trail Making A and moderate impairment on Trail Making B, which again appears to suggest a difficulty in the integration of information between the two hemispheres.

The *Finger Oscillation Test* requires the client to depress a lever as quickly as possible with each index finger. Differences in speed are considered indicative of differences in cerebral hemispheric impairment. Vince's scores suggested adequate fine motor functioning for both hemispheres.

The *Aphasia Screening Test* assesses both language and nonverbal left hemispheric functions (e.g., naming, copying, spelling, reading, and writing) (Lezak, 1983; Selz, 1981). Vince's score on this test indicates mildly impaired functioning, which again may be explained by the intrahemispheric demands of some of the questions.

Overall, the HRNB suggests a deficit in left hemispheric function (D'Amato, 1990; Selz, 1981) or in intrahemispheric functioning (Reitan & Wolfson, 1985). At first glance, the apparent contradiction between the neuropsychological evaluation and the standard school battery seems difficult to reconcile. However, upon closer inspection, some patterns emerge that show how significant and beneficial the information generated from a neuropsychological approach can be. The information from the HRNB lends new insight to the interpretation of the scatter seen on the WISC–R profile, and the other aptitude/ achievement tests in the battery. This new information added by the neuropsychological assessment suggests that Vince's difficulties in math word problems and language could result from a combination of problems. His neuropsychological deficiencies, discrimination of speech and interhemispheric functioning need to be compensated for. His maladaptive defenses related to previous failure and his gaps in knowledge due to past learning problems need to be remediated. To adequately deal with these behaviors, a plan for compensatory education based on Vince's strengths and remediation based on his educable weaknesses will need to be developed.

Personality.   Since learning disabilities do not exist in isolation, understanding and documenting the child's coping style and emotional status is essential in any attempt to understand and rehabilitate. Among the most important factors to assess are the emotional overlay that is often associated with learning disabilities and serious psychopathologies, so that they do not interfere with rehabilitation efforts (Teeter, 1989). Often emotional overlay cannot be separated from cognitive functioning (Dean & Rattan, in press). Vince does not appear to have any evidence of severe psychopathologies; however, background information and behavioral observations as well as objective and projective personality assessment suggest that emotional stress is interfering with Vince's ability to achieve to his greatest potential. It is not unusual for children with learning problems that go unnoticed this long to have emotional reactions to learning failure.

Vince's background information suggests that academic work has become progressively more difficult through time. It further suggests that he has learned to use avoidance and misbehavior to cope with and defend against recognition of his learning problems. Behavioral observation shows him to become frustrated if he cannot easily accomplish his schoolwork. He appears to be unwilling to try and accomplish tasks unless he is fairly certain of his success. He stated that he could get good grades if he wanted to; however, his behavior implies that he is often afraid to try due to fear of failure.

On the *Piers–Harris Children's Self-Concept Scale* (Piers–Harris) and the *Children's Manifest Anxiety Scale* (CMAS), Vince's scores indicate that he does not feel good about some of his abilities. The Piers–Harris indicated that Vince felt his behavior and intellectual ability may be problematic. The results also suggested that he felt as good about his physical appearance and abilities as do other children his age. The CMAS indicated high levels of anxiety in areas related to attention, task orientation, and social acceptance. The *Vineland* is a behavioral measure that assesses adaptive behavior in children by conversation with the primary caretaker, usually the mother. It renders information on how the parent sees the child's adaptation to his or her environment. As could be expected, given his mother's propensity to ignore Vince's difficulties, there were no problems noted by her on the Vineland. The *Behavior Evaluation Scale* is filled out by the student's teachers to assess the child's adaptation to the school environment. Vince appears to have the most trouble adapting to his Family Living class, as evidenced by his teacher's report of inability to learn, poor peer relations, depression, and overall lowered ability in that class. English is the next most problematic class, where he is listed as having an overall inability to learn.

Overall, Vince's responses on subjective personality measures indicate that he is anxious and fearful of academic failure, especially in language-intensive areas. Vince seems to worry about his future, and he appears to need high levels of acceptance that he may not currently be receiving. His responses also indicated that he realizes his current behavior is not appropriate.

Vince's problems appear to be exacerbated by his mother who does not seem to be able to understand or accept how Vince feels. In fact, the Vineland, which was based on an interview with his mother, shows none of the problems expressed by Vince and his teachers. She seems to believe that everything is all right, which puts Vince in a double bind. Not only does he need comfort and support as he works out his feelings about his father, but his mother, his only security, may not empathize with his experience or his feelings. Vince's emotional evaluation further suggests that he is distressed about his parents' divorce and currently has no avenue to express his frustration. He appears to resent the stepfather's presence in his life, but tolerates him because the stepfather seems to make his mother happy. It is not surprising that he has overall behavior problems in his Family Living class considering his desire to reunite his family and his feelings that his current family is not a real family.

SUMMARY AND INTERVENTION RECOMMENDATIONS

Vince's intelligence as measured by the WISC–R was 108 +/− 6, which falls in the average range of intellectual functioning for children his age. The 22-point difference between his verbal and perceptual abilities suggest that he may have some neuropsychological impairment. Vince's perceptual abilities fall at the 50th percentile and are a weakness compared to his overall ability. This suggests that his impairment could be either a right hemisphere dysfunction, or an interhemispheric problem. Vince displayed a strength in his verbal problem-solving ability (95th percentile), suggesting that if he can learn to compensate for his verbal auditory discrimination problems, he may be able to be successful at verbally mediated tasks. Vince's achievement scores on the WJTA were not commensurate with his intellectual abilities in the areas of written language and general knowledge. This difference is large enough to qualify him for special education services. However, junior high school would seem too late for an initial placement in special education if academic rehabilitation can be accomplished in a less restrictive environment. Vince's scores on the HRNB suggest that he has some mild overall impairment in neuropsychological functioning in the area of nonverbal problem solving, moderate impairment in verbal auditory discrimination, and mild to moderate difficulties in interhemispheric processing. These results concur with his current academic difficulties in language-intensive subjects and in math as well. Neuropsychological weaknesses in language processing have been shown to interfere with mathematics reasoning ability, especially the ability to apply mathematical functions correctly (Telzrow, 1989). This fits with the problems noted in Vince's profile—his language disability is now beginning to circumscribe his math achievement as he is required to apply concepts rather than just compute a set of numbers.

Personality measures indicate that Vince's high level of emotional stress could be affecting his academic achievement. There are also indications of avoidance—trying to avoid attempting tasks without first trying to see if he can accomplish them. His tendency to downgrade or negate the importance of activities that are difficult for him confounds his academic achievement. Moreover, his acting out behaviors seem to negatively influence his school achievement as well. Vince's current level of stress seems to stem from two main sources: first, the emotional impact of dealing with an undefined learning disability and second, the increasing stress in his family relating to his parents' divorce and present living circumstances. These dilemmas are seriously compounded by Vince's hurt and feeling of rejection, and his mother's difficulty in recognizing his learning problems.

Based on the results of Vince's neuropsychological evaluation a threefold plan is recommended for Vince's academic rehabilitation that takes into account remediation, compensation, and counseling. Remediation is a process whereby a child is taught specific skills and ideas and is encouraged to practice them until mastery. Rehabilitation is useful for skills a child needs more time to master (e.g., developmental lag), needs more encouragement to master (e.g., motivational lag), or has not tried to master because of emotional overlay (e.g., fear of failure). Remediation efforts rest on the assumption that further or more extensive exposure to a subject through individualized instruction to strengthen specific areas of weakness will enable a child to learn needed information and skills. Compensation, on the other hand, is based on the premise that a person is unable to perform a certain skill because of underlying cerebral impairment and therefore must try to accomplish the overall objective of learning another way. Compensation is the basis for teaching a blind child to read by braille. No matter how long a blind child is taught the rules of reading and sits and stares at a regular printed book, she or he will not learn to read until the nature of the task is changed such that his or her processing limitations are overcome. For some areas of neurological deficits retraining is feasible (i.e., for very young children or older clients who have sustained a cerebral impairment), but for the most part teaching of compensatory skills is the most efficient and usually the only way to overcome significant neuropsychological limitations.

I. Remediation should be attempted in those areas in which Vince does not achieve commensurate with abilities because he has quit trying or because he has learning deficits which resulted from past hearing or learning problems (i.e., verbal skills, organizational skills, deficits in knowledge, and misbehavior).

II. Compensation techniques need to be taught in the areas of neuropsychological impairment. Vince's relative strengths and weaknesses defined by his overall achievement/ability profile suggest that the areas of verbal auditory discrimination, and interhemispheric processing should be dealt with by teaching compensation skills.

III. Counseling appears necessary for Vince and his family to help him integrate the emotional and social aspects of his life, which seem to be interfering with his ability to learn.

I. Remediation. Areas that appear to require remediation for Vince are all skills that are language-intensive, deficits in knowledge, organizational skills, and behavior. It seems that Vince has come to believe that he still cannot succeed in tasks that require language abilities, but there is no indication in this assessment that he has neuropsychological impairment that would prohibit global language functions except as they are circumscribed by his discrimination and processing disabilities. Therefore, it is recommended that:

1. Vince be given a complete assessment of subskills in all language-intensive areas by a speech or language specialist. Nothing should be taken for granted, since we know that Vince was not able to hear adequately as a child. Therefore, it cannot be assumed that acquisition of language skills followed a natural progression. After the assessment, a private tutor who is certified to work with learning disabled students is recommended to assist Vince. The recommendation for tutoring outside the school system is made because of the extent of emotional overlay present, which appears to be affecting his educability. It is felt that tutoring outside of school would be less stigmatizing for Vince. If a private learning disability tutor is not available, a part-time language referral to the speech language pathologist, or a referral to a resource room learning disabilities program, might be more beneficial than trying to give this level of remediation in the regular education classroom. Since Vince is currently in junior high school, perhaps this remediation could be offered instead of a study hall so that there is as little social stigma attached as possible.

2a. Whoever works with Vince on his language problems needs to carefully list the deficits found in his comprehensive assessment. Beginning with the most basic deficits, plan a remediation program of individualized instruction and rehearsal. Concrete manipulables should be used as much as possible. Concrete manipulables can be devised for language with some ingenuity. Things such as scrambled word games, analogy games, crosswords, and word search puzzles have been shown to be helpful ways to enhance language abilities. To teach Vince proper sentence structure, sentences that have been cut apart may be helpful. The sentences can be cut in such a way that the words fit together like a puzzle—this way Vince can self-correct at the beginning. As he becomes better at the process, perhaps the words of the sentences could be cut so that there were several obviously wrong ways that would physically fit, but only one grammatically correct way. The same process could be used when teaching Vince other skills.

2b. If the assessment shows that Vince does not use rules of oral or written language appropriately, actively teach Vince the rules of speech. Emphasize the parts of speech and the roles words play in our language. Help Vince to understand and improve his speaking skills by using a tape recorder to practice for oral presentations. Given Vince's history of hearing and articulation problems, he may not have a realistic notion of his current speaking abilities. Taping his own voice will help Vince to improve his speech and enable him to hear the improvement.

3. Vince's teachers should encourage him to engage in pleasure reading at his reading level or a little below to build confidence and allow Vince to catch up to his age mates in general written language skills and working vocabulary. Great effort should be made to find books at this reading level that interest him.

4. Although math appears to be Vince's area of academic strength, math word problems may be problematic for him. Given the nature of Vince's problems it would appear that he might benefit from direct teaching of all the concepts involved in word problems, as well as active teaching of how to decide what is important (i.e., necessary and sufficient) to consider in solving these problems. Make drill, and practice as interesting and as concrete as possible by using a variety of familiar and interesting experiences. Vince may enjoy such things as figuring batting averages, won–lost percentages, bowling averages, and approximate costs of groceries or other home expenses.

5. In all subject areas, grade level concepts should be continued to be taught with emphasis upon visual aids and concrete demonstrations. This is important, given Vince's problems in processing between hemispheres. He needs as much discrete information as possible directed to each hemisphere individually. Therefore, present information verbally and nonverbally, simultaneously and sequentially and use pictures as well as words in separate activities.

6. Teach Vince how to organize his life as concretely as possible; he needs to be told what is expected of him; do not expect him to get the "big picture"

by himself. Verbalize as much as possible and encourage Vince to ask questions and to practice generalizing concepts he learns to many familiar situations. Part of Vince's difficulty in organization and planning appears to be an impulsive response pattern that he employs when confronted with tasks he finds difficult. Teach Vince to use basic concentration and study skills (reading for main idea, note taking, highlighting, outlining, summarizing, studying in an appropriate environment) by breaking down larger tasks into smaller tasks and teaching the smaller tasks individually. Having Vince play games that require increasing levels of concentration might also be helpful. Video games or computer chess might be beneficial in helping him to develop planning abilities and strategies. Give appropriate positive reinforcement for any small success in weighing alternatives before acting. Discourage wild guesses, by reinforcing pauses to consider alternatives. To aid in general organization and planning have Vince map out alternate routes to well-known locations within the community; extend to outlining routes for short trips within a 20-mile range. Have Vince, in a group at first and later alone, make planned, sequential activities for class projects, parties, or plays. He could also write instructions for common activities or make rules for a new game or sequentially list rules for familiar games.

7. As a small child in a rigid school situation, Vince's acting out behaviors may have been necessary to avoid work he may not have understood. However, now these tactics are educationally detrimental and need to be curtailed. Make certain that Vince's acting out behavior (e.g., forgetting papers), does not work to get him out of nonpreferred activities. Speak to Vince and explain what he is doing and how he could handle the situation more appropriately. Be supportive of Vince's underlying frustrations and problems but be firm in not allowing inappropriate behaviors to have positive rewards. Enforce adherence to rules by insisting that work not finished at appropriate times be finished during breaks, study hall, or after school. Present tasks in as pleasant a way as is possible, and try to put assignments in terms of a challenge rather than as projects related to success or failure.

II. Compensation. Compensatory skills need to be taught to Vince and used by his parents and teachers to circumvent Vince's neuropsychological impairments in the areas of auditory discrimination of human speech and interhemispheric processing difficulties. Because Vince's auditory reception has improved so steadily and drastically it may be easy for significant others to be unaware of Vince's subtle, but chronic, inability to differentiate between some of the normal sounds of human speech. It is not known currently whether Vince's deficiency in the area of verbal discrimination is neuropsychological and needs compensation or is an educational lag due to his chronic ear problems as a child coupled with his poor nonverbal problem-solving skills. Therefore, to ease some of Vince's current stress his verbal discrimination problems will be handled in a compensatory manner while exploring his skills in this area.

8. Evaluate the appropriateness of task assignment, given Vince's learning problems. A mastery learning approach might work very well for Vince.

Make sure that he can reasonably accomplish all tasks he is assigned. Give Vince assignments that circumvent his difficulties, and that he would enjoy doing. Gradually work in activities that are more difficult as he has time to work on these areas. Do not try to force Vince to attempt tasks that he feels he will fail at, such as speaking in public at the beginning. Gradually, as he works on his self-esteem and language skills, begin to give him opportunities to speak in front of others, and to experience success in other areas as well. Allow him appropriate decision-making opportunities relative to class work.

9. Significant others (parents and teachers) should give directions in a variety of ways to be sure Vince understands what is expected of him. Be as careful as possible to enunciate clearly, use simple instructions, and test for understanding. Make sure he is attending before beginning instructions. Make sure that verbal instructions are given in a helpful, nonthreatening way, and that Vince feels comfortable asking for clarification, if there is anything that he is not sure he understands. This may best be accomplished by approaching Vince in an adult-to-adult manner so that he doesn't feel patronized. Teach Vince when to ask questions, how to ask questions, and what kinds of questions elicit what type of information. Be patient and helpful when Vince asks a question. This may be difficult for him to do at first. Many of the questions he needs to ask may imply that he isn't listening. This may not be the case; he may be listening but not understanding. Often Vince may not realize that he has missed a key word or point, so review with him often to determine his level of understanding before he fails at a task.

10. As previously detailed, many different modalities of presentation may be helpful for Vince to comprehend the nuances and complexities of verbal language-intensive information. However, Vince's assessment results also suggest that he may benefit from as much constancy as is possible. Vince's language problems became more pronounced in seventh grade; thus it seems highly unlikely, given his profile, that it was merely coincidence that this was also the time that he had to hear and understand five new teachers instead of one or two. If it is possible, Vince may be more academically successful the fewer people he needs to hear and understand and the more familiar he is allowed to become with their voice and styles of classroom management. It might be beneficial if Vince's new teachers would interact frequently with Vince to help him familiarize himself with their voices and routines. Familiarity and consistency are important for Vince.

11. The interhemispheric demands of academic work increase over time. As the nature of the information learned becomes more abstract the more integration between the two hemispheres is required for mastery of information and skills. Vince might benefit from special effort being made to keep instruction as intrahemispheric as possible. As detailed previously, information using different modalities that affect the same hemisphere would be most beneficial.

12. Use a three-step approach when giving Vince information. Tell him in general terms what you are going to tell him. Tell him the specific information and then tell him what you told him in a summary. After this, ask him to explain to you, in his words, what you have said. This will reinforce the learning and will give him another modality (i.e., speaking or writing the information) to aid in his understanding and retaining the material. His teachers could have Vince write instructions at the top of the page, to enable them to check his comprehension of orally presented information.

III. Counseling. Learning disabled children often deal with their feelings of failure when they cannot succeed in academic areas by withdrawing, becoming reckless in their responses, or by exhibiting behaviors inappropriate to the situation (Dean & Rattan, in press). These reactions appear to be quite similar to aversive phobic responses and often extend or generalize far beyond the limitations of the child's original handicapping condition. Vince seems to display some of these emotional reactions to his academic and family stress. Therefore, an essential part of Vince's rehabilitation plan should be to modify his negative emotional responses by working with parents and teachers to relieve some of the stress in his life, while working closely with him individually as well.

13. Individual therapy is recommended for Vince. His self-image is currently negative and effort should be made to help Vince feel better about himself. Help Vince understand that succeeding in school and being liked by his peers are compatible goals. Diagnosing talents, aptitudes, and interests will help Vince understand where his aptitudes are and that he can succeed. Individual counseling could focus on explaining to Vince that his feelings and worries are not unusual given his circumstances. Help Vince to work through his parents' divorce, and get a more realistic picture of both his parents.

14. Family therapy is recommended to work on unresolved issues concerning his parents' divorce, his unrealistic notions about his parents, and his current family relationships. Family therapy could also help Vince's parents learn how to encourage him successfully. All individuals who work with Vince should sympathize with his uncomfortable feelings. Do not employ sarcasm or ridicule, as this has been shown to be ineffective with Vince.

15. Due to Vince's history of his father promising and not following through, and his mother and teachers threatening punishment and not following through, it is recommended that teachers and parents begin a consistent behavior modification program for Vince that enforces positive and negative consequences for his behavior. Such a program could be developed and monitored by the school psychologist.

16. Teachers and parents could help Vince to understand that he can be happy with his best efforts, and he should be made aware that he has difficulties that the other students do not have. Be sure that Vince understands that this does not make him stupid, that it just means that through no fault of his

own, schoolwork *is* harder for him than it may be for his friends. Reinforce acceptance of his real limitations and strengths. Emphasize individual differences and point out that everyone has strengths and weaknesses. Emphasize personal improvement over competition. Reinforce Vince for improvement, don't wait for perfection. Provide Vince with tasks he can be successful at and gradually increase the difficulty level of the tasks. Allow Vince to participate in activities in which he can excel. Minimize grading or other comparative procedures if possible and if not, modify the expectations of the school and home so that Vince can learn without such high levels of stress.

17. Vince should be able to successfully complete high school if he is given the rehabilitation outlined in these recommendations. He also may be able to successfully complete a baccalaureate degree at a university that is willing to work with learning disabled students. It is recommended that Vince begin now to explore career options that focus on and use his strengths. There are several good interest inventories available that could help him evaluate career strengths and interests. Vince should begin soon to give serious consideration to his future. Given more support from significant others and a better understanding of his disabilities, Vince should be quite successful in overcoming his current problems.

REFERENCES

Black, F. W. (1974). WISC verbal-performance discrepancies as indicators of neurological dysfunction in pediatric patients. *Journal of Clinical Psychology, 30,* 165–167.

Boll, T. J. (1974). Behavioral correlates of cerebral damage in children nine through fourteen. In R. M. Reitan & I. A. Davison (Eds.), *Clinical neuropsychology: Current status and applications.* New York: Wiley.

Chittooran, M. M., D'Amato, R. C., & Dean, R. S. (1990). *Factor structure of psychoeducational and neuropsychological measures with learning disabled children.* Manuscript under review.

D'Amato, R. C. (1990). A neuropsychological approach to school psychology. *School Psychology Quarterly, 5,* 141–160.

D'Amato, R. C., Chittooran, M. M., & Whitten, J. D. (in press). Neuropsychological implications of malnutrition. In L. C. Hartlage, D. Templer, & W. G. Cannon (Eds.), *Preventable brain damage: Brain vulnerability and brain health.* New York: Springer.

D'Amato, R. C., & Dean, R. S. (1988). School psychology practice in a department of neurology. *School Psychology Review, 17,* 416–420.

D'Amato, R. C., Dean, R. S., & Holloway, A. F. (1987). A decade of employment trends in neuropsychology. *Professional Psychology: Research and Practice, 18,* 653–655.

D'Amato, R. C., Gray, J. W., & Dean, R. S. (1988). A comparison between intelligence and neuropsychological functioning. *Journal of School Psychology, 26,* 282–292.

D'Amato, R. C., Hammons, P. F., Terminie, T. J., and Dean, R. S. (1990). *Neuropsychological training in American Psychological Association-approved and non-approved school psychology programs.* Manuscript under review.

Das, J. P. (1973). Structure of cognitive abilities: Evidence for simultaneous and successive processing. *Journal of Educational Psychology, 65,* 103–108.

Dean, R. S. (1981). Cerebral dominance and childhood learning disorders. *School Psychology Review, 10,* 373–380.

Dean, R. S. (1982a). Providing psychological services to school age children. In G. D. Miller (Ed.), *Differentiated levels of student support services: Crisis, remedial and developmental approaches* (pp. 98–123). St. Paul, MN: Pupil Personnel Services, MN State Department of Education.

Dean, R. S. (1982b). Neuropsychological assessment. In T. R. Kratochwill (Ed.), *Advances in School Psychology* (Vol. 2, pp. 171–201). Hillside, NJ: Erlbaum.

Dean, R. S. (1984). Functional lateralization of the brain. *Journal of Special Education, 18*, 239–256.

Dean, R. S. (1985a). Neuropsychological assessment. In J. D. Cavenar, R. Michels, H. K. H. Brodie, A. M. Cooper, S. B. Guze, L. L. Judd, G. L. Klerman, & A. J. Solnit (Eds.), *Psychiatry* (pp. 1–16). Philadelphia, PA: Lippincott.

Dean, R. S. (1985b). Foundation and rationale for neuropsychological bases of individual differences. In L. C. Hartlage & C. F. Telzrow (Eds.), *The neuropsychology of individual differences: A developmental perspective* (pp. 7–39). New York: Plenum.

Dean, R. S. (1986a). Perspectives on the future of neuropsychological assessment. In B. S. Plake & J. C. Witt (Eds.), *Buros-Nebraska series on measurement and testing: Future of testing and measurement.* (pp. 203–241). Hillside, NJ: Erlbaum.

Dean, R. S. (1986b). Neuropsychological aspects of psychiatric disorders. In J. E. Obrzut & G. W. Hynd (Eds.), *Child neuropsychology* (Vol. 2, pp. 10–34). New York: Academic.

Dean, R. S. (1986c). Lateralization of cerebral functions. In D. Wedding, A. M. Horton, & J. S. Webster (Eds.), *Handbook of clinical and behavioral neuropsychology* (pp. 80–102). New York: Springer.

Dean, R. S., & Rattan, A. (in press). How learning disabled students cope with failure. *International Journal of Neuroscience.*

Gaddes, W. H. (1985). *Learning disabilities and brain function.* (2nd ed.). New York: Springer.

Gibson, W. C. (1962). Pioneers of localization of function in the brain. *Journal of the American Medical Association, 180*, 944–951.

Golden, C. J., Hammeke, T. A., & Purisch, A. D. (1980). *Luria-Nebraska neuropsychological battery.* Los Angeles: Western Psychological Services.

Gray J. W., & Dean, R. S. (1989). Approaches to the cognitive rehabilitation of children with neuropsychological impairment. In C. R. Reynolds & E. Fletcher-Janzen, (Eds.), *Handbook of clinical child neuropsychology,* (pp. 397–408). New York: Plenum.

Gray, J. W., Dean, R. S., & Rattan, G. (1987). Assessment of perinatal risk factors. *Psychology in the Schools, 24*, 15–21.

Hartlage, L. C., & Telzrow, C. F. (1983). The neuropsychological bases of educational intervention. *Journal of Learning Disabilities, 16*, 521–528.

Hartlage, L. C., & Telzrow, C. F. (Eds.). (1985). *The neuropsychology of individual differences: A developmental perspective.* New York: Plenum.

Hynd, G. W., & Obrzut, J. E. (1981a). School neuropsychology. *Journal of School Psychology, 19*, 45–50.

Hynd, G. W., & Obrzut, J. E. (Eds.). (1981b). *Neuropsychological assessment and the school-age child: Issues and procedures.* New York: Grune & Stratton.

Hynd, G. W., Quackenbush, R., & Obrzut, J. E. (1980). Training school psychologists in neuropsychological assessment: Current practices and trends. *Journal of School Psychology, 18*, 148–153.

Hynd, G. W., & Willis, W. G. (1988). *Pediatric neuropsychology.* New York: Grune & Stratton.

Kalat, J. W. (Ed.). (1984). *Biological psychology* (2nd Ed.). Philadelphia: Wadsworth.

Kastrup, E. K., & Olin, B. R. (1987). *Drug facts and comparisons.* St. Louis: Lippincott.

Kaufman, A. S. (1979). *Intelligent testing with the WISC–R.* New York: Wiley.

Kaufman, A. S., & Kaufman, N. L. (1983a). *Kaufman Assessment Battery for Children: Administration and scoring manual.* Circle Pines, MN: American Guidance Service.

Kaufman, A. S., & Kaufman, N. L. (1983b). *Kaufman Assessment Battery for Children: Interpretive manual.* Circle Pines, MN: American Guidance Service.

Leavell, C. & Lewandowski, L. (1988). Neuropsychology in the schools: A survey report. *School Psychology Review, 17,* 147–155.

Lezak, M. D. (1983). *Neuropsychological assessment* (2nd ed.). New York: Oxford University Press.

Luria, A. R. (1966). *Higher cortical functions in man.* New York: Basic Books.

Naglieri, J. A., & Das, J. P. (1988). Planning-arousal-simultaneous-successive (PASS): A model for assessment. *Journal of School Psychology, 26,* 35–48.

Osofsky, J. (1979). *Handbook of infant development.* New York: Wiley.

Parks, R. W., Crockett, D. J., & McGeer, P. L. (1989). Systems model of cortical organization: Positron emission tomography and neuropsychological test performance. *Archives of Clinical Neuropsychology, 4,* 355–349.

Puente, A. E. (1989) Historical perspectives in the development of neuropsychology as a professional psychological specialty. In C. R. Reynolds & E. Fletcher-Janzen (Eds.), *Handbook of clinical child neuropsychology* (pp. 3–16). New York: Plenum.

Reitan, R. M. (1955). An investigation of the validity of Halstead's measures of biological intelligence. *Archives of Neurology and Psychiatry, 73,* 28–35.

Reitan, R. M. (1989). A note regarding some aspects of the history of clinical neuropsychology. *Archives of clinical neuropsychology, 4,* 385–391.

Reitan, R. M., & Wolfson, D. (1985). *The Halstead-Reitan Neuropsychological Test Battery: Theory and clinical interpretation.* Tucson, AZ: Neuropsychology Press.

Rourke, B. P. (Ed.). (1985). *Neuropsychology of learning disabilities: Essentials of subtype analysis.* New York: Guilford.

Rourke, B. P., Bakker, D. J., Fisk, J. L., & Strang, J. D. (1983). *Child neuropsychology: An introduction to theory, research, and clinical practice.* New York: Guilford.

Rubin, H., & Dworkin, P. H. (1985). The language impaired student. In P. H. Dworkin (Ed.), *Learning and behavior problems of school children* (pp. 98–115). Philadelphia: Saunders.

Rutter, M. (Ed.). (1983). *Developmental neuropsychiatry.* New York: Guilford.

Sattler, J. M. (1988). *Assessment of children* (3rd ed). San Diego, CA: Author.

Selz, M. (1981). Halstead-Reitan neuropsychological test batteries for children. In G. W. Hynd, & J. E. Obrzut (Eds.), *Neuropsychological assessment and the school-age child: Issues and procedures.* New York: Grune & Stratton.

Selz, M. J., & Wilson, S. L. (1989). Neuropsychological bases of common learning and behavior problems in children. In C. R. Reynolds & E. Fletcher-Janzen (Eds.), *Handbook of clinical child neuropsychology* (pp. 129–145). New York: Plenum.

Teeter, P. A. (1989). Neuropsychological approaches to the remediation of educational deficits. In C. R. Reynolds & E. Fletcher-Janzen (Eds.). *Handbook of clinical child neuropsychology* (pp. 357–376). New York: Plenum.

Telzrow, C. F. (1986). The science and speculation of rehabilitation in development neuropsychological disorders. In L. C. Hartlage & C. F. Telzrow (Eds.), *The neuropsychology of individual differences: A developmental perspective* (pp. 271–307). New York: Plenum.

Telzrow, C. F. (1989). Neuropsychological applications of common educational and psychological tests. In C. R. Reynolds & E. Fletcher-Janzen (Eds.), *Handbook of clinical child neuropsychology* (pp. 227–245). New York: Plenum.

Telzrow, C. F. (Ed.). (1990). Mini-series on communication disorders [Special issue]. *School Psychology Review, 18*(4).

Volpe, J. J. (1987). *Neurology of the newborn* (2nd Ed.). Philadelphia: Saunders.

Wedding, D., Horton, A. M., & Webster, J. S. (Eds.). (1986). *Handbook of clinical and behavioral neuropsychology.* New York: Springer.

CHAPTER 8

A Moral Developmental Approach to Intervention

Robert D. Enright, Issidoros Sarinopoulos, Radhi Al-Mabuk, and Suzanne Freedman
University of Wisconsin–Madison

A moral developmental approach draws primarily on the organismic or cognitive developmental approaches of Piaget and Kohlberg. There are predictable stage sequences in both justice and forgiveness, which represent increasingly more complex ways of understanding justice or forgiveness. Justice is concerned with what is fair; the basic principle is equality or reciprocity. Forgiveness is concerned with mercy, or more specifically, giving a gift to one who has inflicted deep hurt; the principle underlying forgiveness is love. The stage models and a new social processing model of forgiveness are described and applied to the Vince Chandler case.

Morality is equivalent to the good or right, rather than to the immoral or unethical. Morality exists in society before and after any one person in our community. As we develop we become participants to a greater degree in the good than was the case in our past. Morality is thus grounded in our societal experience for the express purpose of guiding individuals and groups (Frankena, 1973). With time we internalize the good or the moral so that morality in this sense exists within us. Morality can be contrasted with convention or etiquette. Morality on the one hand concerns universal "laws" and principles, whereas convention, although a social dimension, can be more arbitrary and specific to a given culture; convention centers on such issues as appearance, taste, and convenience (Frankena, 1973; Turiel, 1983).

Within morality we can distinguish between the quest for justice (the fair resolution of competing claims) and beneficence (going beyond duty in producing only good and avoiding evil). In justice, our basic principle is equality whether we are considering competing claims, for example, about the distribution of goods or the appropriateness of punishments. Equality does not imply making all people alike, but instead making "prima facie . . . proportionally the same contribution to the goodness of their lives, once a certain minimum has been achieved by all" (Frankena, 1973, p. 51). In beneficence, our basic principle is love, or doing good out of a sense of charity, not duty. Our doing good here may go beyond the justice requirements, as we seek to build up the other. We state elsewhere that such love, unconditionally held, emerges from a sense of justice (Enright & The Educational Psychology Study Group, in press). A beneficent response can include legal pardon, mercy, and forgiveness.

The moral developmental approach to the Vince Chandler case involves first the assessment of whether Vince has a sense of justice and beneficence and how he behaves as a moral person. If he is wanting in either the justice or beneficence domains, we will seek, by definition of the moral, to provide those experiences that will aid his participation in the greater good of society. This will involve guidance and instruction to improve his moral development in these areas. In our view, both Vince and society would benefit by such an intervention. Our first task, then, is to locate effective psychological models that utilize principles of justice and beneficence that allow for such assessment and intervention.

THE MORAL DEVELOPMENTAL MODEL OF JUSTICE

Most practitioners studying justice take a scientific approach. As such, they attempt to describe the way people think about the resolution of competing claims or how they behave in seeking a fair solution to competing claims. Practitioners study justice, for example, by asking people to defend their stated solution to a dilemma, by observing their behavior in justice contexts, or by assessing the degree to which a person has internalized social norms.

The most comprehensive justice model in psychology is Kohlberg's (1969, 1976, 1985). It is his approach that we will focus upon here. Although other systems exist, such as Gilligan's care perspective (Gilligan, 1982), we will not emphasize them here; Gilligan, for example, has deemphasized *stages* of *development* in her recent work, rendering a developmental analysis difficult. As Piagetians, the Kohlbergians emphasize the cognitive aspects of justice, or how people think about resolving moral dilemmas. Because Kohlberg's system of justice specifically centers on justification, he is concerned primarily with the reasons people give for their proposed solution to moral dilemmas. For example, suppose a Kohlbergian told a story of the relatively impecunious Heinz, who must decide to steal or not to steal a drug from a greedy druggist. The drug might save Heinz's wife from death. The competing claims here, requiring a justice solution, are Heinz's claim to his wife's life and the druggist's claim to fair compensation. Kohlbergians would be less interested in the person's proposed solution (e.g., "He should steal the drug") than in the person's telling us why he or she takes such a stance.

The Kohlbergians believe that our justifications of or reasons for our justice stance develop in a predictable, stage-like way, based on age, experience, and education (Rest, 1983). They further claim that moral *reasoning* is central to moral *functioning*. Literature reviews by Nelson, Smith, and Dodd (1990) and Blasi (1980) support the theoretical notion that advanced moral reasoning does relate to competent functioning in society. Those justice stages (together with a set of role-taking and forgiveness stages) are in Table 8.1. We will discuss the forgiveness stages shortly. Each justice stage, in theory, is constrained by a necessary but not sufficient prerequisite role-taking stage (Kohlberg, 1976). Role-taking is the cognitive ability to step inside another's shoes and view the world from his or her perspective.

On stage 1 role-taking, the person can take only one other person's perspective. In justice stage 1, that one perspective is the authority. When a person is predominantly in stage 2 role-taking, he or she can take a reciprocal perspective. This allows for the expression of sharing on justice stage 2. On stage 3 role-taking, a person can take a group perspective. This translates into a conformity to group norms in justice stage 3. We can note similar connections between role-taking level 4 and justice stage 4. A systems or societal perspective allows one to willingly adhere to established laws for the purpose of orderly societal functioning. On role-taking level 5 the person views the system in the specific context of rights and values. This allows stage 5 moral reasoning in which the person sees the self and others as participants in the formation of just laws and norms. Finally, the stage 6 role-taking perspective allows the person to view all people as ends in themselves. This leads to moral stage 6 in which equality of human rights and individual dignity is strongly emphasized. Although Selman (1980) describes a series of role-taking stages, these are taken from Kohlberg (1976), since it is his descriptions that underlie each moral stage.

A major point regarding role-taking is that Kohlberg emphasized two domains critical for its development: societal institutions and peer groups. Institutional role-taking requires one to take the perspective of institutional authorities, such as the school principal and teachers in Vince Chandler's case. Peer group role-taking requires one to step inside the shoes of age-mates, understanding contemporary group norms. If one has limited participation in either domain, one's role-taking may be impaired (see especially Power, 1988). Impaired role-taking constrains moral development (Kohlberg, 1976).

A more specific point of the role-taking and justice relationship is this. A person cannot reason in justice development any higher than his or her current role-taking stage (Kohlberg, 1976; Walker, 1980). Kohlberg, in fact, has proposed that one can actually assess a person's moral development by diagnosing the role-taking level used in solving moral dilemmas (Kohlberg, 1976). In our initial assessment of Vince Chandler, and in the absence of a reliable and valid test of moral development, we can garner clues to his stage of justice by examining his complexity of role-taking as brought out in the case.

Current thinking regarding stages of justice development is as follows:

1. As people mature, they slowly progress through the stages, not necessarily experiencing the highest stages (Rest, 1983; Snarey, 1985).
2. The stages appear to be culturally universal through stage 3 only (Snarey, 1985).
3. Theorists no longer see a person's stage as representing a structured whole. By structured whole we mean an internally consistent response to most dilemmas with only one stage response. Research indicates that we use a variety of stage responses in solving any one dilemma (Rest, 1983).
4. Our reasoning patterns, however, will cluster around a predominant stage (Walker, deVries, & Trevethan, 1987).

TABLE 8.1 Stages of Justice and Forgiveness Development

Stages of Role-Taking	Stages of Justice	Stages of Forgiveness
Stage 1: Egocentric Perspective. I do not yet consider the interests of others. I do not yet relate two points of view; there is a confusion of the authority's with my own perspective.	Punishment and Obedience Orientation. I believe that justice should be decided by the authority, by the one who can punish.	Revengeful Forgiveness. I can forgive someone who wrongs me only if I can punish him/her to a similar degree to my own pain.
Stage 2: Concrete Individualistic Perspective. I take a reciprocal perspective with the idea that each person pursues his/her own interests.	Instrumental Justice. I have a sense of reciprocity that defines justice for me. If you help me, I must help you.	Restitutional or Compensational Forgiveness. If I get back what was taken away from me, then I can forgive. Or, if I feel guilty about withholding forgiveness, then I can forgive to relieve my guilt.
Stage 3: Individual in Relation to Others. I take a group perspective with an awareness of shared feelings and expectations among us.	Good Boy/Girl Justice. Here, I reason that the group consensus should decide what is right and wrong. I go along so others will like me.	Expectational Forgiveness. I can forgive if others put pressure on me to forgive. It is easier to forgive when other people expect it.
State 4: Differentiation of Societal Viewpoints. I take a systems perspective (groups interacting). Each person is viewed within this category.	Law and Order Justice. Societal laws are my guides to justice. I uphold laws in order to have an orderly society.	Lawful Expectational Forgiveness. I forgive when my religion demands it. Notice that this is not Stage 2 in which I forgive to relieve my own guilt about withholding forgiveness.
Stage 5: Prior-to-Society Perspective. I view people as rational and aware of the values underlying systems decisions.	Social Contract Orientation. I am still interested in that which maintains the social fabric but I also realize that unjust laws exist. Therefore, I see it as just, as fair, to work within the system for change.	Forgiveness as Social Harmony. I forgive when it restores harmony in society. Forgiveness decreases friction and conflict in society. Note that forgiveness is a way to control society; it is a way of maintaining peaceful relations.
Stage 6: Perspective of a Moral Viewpoint. I now realize that people are ends in themselves and must be treated as such.	Universal Ethical Principle Orientation. My sense of justice is based on maintaining the individual rights of all persons. Conscience rather than laws or norms determines what I will accept when there are competing claims.	Forgiveness as Love. I forgive unconditionally because it promotes a true sense of love. Because I must truly care for each person, a hurtful act does not alter that sense of love. This kind of relationship keeps open the possibility of reconciliation and closes the door on revenge. Forgiveness is no longer dependent on a social context, as in Stage 5. The forgiver does not control by forgiving; he releases the other.

SOURCES: "The Moral Development of Forgiveness," by R. D. Enright and Educational Psychology Study Group (in press) in W. Kurtines and J. Gewirtz (Eds.), *Moral Behavior and Development*, Vol. 1. Hillsdale, NJ: Erlbaum. The role-taking labels from "Moral Stages and Moralization: The Cognitive Developmental Approach," by L. A. Kohlberg (1976), in T. Lickona (Ed.), *Moral Development and Behavior: Theory, Research, and Social Issues* pp. 31–53. New York: Holt, Rinehart & Winston.

5. Stimulus materials and environmental idiosyncracies play a part in our predominant stage (Leming, 1978). We are highest in those areas in which we have been most challenged (Flavell, 1985).

6. The way one reasons about hypothetical dilemmas is often higher than how one reasons about actual dilemmas one faces in one's life (what Power et al., 1989, call *practical* moral reasoning). Participation in democratic environments enhances one's practical moral reasoning (Power, Higgins, & Kohlberg, 1989).

7. Role-taking and educational opportunities have an impact upon rate of growth and highest stage attained (Kohlberg, 1976; Rest, 1983).

8. Stage regression is possible (Rest, 1983), but usually is not dramatic (e.g., one rarely sees a regression of two stages).

There is convincing empirical evidence that the higher moral stages are *psychologically* more adequate than the lower stages. For example, Blasi's (1980) comprehensive literature review suggests that there are more juvenile delinquents on the lower stages; altruistic people are more often on higher stages; those who stand up for moral principles are on the higher stages (see also Candee & Kohlberg, 1987). Slugoski, Marcia, and Koopman (1984) observe that those adolescents higher in justice stage have a more adequate ego identity. Because Vince Chandler seems to lack some of the social skills expected of a 13-year-old, a clinician would do well to consider his moral development as one avenue of promoting psychological maturity.

There also are challenging essays claiming that the higher justice stages are *morally* more adequate than the lower stages (Reed & Hanna, 1982, Kohlberg, 1971; Rosen, 1980; Lapsley, Enright & Serlin, 1989). The higher the stage, the more likely will be a solution based on moral equality (the heart of justice). A person using the higher stages takes more information into account and, as a given, attempts to preserve each person's rights where there are competing claims. The resulting decision, therefore, is likely to be more just. If we can stimulate Vince's stage of justice development, we may be promoting his greater *moral* reflection. Thus he will be more integrated into the good of society.

The Technology of Justice Change

Two basic approaches have emerged in justice education: plus-one exchange and the Just Community (see Enright, Lapsley, & Levy, 1983; Lapsley et al., 1989; Power et al., 1989). The plus-one convention assumes that development is stimulated by cognitive conflict, specifically one stage higher than one's current, predominant stage. Suppose Vince were predominantly on stage 2. The educator would devise a series of dilemmas and consistently argue those dilemmas on stage 3 with Vince. Over time and because of the cognitive challenge, Vince should begin using stage 3 statements more frequently. As we have seen, this should then have an impact upon his psychological and moral maturity. The plus-one technology is the oldest of the moral education approaches (originating with Turiel in 1966) and is powerful in inducing change of about a third of a stage in short-term interventions (see Lapsley et al., 1989). Such an approach is more effective with high school students than those younger (Enright et al., 1983). Thus, it would be appropriate for Vince.

The Just Community approach is more concerned with the moral atmosphere of the school environment than with the student's individual stage of justice development. The crux of the program is to create a democratic environment. Administrators, teachers, and students are all involved in creating rules and adjudicating offenses against them. In terms of role-taking, it allows for the crucial instructional perspective to broaden. Although such programs are very difficult to begin, involving entire schools, they are more easily maintained than the plus-one approaches because of the interest and challenge for the students (Power et al., 1989). There is preliminary evidence that such programs can stimulate students' predominant stage usage (Power et al., 1989). The results, however, are not dramatically different from those found in plus-one programs. An important recent finding is that the Just Community is especially strong for improving *practical* moral reasoning (Power et al., 1989).

The goal of the justice education programs is primarily wisdom, not behavior. A major assumption of Kohlbergian education is that adequate thoughts drive adequate behavior; there is little room for intuition or spontaneous behavior in the theory. Assessment of the individual stage is usually done with Kohlberg's interview (Colby, Kohlberg, Hewer, Candee, Gibbs, & Power, 1987) or Rest's (1979) objective Defining Issues Test. The latter gives either a stage score or the percentage of stages 5 and 6 statements advocated in solving the hypothetical dilemmas.

THE MORAL DEVELOPMENT OF FORGIVENESS

Because forgiveness as a psychological construct is new, a practitioner should proceed cautiously (with continuing assessments) if he or she attempts the approach. A comprehensive discussion of the forgiveness construct is in Enright et al. (in press).

There are two primary purposes in our view for the use of forgiveness in clinical practice: to reduce negative emotions (anger, hatred, resentment, and so forth) and to initiate reconciliation between two or more people. Forgiveness is defined as follows: It is the "overcoming of negative affect and judgment toward the offender, not by denying ourselves the right to such affect and judgment, but by endeavoring to view the offender with compassion, benevolence, and love while recognizing that he or she has abandoned the right to them" (Enright et al., in press, p. 6).[1] One forgives another person who has inflicted deep hurt. The offended person, having a right (justice issue) to condemnation, withholds it. The negative affect, judgment, and behavior toward an offender are replaced with more positive affect, judgment, and behavior. This does not mean the offended party becomes morally blind, no longer seeing the other's faults. It does mean that those faults are no longer the basis for their relationship.

Let us be clear that forgiveness is not the same as reconciliation. Forgiveness is something the offended gives to the offender. Reconciliation is two people coming together again. Further, the offended one does not give up *all* rights in forgiveness. One does give up the right to retaliate for emotional, psychological pain, but can still seek compensation for a damaged car or home, for example. Forgiveness is not condoning or excusing. Instead, a forgiver continues to realize there was wrong done.

When someone forgives there are six changes in his or her psychological system. Hate (or other negative emotions) is reduced or eliminated in the affective system;

condemning judgments are reduced or eliminated in the cognitive system; revenge disappears from the behavioral system. More positive affect (love, compassion) emerge toward the offender in the affective system; positive judgments emerge in cognition; and a *willingness* to reconcile occurs in behavior. In sum, the paradox of forgiveness is that, when a person is willing to absorb the pain of an offense, the forgiver is released from deep hurt. The way to reconciliation also is opened (Enright et al., in press).

The first of two psychological models of forgiveness is in Table 8.1. Because it is a cognitive developmental model following both Piaget and Kohlberg, it is the more straightforward. There is a parallel with the Kohlbergian stages because of the similar, underlying role-taking requirements of each stage. The validity of the stage sequence is supported in two studies in the United States (Enright, Santos, & Al-Mabuk, 1989), one in Korea (Park, 1989), and one in Taiwan (Huang, 1990). A practitioner should realize that only stage 6 captures the subtlety and complexity of forgiveness. All people reasoning on a lower level cast forgiveness into a conditional and incomplete light. A practitioner, however, should also realize that most people do not consistently reason only on one stage. Someone labeled "stage 4," for example, in all likelihood has some percentage of reasoning on stage 6. Thus, many who are not predominantly in stage 6 should be able to understand, even to a small degree, the concept of forgiveness.

We hesitate to introduce the second model of forgiveness because of its complexity and our space limitation here. Yet, as a process model, it provides clues to how a person actually forgives another. At the risk of some distortion we will not present the entire model here, but instead outline the 17 processes involved in a forgiveness response. The processes are gleaned from the case study literature and described more fully in Enright et al. (in press).

Psychological Variables Engaged in a Process Intervention on Forgiveness
 1. Examination of psychological defenses
 2. Confrontation of anger; the point is to release, not harbor, the anger
 3. Admittance of shame, when this is appropriate
 4. Awareness of cathexis
 5. Awareness of cognitive rehearsal of the offense
 6. Insight that the injured party may be comparing self with the injurer
 7. Insight into a possibly altered "just world" view
 8. A change of heart/conversion/new insights that old resolution strategies are not working
 9. Commitment to forgive the offender
 10. Reframing, through role-taking, who the wrongdoer is by viewing him or her in context
 11. Empathy toward the offender
 12. Awareness of compassion, as it emerges, toward the offender
 13. Acceptance/absorption of the pain
 14. Realization that self has needed others' forgiveness in the past
 15. Realization that self has been, perhaps, permanently changed by the injury
 16. Awareness of decreased negative affect and, perhaps increased positive affect, if this begins to emerge, toward the injurer
 17. Awareness of internal, emotional release

The basic points are these. First, for a person to forgive, his or her rigid psychological defenses must allow for the conscious expression of anger or resentment. A deep, unjust offense must be recognized as such (Linn & Linn, 1978; Smedes, 1984). Points 3–7 show how people sometimes experience added psychological pain by sensing shame, attaching too much emotional energy to the hurtful event (cathexis), and playing the scene over and over in one's mind (cognitive rehearsal). Sometimes the person begins comparing his or her own unfortunate state with the offender's more fortunate one, exacerbating psychological distress. For example, Kiel (1986) describes comparing his own paraplegic state with the ambulatory one of the robber who shot him. It incurred Kiel's wrath. This can lead to the conclusion that life is profoundly unfair (point 7).

The eighth and ninth are turning points. The person, through counseling help or on his or her own, realizes that coping strategies are not working. There is a "change of heart" toward the hurtful events and the people in the hurt person's life. A commitment to forgive is usually a cognitive *decision* to forgive the offender.

Points 10–16 are the active, therapeutic regimen and will be discussed more fully later in the Vince Chandler case. Point 17 signifies an inner healing from the stressful event. The seventeen points are not rigid, step-like progressions. In all likelihood some people do not experience some of the processes described. Others circle back, working again through some of the issues. We believe there are considerable individual differences in how people forgive.

MORAL DEVELOPMENT
IN THE VINCE CHANDLER CASE

Justice Issues

First, let us examine Vince's justice development, particularly his *practical* reasoning. In the absence of a valid measure of justice development, and following Kohlberg, we will estimate Vince's stage of justice by examining his role-taking as expressed in the case. One thing is clear: Vince is not predominantly stage 1 in justice reasoning. Someone predominantly reasoning on stage 1 looks to authority for guidance; punishment is an issue. Vince is almost casually unconcerned about discipline as seen in his constant challenges to his stepfather. He says, "That's not fair. You can't make me do that! I don't see why I should listen to you." The fact that Mrs. Kirk feels "powerless" in disciplining Vince is further evidence of his disregard for authority. Further, Vince's general "inability to relate appropriately to adults" is yet another indicator of his failure to reason in a stage 1 way. This lack of stage 1 adherence to authority is not unusual for a 13 year old. Often, those in the early teenage years go beyond stage 1, with characteristic challenges, especially around puberty and especially in the home (see Steinberg, 1981, 1987 regarding challenge to parental authority).

It is not typical, however, for such cavalier unconcern with authority to manifest itself as early as fourth grade. Yet, even then Vince's "reactions to and defiance of the rules could no longer be tolerated." He was cited for "not following rules" in fourth grade. Apparently, his challenges cannot be seen as going *beyond* stage 1, but instead might be seen as a failure to coalesce on that stage. We say this because there is no evidence that he ever obeyed in any normative sense, even in childhood. This is the case especially in the institutional setting of the school.

It is further not typical for the cavalier unconcern to be so pervasive in both home and school. Even now, Vince "does not hand in written work"; he "may argue" and he shows "disrespectful behavior" to teachers. Without consolidated reasoning on stage 1 it is not at all surprising that attempts to punish Vince are not working. His basic philosophy of the world does not include a sense of the authority's importance. Therefore, it is not surprising either that Vince stares at a teacher who gives detention or fails to report to detention. We can see in a general, clinical way Kohlberg's concept of the "structured whole" operating in Vince's case. He is pervasively unconcerned with the authority of the mother (who feels powerless), of the stepfather (who battles), and of the teachers (who try to punish). Such structured wholeness is not as typical as once believed, but does seem to hold in this case. From a justice perspective one thing is clear: If Vince is to be a functioning member of society, he must *understand* what an authority position is and must willingly consent to an authority's leadings, within reasonable limits; otherwise, Vince is outside the social nature of morality. Because the Kohlbergian position is a cognitive one, it assumes that Vince first needs *wisdom* if he is to become just. It also assumes that Vince will need to be an active *participant* in institutionalized settings if the institutionalized role-taking is to develop. Right now, Vince is on the fringe of the institution, not a mainstream participant. It might be argued that Vince has gone beyond stage 1 in that he acknowledges the authority's *right* to make rules. Yet, we do not see such acknowledgment in his stares and his defiance. Also it might be argued that he has gone beyond stage 1 in that he breaks rules *when he can get away with it* (which characterizes stage 1 thinking), but he does not get away with his rule violations and continues with the infractions nonetheless.

There is other evidence suggesting that Vince does use stage 2 reasoning, but not consistently. He primarily uses stage 2 with peers and Bea, his stepsister. Such reasoning is conspicuously absent with authority figures. We see stage 2 reciprocity especially with Bea when Vince says, "She stands by me and I'll protect her." This is classic stage 2, I'll scratch your back if you'll scratch mine. We see it with the peer group when he says that a friend is "someone you could do things with and who you can count on." The give-and-take theme of stage 2 seems evident. He also shows an understanding of reciprocity with his mother, but from an earlier time: "We used to help each other a lot, but I guess things change." Because, within peer groups and with a stepsister, there is no adult authority who punishes, we can see why his stage 2 reasoning is expressed most fully within these relationships.

Because he is a participant in a peer group, but on the fringe of the institution, we have the case where one kind of role-taking (peer) is advancing while the other (institutional) is stagnant. His moral reasoning may be more advanced with peers because of his participation in such a group. His moral reasoning with authorities may be lower because he is disenfranchised in the institution. His familial "institution," we must realize, has been broken apart. As we will see, this has caused Vince much hurt.

It is not clear whether Vince has some stage 3 reasoning in justice. We know he did not have such an ability in sixth grade. At that time his writing was "egocentric"; he had difficulty writing for an audience (a clear stage 3 group perspective). He had difficulty explaining himself to others (stepping inside their shoes to see what they need to understand him). Because there are no unambiguous stage 3 statements and several clear stage 2, we will tentatively conclude that Vince has the capacity for stage 2 thinking, but in all likelihood he is not consolidated on that stage. We say this because of the hierarchical nature of the stages; one stage builds on another. Vince shows no consolidation on stage 1, which could have been a basis for consolidation on stage 2. Because he does show potential for stage 2, we must conclude that he has potential for stage 1 as well, given the assumption of hierarchy. Yet, stage 1 is conspicuously absent. It will become a focus for intervention, along with stage 2 reasoning. Institutional role-taking must be a part of any such program, given the particular nature of Vince's case.

Does this tentative diagnosis place him within the appropriate age norms? First, we cannot talk literally of age norms because justice development is idiosyncratic to us all. The key is growth *within* a person, not comparisons between. With this caution in mind we can state in a general way that he is behind what we usually see for someone almost 14 years old in the United States. Many are approaching stage 3 (Kohlberg, 1969; Rest, 1983; Colby, Kohlberg, Gibbs & Liberman, 1983). Vince appears to be somewhere between stages 1 and 2. We are concerned about his institutional role-taking opportunities, which at present are not allowing for acceleration.

His slow growth in justice development is not surprising. He has many of the classic features associated with slower growth patterns. His early hearing and articulation problems are related to a lag in moral development (Lutz, Termini, & Cramer, 1988). Because wisdom in justice occurs through human verbal interaction, Vince was constrained here in his earliest years. His restriction to the home at age five is a further inhibitor to justice development. Piaget (1932/1965) knew that peers are powerful change agents in moral reasoning because of the equality of each person's status relative to an adult–child relationship. Peers are more free to sift and winnow, which stimulates moral reasoning. When we combine this with Vince's resistance to "communication with children and adults" we see an apparent lack of give-and-take that promotes moral judgments to higher stages. Further, divorce has been shown to predict lower moral reasoning in adolescents (Parish, 1980; Schenenga, 1983). The fact that he is so disruptive in school is a sign that he might become rejected by peers (other than his immediate group). This would further reduce peer contact and the opportunity to mutually struggle with moral dilemmas. His slow beginning may have contributed to Vince's being on the periphery of the institution. Such peripheral involvement can become the proverbial vicious cycle as he challenges, is rejected, challenges again, and is further rejected. Vince's life history points to slow development in understanding justice.

Forgiveness Issues

We will refrain from a diagnosis of Vince's forgiveness *stage* because of lack of data in the case. It would be important to eventually get some indication of stage because one's stage does have a bearing upon one's capacity to actually forgive (Park, 1989; Trainer, 1981). We expect that a thorough assessment might place Vince near stage 1 because of his tendency to "get even" when wronged. We nevertheless can establish that an intervention with the process model of forgiveness (as described on p. 143) is desirable. There is ample evidence to suggest that Vince suffers deep, emotional hurt from unjust (in his view) behaviors of others. Whenever a person so suffers, an intervention focusing on forgiveness usually is justified.

Our first point, then, centers on his parents' divorce when he was eight years old. For a child, the parents' divorce is unjust, primarily because the child did nothing to warrant his father's continual and permanent absence. If it is a deep hurt, the child may react with characteristic psychological defenses at first, and then become angry. Vince is angry and he is in denial to a point. In fact, his anger is one of the pervasive themes of the case. He is "unable to inhibit his behavior when frustrated." Even in early elementary school this frustration was apparent. Such patterns are not uncommon even *before* the parents divorce, as a response to the tension in the home (Block, Block, & Gjerde, 1986). It is important to note that Vince's "acting out appeared to increase as he moved through the various grade levels." He did not find a way to cope, but instead apparently got angrier.

We see anger in the form of displacement when he was cited for "student harassment." We see it in his Bender–Gestalt test where themes of "explosiveness, anxiety, impulsiveness, and aggressiveness" are apparent. We see it in his Sentence Completion test where he will "get even" if someone plays a practical joke on him. As already discussed, his anger is apparent in his pervasive resistance to authority.

That his anger is related at least in part to his parents' divorce is clear in several places: For example, on the TAT "elements of discord were frequently related to divorce—and divorce was seen as the cause of great tension." His first of Three Wishes was "his father would remarry his mother." On the Behavior Evaluation Scale his scores obtained from the Family Living teacher were consistently below average.

Vince's anger is also related to his biological father's infrequent visits. "Vince does not understand why his Dad has broken away as much as he has since the divorce." He apparently blames this, in part, on his stepfather. "If my stepfather would let my Mom, she would let me visit Dad more often. He used to invite me all the time; it's just that he got tired of asking." We thus see three sources of deep anger for Vince: his parents' divorce, his father's lack of responsiveness, and his tension with his stepfather.

Besides anger, we see the characteristic psychological defenses that operate so strongly in the early phases of forgiveness. We see them in his "frustration that he had to be evaluated." He claims that "if he wished to have better grades, he could achieve them" even though he is currently scholastically ineligible for junior varsity sports. He told another student that a surprise math quiz was "no problem," but received a "C" on his paper (which he crumpled up). In his own view he is "doing just fine."

Discussion of Findings

In justice and forgiveness development, Vince needs educational and counseling work. For a variety of reasons, he is below average in his justice reasoning. This needs to be rectified if he is to be a contributing member to the moral sphere of society. Even more stark to us is Vince's deep emotion hurt. We see him less as a behavioral problem and more as someone who, at a young age, received the unjust blow of his parents' divorce, from which he has not yet recovered. In all likelihood, he is reacting so harshly, not because he is insensitive, but because he *is* sensitive and caring. Because he loves his mother and father, he is hurting. As we fail to understand this and as we fail to recognize the beneficence side of morality, we may see him as unjust, as a troublemaker, as a behavioral problem, as an emotionally troubled adolescent, or any other label on the justice side of the issue. Yes, Vince is acting unjustly, but in our view, this is due in part to his caring. It is his capacity to care (and be hurt) upon which we would like to first focus. Only as these wounds are bound can Vince think clearly about justice issues, including the just behavior of completing school assignments. One can hardly be cajoled into acting justly as a 13 year old when one sees the world as so unjust.

RECOMMENDATIONS
AND SUGGESTED INTERVENTIONS

If this were an ideal world we would recommend first that Vince cry on a reliable and good friend's shoulder regarding his parents' divorce. In our view, this would help break down his psychological defenses and help him face the pain. Not being in an ideal world, he may have to purchase that friendship. It is our hope that he sees a counselor who understands and has studied not only justice, but also beneficence. Such a counselor, in our view, must have read Smedes (1984), Kaufman (1984), Fitzgibbons (1986), and Hope (1987). Such a counselor should have read North's (1987) sensitive piece on forgiveness and struggled with the philosophical objections to forgiveness in Enright et al. (in press). Such a counselor should know the characteristic, unfolding pattern when a person forgives.

The treatment regimen, then, would consist of bringing Vince through the forgiveness processes first, directed specifically at his parents and the divorce. Eventually, he should also focus on his stepfather, given the deep anger there. He may then have to focus on teachers who call him "lazy and stupid." Following his exploration of forgiveness, Vince should then begin a program to help him with his stage 1 justice issues, particularly in institutionalized settings. Moving him up the stage ladder should also be a goal of the program. We suggest forgiveness first because of Vince's deep anger, which may adversely affect his cerebral sifting and winnowing in justice. Forgiveness issues are also the most pressing, given his pervasive anger.

In initiating the forgiveness process, a counselor should get an indication of Vince's percentage of responses on each forgiveness stage, to assess whether he is capable of understanding what forgiveness is. It would not be healthy for him to erroneously imagine that, if he could only get back at his parents, then he could forgive. Such an assessment of stage would follow Enright, Santos, and Al-Mabuk (1989). Let us presume that Vince does see, even if dimly, that forgiveness is an unconditional drawing of another in love, without bitterness or hatred.

The counselor would then focus on Vince's psychological defenses, his awareness of his anger, and the painful attempts to solve the problem (through cathexis, cognitive rehearsal, and comparisons of pre- and post-divorce circumstances). This could take weeks and should not be rushed. Only when he sees his own emotional pain should the topic of resolution strategies and commitment to forgive be broached. Only if Vince decides that forgiveness is worth exploring should steps 10–16 listed on page 143 be implemented.

Reframing (point 10) consists of viewing his mother and father within new contexts. He must see more fully the pressures they were under at the time of divorce. He must view them within their own developmental contexts—the difficulties they brought to the marriage. He must view anew their reactions to him, lest he believe he is the cause of the divorce. The point is to more thoroughly understand the divorce so that he can eliminate stereotypical myths he may be harboring. Once he sees his parents as fallible and human, empathy (point 11) is more likely. He would step inside his parents' shoes (of five years ago and now) and see that they, too, were emotionally hurt by the divorce; he is not alone in his suffering. This may lead to greater compassion, or a suffering along with them (point 12). Eventually, Vince must take the courageous step of shouldering the pain he feels (point 13), knowing his parents are imperfect. The pain they caused him must be accepted, knowing they did not intentionally want him to so suffer (see Bergin, 1988, on this point).

Points 14 and 15 involve a certain degree of humility because one sees the self as vulnerable. Vince may struggle here because of his characteristic denial. He has a certain pride, as seen in his "special attention" from girls and his "getting even" when hurt. The practitioner's asking for specific, concrete examples of Vince's hurting others or being hurt will be necessary for him to master points 14 and 15. We recommend that a practitioner not discuss points 14 and 15 until points 8–13 are successfully examined. Otherwise, self-blame may emerge as Vince focuses on his own imperfections. As he works on points 8–15, over time he should notice a change in his attitudes toward his parents and the divorce.

In the forgiveness journey, Vince should be allowed to consider only one parent at a time. He should choose the one upon whom he will first focus. If the counselor observes success in that Vince's affect, cognition, and behavior are changed (toward emotional release), the process can continue with the other parent, the stepfather, and then perhaps a teacher. Within each of these journeys, the counselor must realize that pacing is idiosyncratic for each person and that the steps of forgiveness are idealized. Not everyone goes through all, nor in the same order.

Over time, the changes in his affective, cognitive, and behavior systems (discussed previously) should be observable. For example, his statements toward his mother may have a less condemnatory ring than now. His judgments of both parents should grow even more positive. His attempts to reconcile should be observable (in contrast to his present sense of separateness from his mother).

Perhaps the major indicator that forgiveness is occurring for Vince is his anger reduction. This should be seen on the TAT, Bender–Gestalt, and Sentence Completion tests. This should be seen in his verbal statements about home and school events. We do not expect a complete elimination of anger, of course, but rather a reduction in the dysfunctional anger so pervasive in the case study report.

If the counselor observes such anger reduction, we next recommend justice education. Although a Just Community approach in its classical sense (Power et al., 1989) is impractical, we recommend a variant of it. Vince needs greater participation in the institutions of school and family where authority issues are so difficult for him. Vince needs to improve his practical reasoning toward authorities and the Just Community is especially strong for such reasoning (Power et al., 1989). We recommend the perhaps paradoxical idea that Vince contribute to the rules governing his academic requirements. With each teacher he should contractually agree to what will be accomplished and when. Here he is treated as a moral equal (the epitome of justice) and he may see the authority as less autocratic and punishing. This, of course, would need the full cooperation of teachers. We should note that a similar approach has been popular for decades in behavior modification—contingency contracting. The difference is that Vince gets no tangible reward here; his reward is the participation. We recommend a similar approach in the home. Rules should be negotiated, expectations discussed. The parents may require some instruction in Just Community theory. The point is to increase Vince's mainstream participation in institutions for the purpose of stimulating his institutional role-taking. Over time, he may change his moral judgments about authority figures, becoming more cooperative. As such, he is becoming more moral as he can participate in the institutional and moral requirements of society.

The plus-one exchange also could be used. Following a reliable assessment of Vince's justice development, the counselor could begin with a series of dilemma discussions. Starting on the level of hypothetical dilemmas and then moving to more personal issues may prove less threatening as Mosher and Sprinthall (1971) suggest. We recommend that the practitioner initially center such dilemmas on sporting events because of the following school observation: "Questions from the class as to what would be acceptable topics seemed to awaken Vince's interest—especially when one boy asked about sporting events." As Power et al. (1989) note, dilemma discussions can grow wearisome. Focusing on high-interest dilemmas may spark Vince's motivation. When the counselor moves to Vince's own dilemmas at home and school he should be well engaged in this process.

The counselor might begin, not with plus-one, but with consolidation exercises designed to induce more subtle reasoning on stage 1. The counselor could present a dilemma, for example, in which a boy is constantly breaking the rules during junior varsity basketball practice. The consequences of such could be the basis of discussion. The counselor could then generalize this kind of thinking to Vince's current disobedience in school.

Plus-one exercises could eventually occur on stage 3. The importance of following rules so all can get along should be emphasized. The point is to provide rationales that Vince can understand and appreciate, for cooperation in his various environments. An important point of stage 3 is that prosocial norms are emphasized and relationships are valued for their own sake. Pointing out parallels among the cooperation and prosocial norms of athletics, school, and home in general should be implemented. Over time (and without the excessive anger blocking his thoughts), Vince may begin developing the wisdom needed for justice. Were such a program successful, we could see it in his cooperation with authorities at home and in school. The practitioner might also instruct the parents in democratic communication patterns to further foster such cooperation.

A Closing Perspective

The point of the moral perspective is to enhance the sense of the good in people. We try to enhance this good so that people can interact in ways that build one another up, not tear down. Morality, then, is a social enterprise, enacted for each person's and society's good. Because morality exists apart from Vince Chandler, he must learn that which has existed before him and will continue to exist after him, if he is to contribute to his society.

At the moment, Vince is not participating in the good or the right to the extent that his potential suggests. He is not building others up in his environment. In fact, his anger seems more often to tear down. In contrast to Kohlberg's view, we do not see the cause of his difficulties as a lack of wisdom. We agree that he lacks that wisdom, but to us it is his lack of participation in the more affective moral domain of love that is the central issue.

Vince must be introduced to love, not in a possessive or romantic sense, but in the sense of going beyond duty and stepping outside himself to others. We are concerned that his current environments, both school and home, are not providing the lessons of love. His group in school seems on the fringes of the school's mainstream. What one can get in terms of attention and prestige is more emphasized than giving to others. Vince's current home is a battleground of discord, discontent, and authoritarianism (this family "is not a real family" he says on the Sentence Completion test). Yes, his stepfather may be doing his best, but we do not see the *agapism* of which Frankena (1973) speaks. As a consequence, Vince is learning to fight, mostly in a verbal and behaviorally passive way.

If Vince is to learn love, he must experience it. If this means counseling, then so be it, as long as the counselor understands love as a moral principle. Of course, it would be far better if Vince could get a consistent, continuing lesson of love within his own community. His learning would not have to be generalized outside the therapeutic encounter and his models may be those he has admired for years. It is a sad commentary that such love is too little available for the Vince Chandlers of the world; it was so in Freud's day, too. He understood that many came to him trying to learn how to work and to love.

Perhaps we can all learn a lesson from the Just Community approach. As adolescents benefit from an environment that stresses democracy, so too would they benefit from environments that emphasize the moral principle of love. As the Just Community seeks first to change the environment, so too should we begin thinking of ways to transform environments based on the principle of love. A first step is to explore such a principle with authorities. We wonder how many authorities have actively, consciously struggled with the principle of love and its concomitant action of forgiveness. Were such a principle and action a conscious part of institutions (families, schools, and beyond), we are convinced that the Vince Chandlers of the world would be far fewer in number. Lest the reader see us as utopian idealists, we must remember that the Kohlbergian Just Community has been concretely and successfully implemented in a variety of environments (see Hickey & Scharf, 1980; Power et al., 1989; Scharf, 1973; Wasserman & Garrod, 1983). Educating authorities toward this end may pay more dividends than we now realize.

NOTE

1. We are indebted to North (1987) for much of this definition.

REFERENCES

Bergin, A. E. (1988). Three contributions of a spiritual perspective to counseling, psychotherapy, and behavioral change. *Counseling and Values, 33,* 21–31.

Blasi, A. (1980). Bridging moral cognition and moral action: A critical review of the literature. *Psychological Bulletin, 88,* 1–45.

Block, J. H., Block, J., & Gjerde, P. F. (1986). The personality of children prior to divorce: A prospective study. *Child Development, 57,* 827–840.

Candee, D., & Kohlberg, L. (1987). Moral judgment and moral action: A reanalysis of Haan, Smith, and Block's (1968) free speech movement data. *Journal of Personality and Social Psychology, 52,* 554–564.

Colby, A., Kohlberg, L., Gibbs, J., & Liberman, M. (1983). A longitudinal study of moral judgment. *Monographs of the Society for Research in Child Development, 48* (No. 1–2).

Colby, A., Kohlberg, L., Hewer, A., Candee, D., Gibbs, J. C., & Power, C. (1987). *The measurement of moral judgment, Vol. 2: Standard issue scoring manual.* New York: Cambridge University Press.

Enright, R. D., & The Educational Psychology Study Group (in press). The moral development of forgiveness. In W. Kurtines and J. Gewirtz (Eds.), *Moral behavior and development* (Vol. 1). Hillsdale NJ: Erlbaum.

Enright, R. D., Lapsley, D. K., & Levy, V. M. (1983). Moral education strategies. In M. J. Pressley & J. R. Levin (Eds.), *Cognitive strategy training: Educational, clinical, and social applications.* (pp. 43–83). New York: Springer.

Enright, R. D., Santos, M., & Al-Mabuk, R. (1989). The adolescent as forgiver. *Journal of Adolescence, 12*, 95–110.

Fitzgibbons, R. P. (1986). The cognitive and emotive use of forgiveness in the treatment of anger. *Psychotherapy, 23*, 629–633.

Flavell, J. H. (1985). *Cognitive development* (2nd ed.). Englewood Cliffs, NJ: Prentice Hall.

Frankena, W. K. (1973). *Ethics* (2nd ed.). Englewood Cliffs NJ: Prentice Hall.

Gilligan, C. (1982). *In a different voice: Psychological theory and women's development.* Cambridge, MA: Harvard University Press.

Hickey, J., & Scharf, P. (1980). *Toward a just correctional system.* San Francisco: Jossey-Bass.

Hope, D. (1987). The healing paradox of forgiveness. *Psychotherapy, 24*, 240–244.

Huang, S. T. (1990). *Cross-cultural and real-life validations of the theory of forgiveness in Taiwan, the Republic of China.* Unpublished doctoral dissertation, University of Wisconsin–Madison.

Kaufman, M. E. (1984). The courage to forgive. *Israeli Journal of Psychiatry and Related Sciences, 21*, 177–187.

Kiel, D. V. (1986). I'm learning how to forgive. *Decisions,* February, 12–13.

Kohlberg, L. (1969). Stage and sequence: The cognitive-developmental approach to socialization. In D. A. Goslin (Ed.), *Handbook of socialization theory and research.* (pp. 347–480). Chicago: Rand McNally.

Kohlberg, L. A. (1971). From *is* to *ought*: How to commit the naturalistic fallacy and get away with it in the study of moral development. In T. Mischel (Ed.), *Cognitive development and epistemology.* (pp. 151–235). New York: Academic.

Kohlberg, L. A. (1976). Moral stages and moralization: The cognitive developmental approach. In T. Lickona (Ed.), *Moral development and behavior: Theory, research, and social issues* (pp. 31–53). New York: Holt, Rinehart & Winston.

Kohlberg, L. A. (1985). A current statement on some theoretical issues. In S. Modgil and C. Modgil (Eds.), *Lawrence Kohlberg: Consensus and controversy.* (pp. 485–546). London: The Falmer Press.

Lapsley, D. K., Enright, R. D., & Serlin, R. C. (1989). Moral and social education. In J. Worell and F. Danner (Eds.), *The adolescent as decision-maker: Applications to development and education.* San Diego: Academic.

Leming, J. S. (1978). Cheating behavior, situational influence, and moral development. *Journal of Educational Research, 71*, 214–217.

Linn, D., & Linn, M. (1978). *Healing life's hurts.* New York: Paulist Press.

Lutz, D. J., Termini, P. V., Cramer, R. E. (1988). Distributive justice reasoning in hearing and hearing-impaired children. *Journal of Applied Developmental Psychology, 9*, 275–285.

Mosher, R. L., & Sprinthall, N. A. (1971). Psychological education: A means to promote personal development during adolescence. *The Counseling Psychologist, 2*, 3–82.

Nelson, J. R., Smith, D. J., & Dodd, J. (1990). The moral reasoning of juvenile delinquents: A meta-analysis. *Journal of Abnormal Child Psychology, 18*, 231–239.

North, J. (1987). Wrongdoing and forgiveness. *Philosophy, 62*, 499–508.

Parish, T. J. (1980). The relationship between factors associated with father loss and individuals' level of moral judgment. *Adolescence, 15*, 535–541.

Park, Y. (1989). *The development of forgiveness in the context of friendship conflict.* Unpublished doctoral dissertation, University of Wisconsin–Madison.

Piaget, J. (1932/1965). *The moral judgment of the child.* Glencoe, IL: Free Press.

Power, C. (1988). The just community approach to moral education. *Journal of Moral Education, 17*, 195–208.

Power, F. C., Higgins, A., & Kohlberg, L. (1989). *Lawrence Kohlberg's approach to moral education.* New York: Columbia University Press.

Reed, T., & Hanna, P. (1982). Developmental theory and moral education: Review essay. *Teaching Philosophy, 5*, 43–55.

Rest, J. R. (1979). *Development in judging moral issues.* Minneapolis: University of Minnesota Press.

Rest, J. R. (1983). Morality. In J. Flavell & E. Markman (Eds.), *Handbook of child psychology, 3*, 556–629. (P. Mussen, Gen. ed.). New York: Wiley.

Rosen, B. (1980). Kohlberg and the supposed mutual support of an ethical and psychological theory. *Journal for the Theory of Social Behavior, 10*, 195–210.

Scharf, P. (1973). *Moral atmosphere and intervention in the prison.* Unpublished doctoral dissertation, Harvard University.

Schenenga, K. (1983). Father absence, the ego ideal and moral development. *Smith College Studies in Social Work, 53*, 103–104.

Selman, R. L. (1980). *The growth of interpersonal understanding.* New York: Academic.

Slugoski, B., Marcia, J. E., & Koopman, R. F. (1984). Cognitive and social interactional characteristics of ego identity statuses in college males. *Journal of Personality and Social Psychology, 47*, 646–661.

Smedes, L. B. (1984). *Forgive to forget: Healing the hurts we don't deserve.* San Francisco: Harper & Row.

Snarey, J. R. (1985). Cross-cultural universality of social-moral development: A critical review of Kohlbergian research. *Psychological Bulletin, 97*, 202–232.

Steinberg, L. (1981). Transformation in family relations at puberty. *Develomental Psychology, 17*, 833–840.

Steinberg, L. (1987). Impact of puberty on family relations: Effects of pubertal status and pubertal timing. *Developmental Psychology, 23*, 451–460.

Trainer, M. (1981). *Forgiveness: Intrinsic, role-expected, expedient, in the context of divorce.* Unpublished doctoral dissertation, Boston University.

Turiel, E. (1966). An experimental test of the sequentiality of developmental stages in the child's moral judgments. *Journal of Personality and Social Psychology, 3*, 611–618.

Turiel, E. (1983). Domains and categories in social-cognitive development. In W. Overton (Ed.), *The relationship between social and cognitive development* (pp. 53–90). Hillsdale, NJ: Erlbaum.

Walker, L. J. (1980). Cognitive and perspective-taking prerequisites for moral development. *Child Development, 51*, 131–139.

Walker, L. J., deVries, B., & Trevethan, S. D. (1987). Moral stages and moral orientations in real-life and hypothetical dilemmas. *Child Development, 58*, 842–858.

Wasserman, E., & Garrod, A. (1983). Application of Kohlberg's theory to curricula and democratic schools. *Educational Analysis, 5*, 17–36.

CHAPTER 9

A Cognitive-Behavioral Approach to Intervention

Jan N. Hughes and Sylvia M. Kemenoff
Texas A&M University

A cognitive-behavioral approach recognizes that a person's cognitions (thoughts, beliefs, problem-solving processes, interpretations of experience) affect a person's behavioral response to the environment. Cognitive behaviorists assume a dynamic interrelationship among behavior, environmental influences, and person variables (affect and cognition). Maladaptive cognitive processes are assumed to produce dysfunctional behavior. Thus, a direct focus on changing these cognitive processes is recommended. Cognitive behavioral therapy encompasses a diverse range of specific procedures and techniques and includes both strategies to directly modify behavior as well as strategies to modify cognitive processes, such as attributions, expectancies, self-control processes, and problem-solving skills.

Cognitive behavior therapy is an evolved behavioral paradigm which, unlike traditional behavior therapy, incorporates internal processes (i.e., cognitions) into the assessment and treatment of psychological disturbance. However, due to cognitive behavior therapy's inherited empirical tradition, the utility of cognitive constructs in mediating behavior change must be empirically validated and, as a result, the "mentalism" of cognitive behavior therapy is firmly grounded in the scientific realm.

Cognitive behavior therapy evolved from traditional behavior therapy over a period of two decades. During the late 1960s and early 1970s mental phenomena were reintroduced into American experimental psychology, as research developments in various areas of psychological inquiry led to the incorporation of cognitive concepts into theories of psychological phenomena (Dember, 1974). As American experimental psychology turned cognitive (Dember, 1974), behavior therapists began to incorporate cognitive constructs into therapeutic techniques and to empirically validate the utility of these applications (Dobson & Block, 1988; Hughes, 1988a). Cognitive behavior therapy gradually emerged from this union of behavior therapy and cognitive psychology. However, the evolution of cognitive behavior therapy was neither immediate nor the result of a single event. Rather, this evolution of cognitive behavior therapy was a progressive phenomenon influenced by a variety of contributing historical events.

HISTORICAL ANTECEDENTS

Dissatisfaction with Current Therapeutic Models

Although the behavior therapy movement was the dominant model for clinical intervention during the 1960s and 1970s, dissatisfaction with behavior therapy took root in the late 1960s and continued to grow. During this time, increasing amounts of data emerged that could not be explained by the strict S-R, nonmediational model of human behavior (Dobson & Block, 1988). A major challenge to the S-R model was Bandura's (1965, 1971) reports of vicarious learning. As Wessler (1987) notes, "the key concept in vicarious learning is that of expectancy of reinforcement. The notion of expectancy of reinforcement is clearly cognitive, and therefore antithetical to radical behavioral approaches" (p. 5). Likewise, the behavioral model could not adequately explain children's language acquisition. According to the behavioral model of language acquisition, children learn words, syntax, and grammar through overt reinforcement. However, children acquire grammatical rules well beyond most caregivers' ability to overtly reinforce (Vygotsky, 1962).

While there was a growing dissatisfaction with a strict behavioral model of behavior, there was continued disenchantment with the psychodynamic model. Not only were the theoretical assumptions and tenets of this model being disputed (Dobson & Block, 1988), but there was an accumulating body of empirical evidence that indicated the limited therapeutic effectiveness of psychodynamic therapy (see Dobson & Block, 1988; Meyers & Craighead, 1984).

Research Developments within Cognitive Psychology

Dissatisfaction with current models or theories due to their inability to satisfactorily explain relevant theoretical constructs or empirical findings results in what Kuhn labels a paradigm shift (Kuhn, 1962). During the early 1970s, a paradigm shift occurred in American psychology which Dember (1974) labeled "the cognitive revolution" (p. 161). Dember (1974) summarizes a significant amount of research in the areas of memory, linguistic acquisition, perception and motivation which clearly indicates that "cognitive concepts had begun to pervade many areas of psychological theory" (p. 161).

Social Learning Theory

Bandura's social learning theory (1969, 1977) was perhaps most influential in determining the evolution of cognitive-behavioral therapy (Hughes, 1988a; Meyers & Craighead,

1984; Wilson, 1978). Social learning theory was, in fact, a learning theory of behavior. However, because of its emphasis on cognitive mediation and its rejection of the unidirectional, S–R (stimulus–response) model of behavior, social learning theory revolutionized behaviorism and opened the way for the cognitive behavioral approach (Hughes, 1988a).

Social learning theory is a comprehensive approach to human functioning that incorporates principles of classical conditioning, operant conditioning and, most important, cognitive mediational processes (Bandura, 1969, 1977). According to social learning theory, the influence of environmental stimuli on behavior is largely determined by cognitive processes, whereby such processes determine what environmental stimuli are attended to, how much stimuli are perceived, and whether they will influence future behavior (Wilson, 1978).

However, the central tenet of social learning theory is reciprocal determinism (Bandura, 1977). Bandura postulates that human functioning involves dynamic interrelationships between behavior, environmental influences, and person variables (i.e., affect and cognitions). Bandura delineated two types of cognitive variables: appraisals and expectations. Appraisals can be defined as the value that an individual places in performing successfully in a given situation. Two types of expectations described by Bandura are self-efficacy expectations and outcome expectations. Self-efficacy expectations refer to individuals' beliefs that they can successfully perform the relevant behavior. An outcome expectation is the individual's belief that a behavior will result in a certain outcome (i.e., punishment or reward).

The Emergence of Cognitive Therapies

The underlying assumption of cognitive therapy is that maladaptive cognitive processes produce dysfunctional behavior and, therefore, desired behavior change may be best accomplished by modifying faulty cognitive processes (Meyers & Craighead, 1984). The two major proponents of cognitive therapy are Beck (1976) and Ellis (1962, 1973). Ellis (1962) contends that individuals participate in maladaptive behaviors or experience negative affect because they engage in illogical and irrational cognitive processes. Likewise, Beck (1976) posits that dysfunctional behavior and negative emotions are the result of individuals' cognitive distortions (i.e., irrational beliefs or expectations), which are representations of their irrational underlying assumptions about themselves, the world, and the future.

Beck's Cognitive Therapy. A primary goal of Beck's cognitive therapy is cognitive restructuring, that is, the modification of irrational fundamental assumptions (i.e., In order to be happy, I have to be successful in whatever I undertake), which presumably underlie maladaptive feelings and behaviors (Beck, Rush, Shaw, & Emery, 1979). The primary technique involved in assisting clients to test the validity of their assumptions and, in turn, to replace illogical assumptions, is hypothesis testing (Beck, 1976; Beck et al., 1979). Two types of hypothesis testing are typically employed. In rational hypothesis testing the client's underlying assumptions are challenged through logical reasoning and debates with the practitioner. In empirical hypothesis testing the client's underlying assumptions are challenged by contradictory data obtained by the client's participation in behavioral experiments.

Cognitive therapy combines various behavioral techniques such as activity scheduling, relaxation training, role playing, and contingency management, with various cognitive techniques, including hypothesis testing, cognitive reappraisal, alternative therapy, and reattribution techniques. These techniques are applied in order to initially provide clients with rapid symptom relief and improved self-concept. Subsequently, clients are taught the relation between their affective state and their thoughts, more appropriate problem-solving skills, and methods of identifying and modifying their maladaptive cognitions (i.e., their irrational beliefs and expectations) (Beck, 1976; Beck et al., 1979; Coleman & Beck, 1981).

A review of relevant developmental literature (DiGiuseppe, 1986; Emery, Bedrosian & Garber, 1983) indicates that children in the concrete-operational stage (7 or 8 to 12 years old) have the cognitive capability for the type of logical reasoning required for the kind of hypothesis testing that is central to cognitive therapy. Thus, they are presumed able to participate and benefit from this therapy. However, due to their limited linguistic abilities (e.g., their inability to discuss their thoughts and feelings), it is suggested that the focus of hypothesis testing be empirical rather than rational (Digdon & Gotlib, 1985; Emery et al., 1983).

Ellis's Rational Emotive Therapy.   The goal of rational emotive therapy (RET) is to assist clients to dispute their irrational beliefs (self-statements such as "I should be perfect", "I must be a perfect student") through various rational methods, such as verbal persuasion, rational debate, and logical reasoning (Ellis, 1962, 1973). It is important to note, however, that there are actually two forms of RET: Elegant (Preferential) RET and Inelegant (General) RET (Dryden & Ellis, 1987; Ellis, 1977). The main goal of Elegant RET is to encourage clients to make a philosophical change. The focus of therapy is on rational disputation, with limited reliance on behavioral techniques (except for, perhaps, homework assignments, which primarily focus on cognitive retraining exercises) (Dryden & Ellis, 1987). However, as Dryden and Ellis point out, inelegant therapy is employed when it is evident that the client is either unable to make a philosophical change or resistant to such a change. The goal of inelegant RET is to use cognitive-behavioral methods and empirical hypothesis testing to "effect inferential and behavioral based change" (p. 147).

Dobson and Block (1988) claim that the proponents of cognitive therapy had a significant role in the evolution of the cognitive-behavioral approach. According to these authors, the identification of influential theorists, such as Beck and Ellis, as well as Cautela, Mahoney, Thorsen, and Meichenbaum, with the cognitive-behavioral perspective "had the effect of creating a *zeitgeist* that drew the attention of others in the field" (p. 10).

Self-instructional Training

The theoretical foundation of Meichenbaum's early work on self-instructional training was Luria's (1961) and Vygotsky's (1962) developmental theories of the relation between language and behavior. Basically, these theories suggest that children's ability to develop voluntary control over their own behavior is a developmental progression, whereby children's behavior is initially regulated by adult verbalizations (i.e., parental instructions). Gradually their behavior comes under the control of their own self-instructions, which are at first overt and then become covert (internalized).

Meichenbaum and Goodman (1971) developed a program to teach impulsive second-grade children to use self-instructions to control their behavior. The specific procedures employed in this program were based on the developmental model outlined by Luria (1961) and Vygotsky (1962) and consisted of five stages. First, an adult modeled the task while making the appropriate self-statements. During the second stage, the child performed the same task while the model provided verbal instructions. Subsequently, during the third and fourth stages, the child performed the task while instructing himself or herself aloud and then whispering. Finally, the child performed the task while employing covert self-instructions. The self-instruction program was considered to be successful since the children who received the self-instruction training significantly improved their task performance on a variety of measures, in comparison with the children in the attention placebo and control groups.

The success of Meichenbaum and Goodman's (1971) self-instructional program with impulsive children resulted not only in further investigations on self-instruction training, but also in further applications of self-instructional training in order to decrease aggression, reduce hyperactivity, reduce fears, improve academic performance, and train social competence in children (Meyers & Craighead, 1984).

Problem-solving Training

The incorporation of problem-solving techniques into behavior therapy was introduced by D'Zurilla and Goldfried (1971). According to these authors, the five stages involved in the problem-solving process are (a) possessing a general problem-solving orientation or mind-set, (b) defining the problem and determining what must be accomplished to solve the problem, (c) generating alternative solutions that might be employed to solve the problem, (d) making a decision about the generated alternatives by evaluating their positive and negative consequences, and (e) verifying the outcome of the decision process by determining whether the selected solution is indeed solving the problem. During problem-solving training a client is first taught a range of problem-solving skills by various methods, such as modeling and behavioral rehearsal. Next, the client is assisted in the use of these skills in actual problem situations (Dobson & Block, 1988; Hughes, 1988a).

The initial applications of problem-solving training were conducted by Spivack, Shure and their associates during the early 1970s. These researchers were investigating the assessment and treatment of children's and adolescents' interpersonal cognitive problem-solving (ICPS) skills. Based on their research, Spivack, Platt, and Shure (1976) concluded that effective interpersonal problem solving involves (a) the ability to recognize the various problem situations within the social environment, (b) the ability to generate a variety of solutions to interpersonal problems (alternative thinking), (c) the ability to sequentially plan a series of steps necessary to accomplish a desired goal (means–end thinking), (d) the ability to predict the immediate and long-term consequences of selecting a particular alternative (consequential thinking), and (e) the ability to recognize the motivating factors that determine one's own behavior as well as the behavior of others.

Based on this model, Spivack, Shure, and their colleagues developed programs to teach the various ICPS skills to children and adolescents. The results of these programs were typically positive (for reviews see Hughes, 1988b; Meyers & Craighead, 1984), culminating in an increasing amount of research and applied interest in problem-solving therapies (Dobson & Block, 1988).

Self-Control

Self-control procedures have always been accepted therapeutic interventions in behavior therapy. However, the explanation of self-control processes offered by traditional behaviorists was exclusively operant. For example, Skinner (1953) argued that thoughts were subvocal responses that were, like all other behaviors, ultimately under the control of external factors. Homme (1965) suggested that coverants (thoughts) were subject to the same operant principles as were overt behaviors. Although Homme's explanation of coverants was basically operant, it resulted in numerous investigations of self-control programs designed to change behavior by modifying covert thought processes (Meyers & Craighead, 1984).

During the 1970s there was a growing consensus among behavioral therapists that behavior was at least partially controlled by cognitions, and explanations of self-control became more cognitive. For example, Kanfer (1970; Kanfer & Karoly, 1972) provided an information processing model of self-control. Within this model, self-control processes are divided into three interrelated components: self-monitoring, self-evaluation, and self-reinforcement. According to this model, self-monitoring provides an individual with information about his or her performance which is then compared against a preestablished performance standard. If the individual's performance is consistent with the performance standard, the individual administers self-reinforcement.

As more cognitive explanations of self control were provided, there was a debate within behavior therapy over the importance of internal versus external factors in the self-control process. However, as Mahoney and Arnkoff (1977; as cited by Meyers & Craighead, 1984) indicate, many practitioners and researchers have continued to argue for the significant role of internal processes (i.e., cognitions) within the self-control process, and as a result have placed self-control within the cognitive-behavioral domain.

CRITICAL ASPECTS

Cognitive-behavioral therapy (CBT) includes a wide variety of strategies and techniques for the assessment and treatment of maladaptive behavior. However, the diverse methods subsumed under the rubric of cognitive-behavioral therapy all share the fundamental theoretical assumption that cognitions (i.e., thoughts, images, and perceptions) affect behavior. Consequently, changes in cognitive events produce desired behavior change. The cognitive-behavioral approach does not deny the influence of environmental stimuli, such as antecedent events and reinforcement contingencies. Rather, it emphasizes that individuals, rather than being passive recipients of environmental influences, form cognitions about environmental stimuli, and these cognitions mediate behavior change. It is this emphasis on cognitions and cognitive processes that distinguishes the cognitive-behavioral approach from the traditional behavioral approach. As Dobson and Block

(1988) succinctly state, "Only in instances where cognitive mediation can be demonstrated, and where cognitive mediation is an important component of the treatment plan can be the label 'cognitive-behavioral' be applied" (p. 7).

It is important to note, however, that the cognitive-behavioral approach does not perceive the relation between cognitions and behavior as unidirectional. Instead, this relation is conceived as bi-directional, whereby cognitions simultaneously influence and are influenced by behavior. In fact, the cognitive-behavioral approach views human functioning as even more complex than the joint interaction between cognitions and behavior. Since 1969, Bandura's conceptualization of human functioning, reciprocal determinism, has been the theoretical foundation of the cognitive-behavioral approach. According to reciprocal determinism, human functioning is a complex interaction in which behavior, environmental variables (i.e., antecedent events and reinforcement contingencies) and personal variables (i.e., cognitions and affect) are mutually interdependent (Bandura, 1977). Although the cognitive-behavioral approach emphasizes the complexity of human functioning, the role of cognitions is still considered to be predominant in determining behavior and producing behavior change.

Recently, however, there has been an increasing acknowledgment of the significant role of affect in influencing behavior and effecting behavior change. Three different views related to the role of affect are held: (a) affect is a subsequent reaction to cognitive appraisal of environmental stimuli, (b) cognitions intervene between environmental stimuli and the affective response that they elicit, and (c) cognitive processing and affective responding occur simultaneously. Despite this diversity of opinion, there is a growing consensus that cognitions and affect are somehow interdependent (Dobson, 1988). Consequently, as Braswell and Kendall (1988) explain, the cognitive-behavioral approach can be currently characterized as having an emphasis on "the complex interaction among cognitive events, processes, products, and structures, affect, overt behavior and environmental context and experiences as contributing to various facets of dysfunctional behavior" (p. 167).

INTENDED GOALS

Since the cognitive-behavioral approach regards the role of cognitive events and cognitive processes as primary in mediating behavior change, the goal of cognitive-behavioral therapy is to employ various cognitive and behavioral strategies to modify maladaptive cognitions and, in turn, produce desired behavior change. Dysfunctional behavior, however, can be attributed to cognitive distortions or cognitive deficiencies (Braswell & Kendall, 1988).

Cognitive distortions (errors or misperceptions of environmental events), are causally related to internalizing behaviors, such as depression, phobias, social withdrawal, and anxiety (Braswell & Kendall, 1988). In these cases, cognitive-behavioral techniques are implemented to assist clients in recognizing and testing their misperceptions, irrational beliefs and expectations, and biased attributions.

On the other hand, cognitive deficiencies (an absence of effective cognitive strategies to control behavior) are causally related to externalizing disorders such as hyperactivity, impulsivity, attentional disorders, and various types of behavior difficulties (Braswell &

Kendall, 1988). Cognitive-behavioral techniques, in these cases, are employed to teach the client the use of verbal mediation, effective problem-solving procedures, and self-control techniques.

An important tenet of the cognitive-behavioral approach is its emphasis upon empiricism. Like the traditional behavioral approach, the cognitive-behavioral orientation requires that the usefulness of the therapeutic interventions employed be empirically demonstrated through scientific investigation. Whereas the behavioral approach requires that the therapeutic utility of behavioral interventions be empirically validated, the cognitive-behavioral approach requires that the role of cognitive constructs in producing behavior change be empirically established (see Kendall & Hollon, 1979; Hughes, 1988a).

FUTURE DIRECTIONS

One advantage of the cognitive-behavioral approach is its flexibility. Some approaches, such as behaviorism and psychoanalytic theory, have become stagnant and obsolete as a result of their adherence to rigid theoretical principles. Cognitive-behavioral theory is broad enough to incorporate scientifically valid theoretical and methodological advances from other psychological perspectives into its domain (Kendall & Hollon, 1979). Thus, cognitive behavior theory continues to evolve. The progressive evolution of the cognitive-behavioral approach augurs well for its potential to continue to contribute to our understanding of behavior and our ability to effect behavior change.

CASE ANALYSIS

Aspects of Case Study Relevant
to Cognitive-Behavioral Perspective

Because the cognitive-behavioral approach focuses on a person's cognitions, affect, and behavior as they interact with each other and with the environment, most of the case data is relevant to this theoretical perspective. For example, the historical information provided in the case study is important because one's life experiences affect one's current cognitions (i.e., perceptions, thoughts, attitudes, problem-solving strategies, expectations, and cognitive schemata). The psychometric information is important because Vince's pattern of successes and failures in school is, in part, determined by his cognitive strengths and weaknesses. His history of school failure affects his beliefs about himself as a learner and about the relationship between effort on the one hand, and achievement outcomes on the other. Specifically, the application of the learned helplessness model appears to be of heuristic value when analyzing Vince's case. According to this model, learned helplessness results from learning that one's behavior and the consequences of one's behavior are independent. As a result of this learning, an individual develops the expectation that events are uncontrollable. In turn, this expectancy of lack of control over events tends to reduce the individual's motivation to respond, to perceptions about future events, and to future expectations. (For a more detailed explanation of the learned helplessness model, see Seligman, 1975; or Maier & Seligman, 1976). Due to Vince's history of academic failures, despite his apparent efforts to succeed, Vince seems to expect that his success in school does not depend upon his effort. In turn, this expectancy appears to reduce his motivation to apply himself academically, since he believes that his future successes or failures are independent of his efforts.

In this section, assessment information from each area of the case study is highlighted and the relevance of that information to the cognitive-behavioral perspective is discussed. In the following section, this information is integrated into a clinical model of Vince's difficulties. The clinical validity of this model should be determined based on its usefulness in formulating an intervention plan and the effectiveness of this plan in remediating Vince's problems. The final section will present the intervention plan which is predicated on the clinical model.

Referral Information.   The facts that Vince's academic performance has declined recently and that this decline has been accompanied by an increase in problem behaviors suggest that motivational and other nonintellectual factors (e.g., learned helplessness, negative affective responses, self-concept, attitudes toward learning) are implicated in his learning problems. Additionally, his social and behavioral problems may be consequences of repeated academic failure.

Medical History.   Vince's severe ear infections and resultant temporary hearing loss between the ages of 16 months and 3½ years occurred during a developmental period that is critical to the development of language competence. It is likely that Vince's speech articulation problems, which lasted until at least the end of second grade, are a result, in whole or in part, of his impaired hearing during his preschool years. Language delays during the early school years are associated with behavioral problems, with attentional and disruptive behaviors being most prevalent (Paul, Cohen, & Caparulo, 1983; Rutter, Graham, & Yule, 1970). This fact is not surprising, given the importance of language skills to the adaptive socialization of young children (for review, see Piacentini, 1987). During the early school years, children are making large strides in regulating their own behavior with their newly developed language skills (Vygotsky, 1962). Children with language delays are at a disadvantage in this developmental sequence and are likely to be viewed as more impulsive and less self-controlled. It is likely that Vince experienced frustration when he could not be understood by peers and teachers in kindergarten and first grade, a problem that was exacerbated by the school's requirement that children read and recite publicly.

When Vince was eight years old (second grade), his pediatrician prescribed a psychostimulant medication, Ritalin, to control Vince's high activity level, impulsivity, and aggressive behaviors. Vince continued on the medication for three years. It is not clear from the case study data whether his behavior improved with the medication, but there are several reasons to doubt that the medication was effective: (a) During fourth grade, when Vince was still on the medication regimen, his behavior was highly disruptive, resulting in his being expelled from the private school. During the following year, when he was not on medication, he had the "best year ever." (b) When Vince was diagnosed as having an attention deficit, he was probably experiencing high levels of emotional distress, as his parents' marriage was failing. The initiation of medication therapy occurred the same year his parents divorced. His attentional and behavioral problems could have been a reaction to his parents' divorce. This possibility was not investigated at the time. (c) Vince's behavioral problems may have been a result of inadequate and insensitive instruction (discussed below). Specifically, Vince had an undiagnosed learning disability (the assessment data employed to reach such a conclusion are outlined below under Evaluation Results). According to Public Law 94–142 (Education for All Handicapped Children Act of 1975), a determination of a learning disability is based upon the following criteria: (1) whether the child's achievement level is commensurate with his or her age and ability levels and (2) whether the child has a severe discrepancy between achievement and intellectual ability in one or more of the following areas of academic achievement: oral expression, listening comprehension, written expression, basic reading skill, reading comprehension, mathematical calculation, or mathematics reasoning. Each state determines what is considered to be "severe." For example, Texas has determined that a difference of one standard deviation (15 points) between a child's score on an intellectual measure and on an achievement measure, with equal standard scores, is considered to be a "severe" discrepancy. Also this discrepancy must not be primarily the result of (1) visual, hearing, or motor handicaps; (2) mental retardation; (3) emotional disturbance; or (4) environmental, cultural or economic disadvantage (*Federal Register*, 1977, 42, p. 65082). Recently, there is some evidence indicating that learning disabled students have poorly developed metacognitive strategies and are inefficient users of such strategies (see Keogh & Hall, 1984). Vince's inability to master the academic curriculum due to his learning disability may have resulted in critical responses from teachers rather than supportive responses, adding to Vince's frustration.

Some children who take psychostimulant medications attribute their behavior to the pill, resulting in less of an internal locus of control. When Ritalin is inappropriately prescribed and the source problems (emotional distress, learning problems, speech difficulties) are not remediated, a child is likely to develop the expectations that he cannot depend on adults for emotional support and that he has little control over future rewards and punishers.

Family/Social History.   Vince's parents' divorce is a significant factor in his current difficulties. He was deprived of his father's attentions during his early school years, when acceptance from a responsible and caring adult male is important to a boy's development of a positive self-concept. Although the divorce occurred when Vince was eight years old, his father's withdrawal from the family seems to have begun at least three years earlier. Vince's perceived rejection on the part of his father, combined with his speech problem and school behavior problems, made it difficult for Vince to see himself as a "good" child.

Expecting rejection from adults, Vince responds to authority figures with open defiance and interprets criticism as rejection rather than as feedback. His stepfather responds to Vince with benign neglect, probably because Vince has been "hard to reach."

Vince has a difficult time expressing his feelings. Although his mother reports that Vince was not traumatized by the divorce, Vince's behavior at the time suggests he experienced much emotional distress. He was less outgoing after the divorce and more negative with his mother. It is likely that Vince did not know how to communicate his feelings about the divorce and acted out his distress rather than seeking support from his mother and others. Vince's pattern of denying feelings is apparent now, as he denies having any problems.

A bright spot in Vince's family history is his relationship with his stepsister. His caring, close relationship with Bea demonstrates that he is capable of loving another person. It is important to note that in this relationship, which Vince values highly, he is "in control," and someone else depends on him. Thus, Vince's sense of powerlessness over his life is lessened when he is with Bea. He feels competent, needed, and loved.

Vince's peer relationships have been fairly typical, suggesting adequate peer relationship skills. His generally positive relationships with peers is in marked contrast to his relationships with authority figures. He expects adults to criticize him and to withhold affection.

Educational History. Since kindergarten, given the choice of appearing dumb or appearing silly or ill-behaved, Vince has chosen the latter. This choice reflects his fragile self-concept. When Vince had the bad fortune of having a fourth-grade teacher who used belittling and shaming approaches, his behavior worsened. However, when he had a sensitive teacher the next year, his school achievement and deportment improved markedly. Thus, as recently as fifth grade, Vince was able to respond positively to an accepting, nonpunitive teacher, suggesting that motivational and emotional factors (i.e., perceived rejection, low self-concept, learned helplessness) play a central role in his current learning difficulties. He needs a supportive and reinforcement-rich learning environment in order to put forth good effort.

In reviewing Vince's educational experiences, it is important to recognize that Vince had an undiagnosed learning disability, as discussed below. He has had difficulty in organization and problem-solving strategies since kindergarten, and this difficulty has had the most detrimental impact on his written expression. He received no special education for his handicapping condition, and teachers attributed his disorganization and poor performance to his lack of motivation or effort. They, in turn, probably responded to him with increased criticism as well as with lower rates of interaction (see Clark & Peterson, 1984, for a discussion of how teachers' attributions for students' behaviors influence their interactions with students).

School Observation. Vince engages in high levels of task avoidance behaviors. He finds academic tasks unpleasant (as expected, given his past failures), especially writing tasks. He responds to the unpleasant emotions he experiences (frustration, hopelessness) in achievement situations with task avoidance behaviors (doodling, visiting with classmates, closing his book), which allow him to terminate the negative emotions. The negative feelings he experiences also interfere with his ability to use effective problem-solving strategies.

Vince's repeated academic failures have affected his achievement-related beliefs. Specifically, he believes that he does not have the ability to succeed and that his efforts have little impact on achievement outcomes. Vince was observed to put forth concerted effort on a mathematics assignment. However, after he learned that he had earned a grade of "C" on it, he gave up. It seems he has high standards for himself (a grade of "C" is unsatisfactory) and is quick to conclude that he cannot be successful. His angry response to a classmate who inquired about his performance on the mathematics test suggests he is quite concerned about how others view him.

Evaluation Observations. Vince denies he has problems. His denial suggests he believes his academic and social difficulties are a result of his low ability. Because this prospect is, naturally, disturbing to him, he copes with his failure by denying it or minimizing its importance. He is quick to state that he could do better if he wanted to, which is his way of protecting himself from the unpleasant feelings associated with failure.

Vince's approach to the tests was impulsive and reflected ineffective problem-solving strategies. The impulsiveness is a result of achievement-related beliefs (i.e., success is not dependent on effort) as well as deficits in metacognitive knowledge. This type of knowledge includes awareness of strategies that may be used to enhance performance on specific tasks as well as the knowledge and skill required to apply specific strategies in a variety of situations. These metacognitive weaknesses and ineffective problem-solving strategies were evident in his performance on the cognitive tests, which are discussed below.

Evaluation Results. The factor structure of the WISC–R may often be employed to arrive at an interpretation of a child's performance on the WISC–R. Kaufman (1977; as cited in Kaufman, 1979), in a factor-analytic study of the WISC–R employing the data from the original WISC–R standardization sample, identified three factors, which he labeled as follows: Verbal Comprehension, Perceptual Organization, and Freedom from Distractibility. The first two factors are considered to be in the cognitive domain while the latter is considered to be in the behavioral or affective domain. Although not perfect, there is a close correspondence between the Verbal Comprehension and Perceptual Organization factors, and the Verbal and Performance Scales respectively on the WISC–R (from which the Verbal and Performance IQs are derived) (Kaufman, 1979). Vince's performance on the WISC–R suggested the two-factor interpretation of his test performance is appropriate. Specifically, Vince's distribution of scores suggests that it is justifiable to assign a primary role in interpreting Vince's performance on the WISC–R to the Verbal and Performance IQs and to consider these IQs as good estimates of Vince's Verbal Comprehension and Perceptual Organization abilities. His performance suggested there was insufficient reason to interpret the third factor, which is often referred to as the freedom from distractibility factor. Vince's attention and concentration problems are probably not the result of an attention disorder but a result of achievement-related beliefs, task avoidance, and specific weaknesses in metacognitive knowledge.

Vince's ability to apply verbal skills and information to the solution of new problems and to process verbal information is better developed (Bright Average range, 88th percentile) than is his ability to think in terms of visual images and to manipulate them with fluency, flexibility, and relative speed (Average range, 39th percentile). The 22-point discrepancy between his Verbal and Performance Scale scores is estimated to occur in fewer than 10 percent of the population. Although several interpretations of this difference are possible, in Vince's situation, his lower Performance Scale score is primarily a result of ineffective problem-solving strategies and poor organizational skills.

Additionally, his impulsive response style interferes more with performance on the Performance Scale than on the Verbal Scale.

Vince's difficulties in interpreting and organizing visually perceived material demonstrated on the WISC–R are consistent with his difficulties in diagramming sentences and in spelling. His difficulties in organizing also interfere with his written expression, as he has trouble putting down his thoughts in an organized, coherent fashion.

Deficits in nonverbal reasoning, planning and foresight, and problems with impulsiveness were also reflected in Vince's performance on the HRNB. Additionally, he has some difficulty in integrating auditory and visual information, a cognitive limitation that contributes to his problems in spelling and written expression.

The 28-point discrepancy between Vince's Full Scale score on the WISC–R and his score on a test of written language is indicative of a learning disability in the area of written expression. Vince's overall pattern of performance on the WJTA is consistent with the view that Vince is an "underachiever." Given Vince's achievement-related beliefs and learning disability, it is not unexpected that he would be achieving at levels below his ability level, even in areas not directly implicated in his disability.

Personality testing supports the view that Vince perceives himself as a failure in school. Specifically, on the Piers–Harris, Vince's percentile score of 7 in the area of intellectual and school status suggest that he has a negative self-assessment of his abilities with respect to intellectual and academic tasks. As well, his low score in this area also suggests that Vince has a general dissatisfaction with school and has negative future expectations related to school. Furthermore, his response that school is *bad* on the Sentence Completion Test as well as his wish to be out of school given during the Three Wishes Interview are also indicative of his general dissatisfaction toward school. As well, Vince's standard score of 15 in the Social Concerns/Concentration area (which has a mean standard score of 10) on the Revised Children's Manifest Anxiety Scale suggest that Vince is worried about his problems in concentration and about being accepted by his peers. Vince's feelings of alienation and disengagement from his parents are evident in his short responses to questions about this area, as well as his specific responses. For example, one of his responses on the Sentence Completion Test was, My family *is not a real family*. Similarly, in one of his Thematic Apperception Stories, Vince describes a guy who "made it in life without his parents help." On a positive note, Vince's aspirations are quite typical for his age and suggest he has not given up hope of achieving traditional goals such as having a job and a wife.

Discussion of Findings

When Vince entered kindergarten, he had several characteristics that placed him at risk for subsequent school learning and adjustment difficulties. His delayed language skills and specific cognitive limitations (i.e., difficulty with auditory–visual integration, poor ability to organize visually perceived material) interfered with his ability to learn to read and to spell. He responded to early failure experiences by acting out his frustration. His teachers responded to his disruptive behavior with criticism and disapproval. Vince developed the expectation that teachers were not sources of assistance and support and expected teachers to disapprove and to criticize him. His teachers' reactions to him, coupled with his father's relative absence and his stepfather's benign neglect, caused Vince to expect authority figures to be rejecting and critical. Thus, Vince learned to respond to teachers with defiance and a lack of cooperation. His behavior, in turn, gave teachers more opportunities to criticize and punish him, strengthening his beliefs that teachers were rejecting and that he was bad.

Currently, Vince's school learning and adjustment difficulties are largely a result of specific cognitive limitations as well as his achievement-related beliefs. The cognitive limitations are in the area of metacognitive competence and organizational capabilities. He lacks knowledge of strategies for solving problems and the ability to apply these strategies to specific situations. He starts solving a problem before he has adequately assessed the task requirements or generated and evaluated specific plans for performing the task. He probably does not monitor his performance or use self-reinforcement.

The achievement-related beliefs are both a result of past academic failures and a cause of current failure. When he began having academic difficulties, he responded to failure by acting out his frustrations. Teachers responded to his behavior with disapproval, which contributed to his feelings of hopelessness and inferiority. These feelings and expectations, in turn, increased the probability of future failure. A "failure cycle" was established, in which Vince fell further behind, and external pressures and internal feelings of despair increased. The result of this cycle was defiance and denial of problems. Repeated failures also affected Vince's beliefs about himself as a learner. Due to his specific cognitive limitations, he was often given tasks to perform that were too difficult for him (without additional support or some modification of the task). The experience of repeated failure that was not under his control contributed to his current belief that he does not have the ability to succeed and that efforts have little impact on achievement outcomes. These beliefs result in less effort, which results in more failure, which increases the strength of the original beliefs. Thus, the failure cycle includes both achievement beliefs and academically ineffective strategies (avoidance, denial).

Vince is capable of responsible, loving behavior, as demonstrated with his stepsister. The enjoyment he derives from this relationship suggests that Vince wants to be responsible and helpful to others and will be so if given the opportunity.

Vince's relationship with his stepsister, his handsome physical appearance, and his athletic prowess are sources of good feelings about himself and should be emphasized in the intervention.

RECOMMENDATIONS AND SUGGESTED INTERVENTIONS

Areas of Emphasis

The model of Vince's academic and social difficulties presented above has implications for the selection of treatment goals as well as intervention methods, which will be delineated below.

1. Improved metacognitive competence. Cognitive strategies are the means to achieve cognitive goals. In the area of reading, example strategies include lookbacks, self-questioning, and paraphrasing. Vince's deficits in the use of cognitive strategies interfere with his academic success. He would appropriately be described as an "inactive learner'' (Torgenson, 1980), because he does not spontaneously generate strategies to improve his performance. His failure to use cognitive strategies is a result of a lack of knowledge of when and where strategy use is appropriate as well as a lack of knowledge of how a strategy operates.

2. Attributions. Vince demonstrates an attributional style characteristic of learning disabled and underachieving students. Specifically, he attributes his failures to internal, stable, and general causes (i.e., low ability) and his successes to external, transient, and specific causes (i.e., good luck). Selection of attributions as a treatment focus is based on the finding that students' causal explanations for why they are doing well or poorly are related to persistence, self-esteem, expectancies for future performance, and affective reactions to success and failure (Weiner, 1979). In order for Vince to improve in his academic performance as well as in his attitude toward school learning, he needs to learn to attribute his failures to a lack of sufficient effort or to strategy use rather than to a lack of ability and to attribute his successes to his ability and strategy use.

3. Relating to authority figures. Although Vince's peer relationships appear satisfactory, he has problems in relating to authority figures and expressing feelings. His reactions to teachers increase their negative reactions to him and interfere with his obtaining the assistance he needs from teachers.

4. Expressing feelings. Vince's difficulty in expressing his feelings will interfere with his establishment of close friendships. During adolescence, the importance of self-disclosure and sharing of feelings to close friends increases. Peers, both boys and girls, can serve as important social support systems for Vince, who feels alienated from his family. However, he needs skills for establishing and maintaining close friendships.

5. Conflict resolution skills. Vince's stepfather's comments about his relationship with Vince, most notably his comments that although they "get along," Vince continues to question his authority over behavioral guidelines and that there is continual disagreement about rules, as well as his mother's statement that she feels "powerless" in controlling Vince's behavior, suggest that, within Vince's family, conflicts are not resolved. Indeed, there is a sense of disengagement between Vince and his parents. This lack of adaptive conflict resolution was also evident in the dissolution of Vince's natural parents' marriage. This pattern of lack of conflict resolution is apparently due to the family's very limited, if any, conflict resolution skills. Due to the family's inability to resolve conflicts adaptively, not only do family conflicts remain unresolved, but it also appears that Vince has consequently learned to view conflict and disagreement as criticism or rejection and in turn responds to conflict with maladaptive defiance. Indeed, Vince's responses on the Thematic Apperception Test revealed that Vince idealizes marriage as a relationship that is devoid of conflict. Therefore, an important goal for the practitioner would be to assist Vince's family to develop skills to enable them to more adaptively resolve conflict. Concurrently, Vince would be assisted in developing an acceptance of conflict as a natural and resolvable component of satisfactory relationships.

6. Attitudes and attributions related to divorce and father's absence. Although Vince's mother reports that Vince was relatively unaffected by his parents' divorce, Vince's escalating behavior problems during his father's gradual withdrawal from the family and surrounding the final divorce seem to suggest otherwise. Since the divorce occurred when Vince was approximately eight years old, Vince, as is common for young children, may have attributed self-blame for his parents' divorce. For example, he may have come to believe that if only he had been a "good" boy, Dad wouldn't have left. In turn, Vince may perceive his father's current absence as a rejection. Another possibility is that Vince may be blaming his mother for the divorce and his father's subsequent absence from the home, and that this attribution may be contributing to some unresolved feelings of anger toward his mother. Therefore, Vince's attitudes and attributions regarding his parents' divorce and his father's absence must be assessed and, if determined to be maladaptive, they should be modified.

Program of Change

Cognitive Strategy Instruction.   It is unlikely that Vince would invest himself in learning cognitive strategies unless he felt more positively about learning. Therefore, cognitive strategies that facilitate reading comprehension should be taught in a supportive social context that enhances students' attitudes toward learning. The reciprocal teaching model developed by Palincsar and Brown (1984) would be highly appropriate because students work in small groups with a teacher, and the students share responsibility for teaching. Reciprocal teaching stresses learner control over learning. Students learn to become aware of reading goals and of plans and strategies to foster reading comprehension. For example, they learn and practice procedural knowledge such as paraphrasing, formulating questions to answer in advance of reading a section, and relating new facts to what they already know (i.e., existing knowledge structures). In addition to teaching specific strategies, students learn how to plan which strategies to use for specific reading goals, to monitor reading comprehension, to monitor and self-correct reading failures, to draw inferences from material in the text, and to predict which material might be forthcoming.

Self-questioning is a central aspect of reciprocal reading, and it is taught by having teachers model the following four activities after a segment of text has been read silently by the students: asking a test question about the segment, summarizing the material, discussing and clarifying any troublesome material, and predicting which material might be forthcoming. The students and the teacher take turns modeling these four activities. Initially, of course, the adult teachers provide a great deal of modeling, prompting, and direction. However, as the students demonstrate improvements in their question-asking, summarizing, clarifying, and predicting skills, the teacher concurrently decreases the amount of prompting and feedback given to the students. For a detailed description of the reciprocal teaching method and examples of various reciprocal teaching dialogues, interested readers are directed to Palincsar and Brown (1984). Vince will also receive strategy instruction in the area of written language. Graham and Harris (1989) describe the purpose of cognitive training in written language as "to increase active task involvement during writing, to activate a search of appropriate memory stores for writing content, to establish intentional control over sentence and paragraph production, to facilitate advanced planning, and to boost the quantity and quality of text revisions" (p. 247). Writing is a complex cognitive process that involves at least three main processes (planning, sentence generation, and revision), each of which involves several subroutines. Because Vince has difficulty organizing his thoughts for written expression, the tasks involved in writing need to be broken down into steps, and he should receive instruction in each step. In the cognitive training method, each step is taught independently at first and then combined with other steps. Instruction in each skill follows seven basic steps:

1. *Pretest and commitment to learn*: Student's current functioning on the task of interest is determined, and this information is shared with the student; the student is asked to sign a written agreement to develop a new skill to remedy the weaknesses.
2. *Describe*: The new skill or strategy is described, and the student and teacher discuss why and when the strategy is used.
3. *Model*: The teacher demonstrates the strategy while thinking aloud.
4. *Verbal rehearsal*: The student memorizes the steps in the strategy.
5. *Controlled practice*: Students practice using the strategy with ability-level material; reinforcement and corrective feedback are provided.
6. *Grade-appropriate practice*: Student practice using the strategy with materials and situations drawn from the regular classroom; reinforcement and corrective feedback are provided.
7. *Posttest and commitment to generalize*: A posttest is administered, and students are informed of their progress; the student is asked to agree to generalize the use of the strategy to other settings. (Graham & Harris, 1989, p. 263)

In addition to learning specific steps involved in writing, Vince should also be taught specific strategies for different writing tasks. For example, the strategy for paragraph writing involves teaching students a procedure for writing four types of paragraphs: List or describe, show a sequence, compare and/or contrast, or demonstrate cause and effect. In order to help students remember the paragraph writing strategy, students are taught to remember the mnemonic SLOW CaPS.

Each letter except for the small ''a'' in CaPS is designed to remind the student to carry out a specific action: (S)—show the kind of paragraph in the first sentence; (L)—list the type of details you plan to write about; (O)—order the details; (W)—write the details in complete sentences; and cap off the paragraph with a (C) concluding, (P) passing, or (S) summary sentence. (Graham & Harris, 1988, p. 265)

Cognitive strategy training in reading and writing should occur in a context that both promotes student responsibility for learning outcomes and engenders positive affective reactions. Students are more likely to apply the strategies taught if they feel responsible for using them and if they feel positively about using them. Strategies for accomplishing both of these goals include the following:

1. Contracting with Vince for accomplishing well-defined learning goals (e.g., write a descriptive paragraph that includes a topical sentence and at least three details): The contract should include consequences for successful and unsuccessful completion of the task. For example, if Vince does not complete the task, he engages in additional practice before attempting the task again. If he is unsuccessful, he advances his player on a gameboard. When he reaches the ''finish'' in the game, he gets to play a video soccer game with the teacher for a class period.
2. Learning goals are broken into small, sequential steps, and Vince is provided with visual feedback of his progress in mastering the steps in the program.
3. Learning occurs in a positive social climate. Vince's interest in socializing should be used to increase motivation for learning. The reciprocal teaching process described above permits students to learn from each other, and students get the opportunity to be responsible for teaching their peers.

4. Vince's interest in sports should be incorporated into academic tasks. For example, he should have been encouraged to practice his writing skills by writing about sports.
5. Because Vince has accumulated several years of unpleasant feelings associated with writing, it is important that instruction in writing be offered in ways that are different from his earlier experience. Given Vince's difficulty with handwriting, he should be allowed to write with a word processor. Not only would the word processor minimize the difficulty of the mechanics of writing for Vince, it would also lessen the association between the new writing instruction and his past writing experiences.

Attributions

If Vince believes success is independent of effort, he will not invest himself in the cognitive training and, if he experiences successes in the cognitive training, he will tend to discount them as the result of luck or the ease of the task. Therefore, a comprehensive intervention program for Vince must also include attribution retraining.

Vince's teachers, parents, and counselors would certainly agree that Vince is unmotivated. However, labeling Vince as unmotivated does not suggest any specific intervention to improve his motivation. When Vince's lack of motivation is viewed as a result of his beliefs about himself and about achievement, these beliefs become the target of the intervention. Attribution retraining attempts to change beliefs about one's self-efficacy as a learner and about the relationship between effort and achievement. Students are encouraged to give themselves more adaptive messages about the reasons for their successes and failures.

Attribution retraining for Vince would begin with his being told the results of the psychological evaluation. His above average intelligence would be emphasized, as would his specific cognitive weaknesses. Weaknesses mean that not all types of instruction are equally effective with him, but that he has sufficient intelligence to master school learning tasks if he learns some different ways to go about learning.

To encourage Vince to attribute his failures to effort, his teachers should respond to his failures by attributing them to effort. "No, you didn't get that right. You need to try harder." It is probably not helpful to attribute successes to effort, as this procedure may cause students to infer low ability (Nicholls, 1978). In order to avoid stereotypical feedback from teachers and to emphasize the role of strategy in learning, teachers should combine effort attributions with strategy attributions. "You didn't get that one right. How else could you try to solve that problem? Did you remember to ask yourself questions after each paragraph?" These two types of attributions (strategy deployment and effort) are similar, in that each places responsibility for failure on the student's changeable, controllable responses.

Relating to Authority Figures

Vince expects persons in authority (parents, teachers) to be unaccepting of him. His response to this anticipated rejection is to be aversive, defiant, and uncooperative. Referring to Vince as having a bad attitude toward authority figures does not suggest any specific intervention. However, describing Vince as believing that adults will be unaccepting and critical of him suggests an intervention. Specifically, Vince would benefit from individual counseling, preferably with a male counselor or therapist. Initially counseling sessions might involve playing basketball or pitching a baseball, because Vince is unlikely to participate in counseling sessions that require a great deal of talking. As Vince becomes more comfortable with the counselor and trust is developed, he will be ready and willing to participate in more structured counseling sessions.

The structured counseling sessions should include instruction in skills for dealing with authority. First, the consequences of Vince's behavior on teachers should be highlighted. Vince needs to understand the relationship between his behavior toward teachers and teachers' reactions to him. He has power in relationships with teachers, which he can use in ways that help or hurt him. After he accepts the need to change his behavior with teachers, he needs training in specific social skills for dealing with authority figures. The following list of skills would be emphasized in this training:

accepting criticism

asking for help

questioning rules that are perceived as unfair

negotiating

apologizing

asking for clarification

The social skills training program described by Goldstein, Sprafkin, and Gershaw (1976) would be appropriate, if it were modified to be used in individual counseling. Individual counseling is preferred due to the importance of a positive relationship with an adult counselor to Vince's motivation to improve his interactions with teachers. The steps in teaching social skills are as follows:

1. Define the skill. Give examples of the skill and explain why the skill is useful. Ask Vince for situations when the skill would be called for and examples of situations when he or someone else did and did not use the skill.
2. Describe the skill in terms of the specific steps which make the skill. Make these steps explicit by outlining them on a board and giving appropriate and inappropriate examples of each step.
3. Model the skill in a role-play situation with Vince. Afterward, draw out the specific steps.
4. Have Vince practice the skill in another role play. Select role-play situations that are relevant to Vince, using situations suggested by him when possible. Provide specific feedback to Vince. Feedback should be weighted toward the positive, especially during the early stages of learning a new skill. Use effort and strategy attributions to explain mistakes.
5. Continue steps 4 and 5 until Vince masters the skill in the role-play situations.
6. Plan for generalization. Develop a plan for practicing the skill between sessions. Agree on a reinforcer Vince can award to himself upon completion of the practice assignment.

Communication Skills Training

Vince needs to learn to express his feelings to others. The individual counseling will provide him with an adult model who expresses feelings and a supportive relationship in which to practice self-disclosure and the expression of feelings. After Vince has made some progress in individual therapy, he should participate in group communication skills training. The following skills will be emphasized:

active listening

complimenting others

expressing positive feelings toward others

expressing anger

standing up for your rights

offering support

seeking support

compromising

The same instructional steps as listed above will be used in the group training. An example of the specific steps that make up the skill of expressing angry feelings follows:

Decide if you are angry with someone.

Tell them what they did.

Tell them how it affects you.

Tell them how you feel.

Ask if they understand.

Conflict Resolution

Family therapy is recommended in order to assist Vince's family to develop more adaptive conflict resolution skills. Specifically, Robin and Foster's (1989) program, would be especially useful due to its particular emphasis upon the intrafamily changes associated with adolescence and the need for families to renegotiate relationship rules to accommodate the adolescent's capacity and need for independence and autonomy. Vince's family's unresolved struggle over Vince's attempts for independence and autonomy is evident in the continuing conflicts between Vince and his stepdad over the rules and stepdad's authority and Vince's mother's sense of "powerlessness" to assert any control over Vince's behavior. To enhance the family's ability to resolve conflicts and to respond adaptively to the developmental changes that occur during adolescence, there is a focus within the Robin and Foster program in improving the family's interactional problem-solving skills as well as their receptive and expressive communication skills, and on the substitution of more adaptive beliefs about family interactions. (Detailed guidance for conducting the Robin and Foster program is provided in Robin and Foster's (1989) book, *Negotiating Parent Adolescent Conflict*.)

Modification of Maladaptive Attributions about Parents' Divorce and Father's Absence

In order to assess Vince's attributions regarding his parents' divorce and his father's absence, Vince would be encouraged to discuss his feelings and perceptions about these issues during individual counseling sessions. If Vince's responses reveal that his attributions are maladaptive (e.g., "Dad left because I wasn't good enough," or "Dad doesn't come around because I don't please him") the practitioner would model more appropriate attributions for the failure of his parents' marriage (e.g., emphasizing that divorce is an adult problem and that children are not responsible for divorce) and the absence of his natural father (e.g., stressing that his father's uninvolvement is his dad's issue and not dependent upon Vince's behavior). As well, Vince would be encouraged to read *The Boys and Girls Book about Divorce* (Gardner, 1970), which addresses the issues of young children's attributions of blame, their sense of guilt, and their feelings of anger and rejection after their parents divorce. In this book valuable suggestions are given to children to cope with the above issues.

Evaluating the Model

The proposed intervention is a comprehensive plan. The comprehensiveness of the plan both matches the complexity of cognitive behavioral theory and is directly based on the clinical model of Vince's difficulties. This model hypothesizes that Vince's school learning and adjustment problems are a result of his beliefs about himself and the relationship between effort and outcomes as well as his expectation that teachers will be critical and unaccepting. Additionally, his undiagnosed learning disability and deficits in both procedural and conditional metacognitive skills interfere with his ability to be successful, which contributes to the hypothesized failure cycle. Evidence of the clinical utility of this model will be provided by evidence of the effectiveness of the intervention which is predicated on this model. The plan's effectiveness should be closely monitored, and the evaluative data should be used to refine both the model and the intervention plan. Some of the evaluative data (i.e., Vince's disruptiveness, amount of time engaged in academic tasks) can be collected on a very frequent basis, whereas other types of data should be collected less frequently (i.e., academic improvement, self-concept). Evidence of the effectiveness of the plan would include increased time spent engaged in learning activities, strategy use (based on self-report and observations), improved interactions with teachers and decreased rates of disruptive classroom behaviors (based on teacher report and observations), practitioner's report of increased self-disclosure in therapy sessions, an increased tendency to attribute failure to strategy deployment (based on teacher and therapist probes), an improvement in academic self-concept (Piers–Harris Self Concept Scale), and a decrease in anxiety (Revised Manifest Anxiety Scale for Children). Additionally, at the end of six months of cognitive training, Vince's performance on standardized tests of written expression and reading should show improvement.

REFERENCES

Bandura, A. (1965). Vicarious processes: A case of no-trial learning. In L. Berkowitz (Ed.), *Advances in experimental social psychology* (Vol. 2). New York: Academic.

Bandura, A. (1969). *Principles of Behavior Modification*. New York: Holt, Rinehart & Winston.

Bandura, A. (1971). Vicarious and self-reinforcement processes. In R. Glaser (Ed.), *The nature of reinforcement*. New York: Academic.

Bandura, A. (1977). *Social learning theory*. Englewood Cliffs, NJ: Prentice Hall.

Beck, A. T. (1976). *Cognitive therapy and the emotional disorders*. New York: International University Press.

Beck, A. T., Rush, A. J., Shaw, B. V., & Emery. G. (1979). *Cognitive therapy of depression*. New York: Guilford.

Braswell, L., & Kendall, P. C. (1988). Cognitive-behavioral methods with children. In K. S. Dobson (Ed.), *Handbook of cognitive-behavioral therapies* (pp. 167–211). New York: Guilford.

Clark, C. M., & Peterson, P. L. (1984). *Teachers' thought processes*. East Lansing: Institute for research on teaching, Michigan State University (ERIC ED 251449).

Coleman, R. E., & Beck, A. T. (1981). Cognitive therapy for depression. In J. F. Clarkin & H. I. Glazer (Eds.), *Depression: Behavioral and directive intervention strategies*. New York: Garland STPM.

Dember, W. N. (1974). Motivation and the cognitive revolution. *American Psychologist, 29*, 161–168.

Digdon, N., & Gotlib, I. J. (1985). Developmental considerations in the study of childhood depression. *Developmental Review, 5*, 162–199.

DiGiuseppe, R. (1986). Cognitive therapy for childhood depression. Special Issue: Depression in the family. *Journal of Psychotherapy and the Family, 2*(3–4), 153–172.

Dobson, K. S. (1988). The present and future of cognitive-behavioral therapies. In K. S. Dobson (Ed.), *Handbook of cognitive-behavioral therapies* (pp. 387–414). New York: Guilford.

Dobson, K. S., & Block, L. (1988). Historical and philosophical bases of the cognitive-behavioral therapies. In K. S. Dobson (Ed.), *Handbook of cognitive-behavioral therapies* (pp. 3–38). New York: Guilford.

Dryden, W., & Ellis, A. (1987). Rational emotive therapy. In W. Dryden & W. L. Golden (Eds.), *Cognitive-behavioral approaches to psychotherapy* (pp. 129–168). New York: Hemisphere.

D'Zurilla, T. J., & Goldfried, M. R. (1971). Problems-solving and behavior modification. *Journal of Abnormal Psychology, 78*, 107–126.

Ellis, A. (1962). *Reason and emotion in psychotherapy*. New York: Lyle Stuart.

Ellis, A. (1973). Rational-emotive therapy. In R. Corsini (Ed.), *Current psychotherapies*. Itasca, IL: Peacock.

Ellis, A. (1977). Rejoinder: Elegant and inelegant RET. *The Counseling Psychologist, 7*(1), 73–82.

Emery, G., Bedrosian, R., & Garber, J. (1983). Cognitive therapy with depressed children and adolescents. In D. P. Cantwell & G. A. Carlson (Eds.), *Affective disorders in children and adolescents* (pp. 445–471). New York: Spectrum.

Gardner, R. A. (1970). *The boys and girls book about divorce*. New York: Bantam.

Goldstein, A. P., Sprafkin, R. P., & Gershaw, N. J. (1979). *Skill-streaming the adolescent: A structural learning approach to teaching prosocial behavior*. Champaign, IL: Research Press.

Graham, S., & Harris, K. (1989). Cognitive training: Implications for written language. In J. N. Hughes and R. J. Hall (Eds.), *Cognitive behavioral psychology in the schools*, (pp. 247–279). New York: Guilford.

Homme, L. (1965). Perspectives in psychology: Control of coverants, the operants of the mind. *Psychological Record, 15*, 501–511.

Hughes, J. N. (1988a). *Cognitive behavior therapy with children in schools* (pp. 3–23). New York: Pergamon.

Hughes, J. N. (1988b). *Cognitive behavior therapy with children in schools* (pp. 193–215). New York: Pergamon.

Kanfer, F. H. (1970). Self-regulation: Research, issues, and speculations. In C. Neuringer & J. L. Michael (Eds.), *Behavior modification in clinical psychology*. New York: Appleton-Century-Crofts.

Kanfer, F. H., & Karoly, P. (1972). Self-control: A behavioristic excursion into the lion's den. *Behavior Therapy, 3*, 398–416.

Kaufman, A. S. (1979). *Intelligent testing with the WISC–R*. New York: Wiley.

Kendall, P. C., & Hollon, S. D. (1979). Cognitive-behavioral interventions: Overview and current status. In P. C. Kendall & S. D. Hollon (Eds.), *Cognitive-behavioral interventions: Theory, Research, and Procedures*. New York: Academic.

Keogh, B. & Hall, R. (1984). Cognitive training with learning-disabled pupils. In A. W. Meyers & W. E. Craighead (Eds.), *Cognitive behavior therapy with children* (pp. 163–191). New York: Plenum.

Kuhn, T. S. (1962). *The structure of scientific revolutions*. Chicago: University of Chicago Press.

Luria, A. R. (1961). The role of speech in the regulation of normal and abnormal behavior. New York: Liveright.

Maier, S. F., & Seligman, M. E. P. (1976). Learned helplessness: Theory and evidence. *Journal of Experimental Psychology: General, 105*, 3–46.

Meichenbaum, D. H., & Goodman, J. (1971). Training impulsive children to talk to themselves. *Journal of Abnormal Psychology, 78*, 107–126.

Meyers, A. W., & Craighead, W. E. (1984). Cognitive behavior therapy with children: A historical, conceptual, and organizational overview. In A. W. Meyers & W. E. Craighead (Eds.), *Cognitive behavior therapy with children* (pp. 1–17). New York: Plenum.

Nicholls, J. (1978). The development of the concepts of effort and ability, perceptions of academic attainment and the understanding that difficult tasks require more ability. *Child Development, 49*, 800–814.

Palincsar, A. M., & Brown, A. L. (1984). Reciprocal teaching of comprehension-fostering and comprehension-monitoring activities. *Cognition and Instruction, 1*, 117–175.

Paul, R., Cohen, D. J., & Caparulo, B. K. (1983). A longitudinal study of patients with severe developmental disorders of language learning. *Journal of the American Academy of Child Psychiatry, 22*, 525–534.

Piacentini, J. C. (1987). Language dysfunction and childhood behavior disorders. In B. B. Lahey and A. E. Kazdin (Eds.), *Advances in clinical child psychology* (Vol. 10) (pp. 259–287). New York: Plenum.

Robin, A. L., & Foster, S. L. (1989). *Negotiating parent adolescent conflict*. New York: Guilford.

Rutter, M., Graham, P., & Yule, W. (1970). *A neuropsychiatric study in children*. Lavenham, England: Lavenham Press.

Seligman, M. E. P. (1975). *Helplessness*. San Francisco: Freeman.

Skinner, B. F. (1953). *Science and human behavior*. New York: Free Press.

Spivack, G., Platt, J. J., & Shure, M. B. (1976). *The problem-solving approach to adjustment*. San Francisco: Jossey-Bass.

Torgensen, J. K. (1980). Conceptual and educational implications of the use of efficient task strategies by learning disabled children. *Journal of Learning Disabilities, 13*, 364–371.

United States Office of Education. (1977). Rules and regulations implementing Public Law 94–142 (The Education for All Handicapped Children Act of 1975). *Federal Register, 42*.

Vygotsky, L. (1962). *Thought and language*. New York: Wiley.

Weiner, B. (1979). A theory of motivation for some classroom experiences. *Journal of Educational Psychology, 71*, 3–25.

Wessler, R. L. (1987). Conceptualizing cognitions in cognitive-behavioral therapies. In W. Dryden & W. L. Golden (Eds.), *Cognitive-behavioral approaches to psychotherapy* (pp. 1–30). New York: Hemisphere.

Wilson, G. T. (1978). Cognitive behavior therapy: Paradigm shift or passing phase? In J. P. Foreyt and D. P. Rathjen (Eds.), *Cognitive behavior therapy: Research and application* (pp. 7–32). New York: Plenum.

CHAPTER 10

An Ecological Approach to Intervention

Jane Close Conoley and Gladys Haynes
University of Nebraska–Lincoln

Ecological approaches emphasize interactions of people with all their environments. Attention is paid to the developing biological organism within social and physical contexts. Ecological thinking, therefore, tends to result in interventions that adjust people's attitudes, information, expectations, or behavior across a number of life spheres. The goal is to increase the fit or match between children and their multiple worlds.

Proponents of an ecological orientation take the position that behavior is determined by the *interaction* of individual and environmental characteristics. Although all major approaches to understanding human behavior cite internal and external forces as operating together to produce behavior, they differ significantly in emphasis.

For example, both psychodynamic and biophysical models are concerned for the most part with the definition and understanding of internal forces. Psychodynamic theorists focus primarily on "needs" and "drives" and on the investigation of patterns of behavior that occur at various stages of development. Biophysical theorists, on the other hand, emphasize physiological conditions that may lead to certain typical behavior patterns.

Behavioral and sociological models are concerned mainly with external forces. The behavior theorist tries to understand stimulus–response patterns and the reinforcing and punishing conditions in the environment that produce particular sequences of behaviors. This is a functional analysis of behavior. Sociologists are more concerned with the broader environment including institutions, communities, culture, and society in their efforts to understand conditions that produce individual and group behavior.

Ecological theory maintains an equal emphasis of concern for internal and external

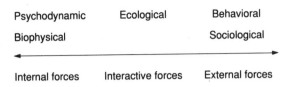

Psychodynamic   Ecological   Behavioral

Biophysical   Sociological

Internal forces   Interactive forces   External forces

Figure 10.1 Internal/External Focus of Major Perspectives in Human Behavior

forces when attempting to understand human behavior. Ecologists assume there is a unique pattern of explanatory forces for each individual case under scrutiny. Gordon (1982), describing ecological theory, has noted:

> While the individual is being examined, the model simultaneously permits the worker to study the environment, seeking beneficial changes in the total structure, redefining the goals, and exploring the ability of the client to survive in that state, as well as the potential of both for changed existence in improved states (p. 110).

Examine Figure 10.1 as a depiction of the relationship of ecological theory to other models of understanding human behavior, especially troubled human behavior.

Ecologists examine ecosystems rather than individuals. Ecosystems are composed of all the interacting systems of living things and their nonliving surroundings. Ecosystems have histories and internal development that make each unique and constantly changing. When a child appears "normal," ecologists see the ecosystem as congruent or balanced. On the other hand, when such congruence does not exist, the child is likely to be considered deviant (i.e., out of harmony with social norms) or incompetent (i.e., unable to perform purposefully in the unchanged setting). When this is the case, ecologists say the system is not balanced, that particular elements are in conflict with one another. Such conflicts are termed "points of discordance," that is, specific places where there is a failure of match between the child and his or her ecosystem.

HISTORICAL ANTECEDENTS

Ecology usually is not seen as a separate discipline, but rather as an area of study within several disciplines. Basic concepts have come from a variety of fields other than psychology, for example, education, biology, sociology, and anthropology. Despite the diversity of disciplines represented, scientists interested in ecology are always concerned about the relationship of individuals to settings and use similar research methods in their inquiries. All human ecologists would agree that behavior is a product of the interaction between internal forces and the environmental circumstances.

Anthropologists may have been the original human ecologists. Their contributions to an understanding of troubled or psychopathological behavior have focused primarily on the cultural contexts in which deviant behavior occurs. Sociologists have added to the knowledge base in human ecology with studies of the significant social conditions that tend to be associated with high rates of deviance. Farris and Dunham (1939) in their classic work, *Mental Disorders in Urban Areas,* described their conceptions of "concentric zone theory'' and social disorganization, and the relationship of those concepts to mental illness. They proposed three things as necessary to have a mentally healthy child: (a) intimacy and affection between the child and some permanent group; (b) a consistency of influence; and (c) some harmony between home and outside situations. They also noted that "insanity" is not defined by a list of actions but rather, by a lack of fit between actions and situations.

Some of the earliest and most important applications of ecological theory to the treatment of special needs children was done by William Rhodes; he suggested that special educators had borrowed a biophysical model and had attempted to apply it to troubled children (Rhodes, 1967). As a result, educators had come to view disturbance as residing totally and completely within the child, and consequently their intervention efforts were based on finding and correcting the neurological, chemical, genetic, and/or psychological flaws within youngsters. Rhodes proposed an alternative view of emotional disturbance that emphasized the reciprocal nature of disturbance and focused on the interchange between a child and the surrounding environment. Although not denying influence from other sources, Rhodes contended that at the very least, both the child and his or her environment were likely intervention targets. The goals and assumptions of ecological theory in treating troubled children have been further developed by Apter (1977, 1982), Hobbs (1966, 1975, 1982), Kounin (1970, 1975) and Swap (1974, 1978).

Ecological psychologists (e.g., Barker, 1978; Lewin, 1951) have analyzed settings in terms of both psychological and nonpsychological forces. Barker and his colleagues developed a comprehensive research program designed to operationalize the concept of life space developed by Kurt Lewin. In their work on behavior settings (small ecosystems that call forth particular behaviors), they have discovered the importance of "synomorphy" (i.e., the fit of individual behavior to the particular setting) and concluded that mental illness is a term used to represent behavior that is poorly fitted to the setting.

Medical ecologists have also contributed to an understanding of human behavior through research into the interaction between individual genetic determinants and environmental differences. Thomas, Chess, and Birch (1968) found that infants are born with varying levels of nine temperamental dimensions (i.e., activity level, approach/withdrawal, intensity of reaction, quality of mood, attention span and persistence, rhythmicity, adaptability, threshold of responsiveness, and distractibility). They suggested that any level of these qualities can result in emotional disturbance under certain environmental conditions, that is, the temperaments (and consequently the behavior) of some children fit better into their environments than do the temperaments and behaviors of other children (Thomas & Chess, 1977).

CRITICAL ELEMENTS

The major assumptions of the ecological model applied to children's difficulties serve as key concepts in developing interventions. In the case analysis that follows this orientation section, note how each of the assumptions will be used to guide assessment and treatment strategies.

1. Each child is an inseparable part of a small social system. Every child lives in a context that is both unique and critical to our understanding of the youngster and our intervention efforts.

2. Disturbance is viewed not as a disease located within the body of the child but rather as discordance in the system. Contrary to psychodynamic or biophysical models in which the disease defined the child, from the ecological position the troubled youngster represents a troubled system. For example, environments may elicit disturbing behaviors and then identify and label such behaviors as symptoms of emotional disturbance or behavior disorders.Which behaviors get labeled depends upon the time, place, and culture in which they are emitted and upon the tolerance of those who observe them (Swap, Prieto, & Harth, 1982; Rhodes, 1967, 1970).

3. Discordance may be defined as a disparity between an individual's abilities and the demands or expectations of the environments—a failure of match between child and system. Some settings are extremely demanding and unresponsive to the individual abilities of a child. In such environments, a child may appear incompetent while in other more nurturing environments the same child will not be identified as deviant. An example may be the so-called "six-hour retarded child"—a child labeled as "retarded" by the school but considered normal in the family and community.

GOALS AND PURPOSES

In sum, the goal of an ecologically based intervention is not a particular state of mental health or particular behavior patterns, but rather an increased concordance between the behavior of a child and the settings in which he or she resides. These goals are reached not through a new set of techniques or treatments but through a framework of using existing techniques in an ecological manner. The treatment plan is guided by the child interacting with all the important elements of his or her life space. The ecological perspective is a useful umbrella under which to organize a variety of intervention efforts into a purposeful attempt to increase the possibility of system change, the competence of individuals, and the congruence of individuals with their settings.

ANALYSIS OF CASE DATA

Relevant Case Data

Because the child's ecosystem or life space (current and past) is the assessment target, data relevant for intervention are potentially quite extensive. Only after the ecosystem is understood can decisions of how and where to intervene be made. Obviously, the smallest change with the greatest likelihood of success is the preferred strategy.

What follows are the case data that would inform treatment planning. The data are presented as elements of Vince's psychological, medical/physical, historical, and social systems. Data gathered in formal assessment are also summarized. Other organizing categories could be constructed. The important purpose is to reach an understanding of Vince in interaction with his significant relationships.

Vince.   Vince is an older-than-average seventh grader from a divorced home. He is failing or close to failing in English, math, science, and social studies. The case referral indicated that Vince is evidencing increasing amounts of frustration, excitability, and troubled relationships with adults. The particular problems he has at school are fairly localized to one or two classes.

Vince appears to be very sensitive to any evaluative comments or situations that are unfamiliar to him. He tends to deny interest in any activity or task that he finds difficult. Vince insists he has no problems and rather defensively externalizes blame for any perceived difficulties. Vince is apparently lacking in problem-solving strategies. He does, however, appear to want to succeed in math, with girls, and as a big brother.

Medical/Physical.   Vince had a seriously high fever as an infant that resulted in convulsions (and perhaps some central nervous system (CNS) involvement). Repeated ear infections caused some hearing impairment and related articulation difficulties as a younger child. There is no current concern about hearing. He was placed on Ritalin at about eight years of age because of teacher complaints about his behavior at school. After three years this was discontinued because of sleeping difficulties. The family continued to medicate him with over-the-counter drugs to decrease his excitability. Currently, Vince is well-built, maturing early, and interested in physical fitness.

Transitions.   Vince has experienced several separations/transitions in his young life. At five years his family relocated and his biological father's and mother's work schedules changed resulting in an increased amount of time with a sitter and a decreased amount of outdoor activity. The parents divorced when he was about nine. He has become increasingly disengaged from his biological father. The biological father moved to another state 18 months ago, is planning a remarriage, and does not foresee increasing his availability to his son. Vince changed elementary schools after fourth grade, being expelled for conduct from a private, parochial school. This was likely related to his being caught masturbating. After one year in the new elementary school, Vince entered middle school.

Social Relationships.   Vince has unusually positive relationships with peers and with his young sister. His current peer group is academically marginal, but he has a history of successful involvement with others of his age. Relationships with his stepfather and most teachers are strained. He expresses more affection toward his mother, but she tends to describe herself as letting Vince have his own way. She had done this historically to make up for his absent father and his medical problems and now feels that she has no control over his behavior. Vince is resisting his stepfather's authority as he does most authority, but suggests that he would work for his stepfather upon graduation or dropping out of high school.

Data from Assessment.   A summary of all the assessment approaches used with Vince would suggest that he is of normal to above normal intelligence with some particular abilities in verbal and memory skills. His written language skills are problematic. He seems to have some mild to moderate specific neurological difficulties around abstract reasoning, and auditory perception. He exhibits emotional indicators in several of the tests suggesting problems in planning, anxiety (especially related to school and behavior), and accepting his family situation. He seems self-confident about his relationship with girls and his physical attributes.

Vince may have idealized notions of what a future family life would be like for him (not too unusual for a teen) and a tendency to understand relationships in rather simplistic terms, for example, good families stay together and live happily ever after. Unfortunately, his understanding of happiness does not match his current situation.

Analysis

Figure 10.2 is a schematic representing a way of organizing the extensive data collected about Vince.

How does Vince "fit" with each aspect of his ecosystem? This is the key ecological question. An analysis of the available data should provide a map of possible treatment targets and methods.

Figure 10.2 is an example of a jumping-off place to investigate Vince's relationships with each of the important components in his life. For example, although sports and peer groups are possible strengths to be developed with Vince, his construction of his absent father and the tensions with his stepfather could be targets for remediation.

Absent Father.   Vince seems to "fit" well with his biological father, but only in an idealized way. His limited experience with the father and the father's assertion that he lacks the resources to increase his interaction with Vince suggests the father may not be a fruitful intervention route. His memories of his father are positive models, however, in terms of seeing the importance of working hard, providing high career aspirations, and a belief in the father's caring for him.

Stepfamily.   The stepfamily system is complex in terms of its match to Vince. Mother matches Vince's teen understanding of caring; that is, she is fairly lax in her expectations

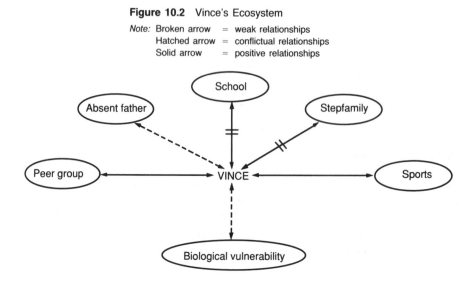

Figure 10.2   Vince's Ecosystem

Note: Broken arrow   = weak relationships
Hatched arrow = conflictual relationships
Solid arrow   = positive relationships

of him, so she's okay. Stepfather and Vince are discordant, but perhaps only because Vince lacks in-depth experience with the stepfather; that is, he has not yet identified the stepfather as deserving his loyalty because he is unsure of the stepfather's loyalty, caring, and commitment to him. Vince has been hurt before due to separations and transitions and may be resistant to committing to another adult. Vince is unusually attached to his little sister. The sister seems to meet a need Vince has to be looked up to, to be needed, to be loved unconditionally. The danger of this match, however, is that the sister's unwavering love is destined to be subject to her own developmental path. She is likely to become more evaluative toward Vince as she grows older and is generally more critical of her surroundings.

School.   Despite the school being the key point of discordance for Vince, the match of skills and abilities to the school environment is rather positive. He is of normal intelligence in areas most critical to schooling; he likes to succeed, to play sports, and be around peers. He has had at least one very successful year with a fifth grade teacher who recognized some of Vince's special needs and strengths. His historical problems with schools seem related more to system inflexibility to normal development and to Vince's particular problems with attention and impulse control than to any serious deficit in Vince.

Peers/Sports.   Vince is particularly well-matched with his current group. His interests in sports and physical fitness are important strengths. These attitudes may allow for the construction of alternative groups for Vince—groups whose academic values are more in line with school expectations. The current group appears to be a support for Vince's self-esteem and his access to girlfriends. Both of these are important outcomes so that no active attempts should be made to disengage Vince from his peer group.

Biological Vulnerability.   Vince seems to have some residual damage from his seizures, hearing impairment, and a generally reactive temperament (i.e., high activity, tendency to withdraw, intense reaction to frustration, impulsive problem solving, low attention span, and high distractibility). These factors would predict that he would be a difficult child to raise. He would need highly skilled adults who were able and willing to monitor his behavior very closely and provide very nurturing responses to his difficulties.

Discussion

Vince's ecosystem contains both supporting and inhibiting forces in terms of his match with his various settings. In Table 10.1 is a summary of these forces.

    An analysis of supportive or driving forces suggests areas of intervention involving enhancement, while an analysis of inhibiting forces suggests areas for remediation. The analysis also pinpoints the people in Vince's life whose behaviors or attitudes interact with his behavior and attitudes. Some of Vince's difficulties are fairly predictable and obvious (e.g., teenage problems with authority; behavior problems associated with divorce/single parenting; resentment toward stepfather's encroachment into the family unit).

    Despite the presence of some signs of neurological involvement in the current testing, Vince's past history suggests his problems with matching the expectations of his various settings, although affected by physiology are, perhaps, explained more

TABLE 10.1   Supportive and Inhibiting Forces in Vince's Ecosystem

Supportive Forces	Inhibiting Forces
	School
Normal intelligence	Written language disability
	Lack of problem-solving strategies
Math aptitude	Undeveloped academic motivation
Some school success	Current problems in school
Desire to excel	Fear of failure/evaluation
	Peers
Circle of friends	Low-achieving peer group
Interest in girls	Immature understanding of relationships
Interest in sports	Problems with authority
	Family
Concerned mother	Disengaged biological father
Concerned stepfather	Conflict with stepfather
Affection for sister	History of disappointment with relationships
Affection toward father	Idealized memories of father
	Medical
Well-built, muscular	Some residual central nervous system involvement
	Vince
Specific high esteem	Anxiety about behavior
	Sadness over family structure
Likes to be needed	Hypersensitive to criticism

heuristically by his learning history than by his biology. His trouble with attention and control of acting-out behavior was fairly specific to certain situations in school. His success with friends suggests he was particularly discordant with academic situations, not the general constraints of school life.

An analysis of the driving and inhibiting forces in Vince's life space suggests that interventions are possible in both of Vince's primary settings, home and school. Both settings contain some strengths to build upon as well as some deficits to overcome (in all the people in the settings, not only Vince). Because Vince is unmotivated to accept personal responsibility for his problems, changing the behaviors and attitudes of others may be the first choice for intervention.

RECOMMENDATIONS
AND SUGGESTED INTERVENTIONS

Ecological change efforts are attempts to make small changes in the patterns of behavior, expectations, or attitudes of significant people in several of a child's settings. To effect such interventions, coordinated meetings must occur among parents, teachers, the child, and other significant persons to the child. Careful plans must be constructed, individual responsibilities specified, and evaluation criteria decided upon. Ecological practitioners must be sensitive to each person's unique goals or criteria for success. It is of utmost importance that all members of an intervention team realize they must be ready to adjust their behavior, expectations, or attitudes if success is to be achieved. This realization is in contrast to the more traditional notion that intervention teams meet to plan for how the child must change to meet criteria.

Areas of Emphasis

Home and school are the obvious choices for interventions. In particular, mother's skills in behavior management and stepfather's skills and attitudes in relationship building are likely targets. At school, some adjustment of teachers' behaviors to increase their monitoring of Vince's behaviors (positive and negative) seems in order. For example, they might be given some support to interact with him more frequently, call on him at least several times each class period, and provide him with progress feedback on his work very often. Another school adjustment could be alterations in the structure of his day to include experiences in tutoring younger children and access to sports or physical training activities. A leadership role in some social club or activity are other possible interventions. Vince's skills in problem solving and attending to auditory input need enhancement. Skill development might be accomplished in a group of children especially chosen to receive such training.

Program of Change

Mother.   Vince's mother must assume a more consistent role with Vince in regard to positive and negative contingencies associated with his behavior. Her long history of "making up for" a distant biological father has mitigated her influence with Vince. Vince has a number of preferred activities that could be used to motivate some behavior change. Mother might link improved grades, prosocial interaction with the stepfather, or performance of daily chores to access to activities he identifies as important to him.

It is likely mother will have to establish a regular study time for Vince and his sister. She will have to insist that TV, radio, and phones are off-limits to everyone in the family as they spend an hour each evening reading, doing assignments, assisting each other on homework, or discussing some family plan for an outing or other event.

Vince's mother may also require some information about normal developmental expectations. Her reluctance to provide reasons for the expulsion from the parochial school suggests she may have been (and still may be) uninformed about developing sexuality. She may benefit from knowing which of Vince's behaviors, though irritating, are common to most 13-year-old boys.

Stepfather.   Vince's stepfather may have inadvertently become his primary critic. Stepfather must remove himself as the disciplinarian and establish a positive relationship with Vince. As mother becomes central as the dispenser of rules and contingencies, the stepfather can develop enjoyable pastimes with Vince. Vince responds to (matches well with) an environment that recognizes his strengths. Some joint sporting events, weight lifting, jogging, talks about dating and social activities may help stepfather see Vince's talents. Vince's strengths in math might be useful in the stepfather's business. Such involvement might raise Vince's career aspirations as well as allow both Vince and his stepfather to build a relationship based on mutual admiration.

Teachers.   Despite the urgency of the original referral, only Vince's Family Living teacher reports serious behavior problems. There may be several sources of his discordance with this class. For example, the content concerning family life may arouse anxiety or anger in Vince. Perhaps many written assignments or essay exams are the norm in this class. If so, the task dimensions would be particularly frustrating to Vince on both affective and cognitive grounds. Some further exploration of the class context seems in order.

Teachers in Vince's other classes must become more attentive to Vince's rather passive-aggressive behavior patterns. Obviously, he uses low-level inappropriate behavior to avoid beginning assignments that he evaluates as being too difficult. Strategies to assist him in beginning work might include: (a) physical proximity at the start of the individual seatwork; (b) progress feedback frequently during the period; (c) heavy reinforcement of any contributions from Vince; (d) adaptation of some assignments in terms of written language requirements; (e) development of personal relationships with him that are based on a recognition of his strengths thus inhibiting his fear of negative evaluation; (f) private conferences or confrontations regarding his work or his behavior rather than public discussions; and (g) consistent enforcement of rules and contingencies. On this last point, for example, teachers must not threaten, but follow through on every contingency they mention.

School Setting.   Vince's academics and self-esteem might be improved with opportunities to tutor younger children. He has skills in relating to young children (who tend to be less critical) and needs an increase in settings that recognize his strengths. This access to some cross-age tutoring might occur after school or ideally during the school day.

Vince would likely benefit as well from some interest from an athletic coach or trainer. The current problems with eligibility to play will not be resolved unless he gets "hooked" into some sport. A coach who paid some special attention to Vince in terms of providing an individual tryout, urging him to improve his academics so that he could play a sport, or requesting that he assist in a weight room might be as successful as Vince's fifth-grade teacher was in improving Vince's performance.

In addition, the school psychologist or counselor's group for impulsive problem solvers might be a good setting for Vince to gain some information about strategies to use when faced with novel problems. Vince's poor problem solving seems compounded with some difficulty in processing auditory stimuli. Simple procedures such as looking at those who are speaking, asking people to repeat, reminding himself to slow down and pay attention might be included in a problem-solving curriculum.

If such a group did not exist, the same training could be done as a prerequisite to Vince beginning his tutoring activities. In fact, he might be more open to information if he felt it was targeted at someone other than himself. On the other hand, junior high children are highly motivated to be with peers. A group of boys and girls of varying skill levels brought together to improve their problem solving and increase their reflectiveness in stressful situations could meet some of Vince's social needs as well as his academic deficits.

Community.   Vince has little community involvement. A secondary setting target would be to increase his involvement in organizations such as a church, YMCA, Boys Club, city sporting league, physical fitness club, and so forth. In these settings, he might be able to take a leadership role because of his athletic prowess. In addition, new peer groups could emerge from such activities, perhaps providing friends with higher academic aspirations for Vince.

It is possible that stepfather and Vince could engage in some of these activities together. Access to these experiences should not be contingent on Vince's good behavior or academic improvement at the beginning of the change program. It will be important for the practitioner to see these as components of treatment and develop other rewards and punishments appropriate to Vince's behaviors. It's possible to make even enjoyable experiences aversive to teens by holding them out as "carrots." Vince has a pattern of denying interest in things he's not sure he will achieve. Giving him noncontingent access to these activities early in the treatment plan will increase the likelihood of their motivational strength later.

Expected Outcomes

Five primary outcomes are expected: (a) improvement in Vince's relationship with his stepfather and with his mother; (b) increase in mother's skills in dealing productively with Vince's behaviors; (c) decrease in Vince's negative self-evaluations concerning academic work; (d) decrease in Vince's disruptive behaviors at home and school; (e) improvement in Vince's academic grades. These outcomes would be expected to develop on different timetables. If every adult cooperated in Vince's treatment and every suggested component was initiated (admittedly rare occurrences!), improvements in his behavior would likely precede improvements in his attitudes. His relationship with his stepfather might take several months to improve. A semester would probably pass before significant effects on his grades would be noticed.

Sources of data to measure whether such outcomes are achieved would be the following: (a) reports from stepfather concerning his relationship with Vince (e.g., how many arguments in the last week, how many joint outings in the last two weeks, how many Vince-initiated conversations in the last few days); (b) reports from mother concerning her success with delivering positive and negative contingencies for Vince's behaviors and her consistency in establishing a family study hour (e.g., journal of critical incidents over 10 days); (c) reports from teachers regarding Vince's behavior and grades (e.g., readminister the Behavior Evaluation Scale, quarterly grade report); (d) direct classroom observations; and, (e) Vince's self-esteem (e.g., readminister the Piers–Harris Children's Self-Concept Scale).

What if improvement is not noted on all or any of the above measures? A first step, if outcomes are not developing as expected, is to analyze treatment integrity. For example, stepfather would have to be queried about his efforts to engage Vince positively. Mother's behavioral management skills could be assessed. School personnel's implementation of setting and teacher behavior modifications could be checked. If everyone is doing as planned then a new round of problem identification and solution generation must be implemented.

Many aspects of Vince's life space were not altered in the first treatment package. It is possible the most important components were overlooked. For example, Vince's biological father was excluded from the initial plan because he indicated he lacked the resources to be more involved with Vince. Some work could be done to alter father's attitudes about the seriousness of the problem or his part in the problem. Father could be given some low investment strategies to keep in touch with Vince (e.g., regular phone calls, surprise small gifts). The goal of such a renewed connection with father would be to mitigate any negative self-evaluations Vince suffers because of a perception he is unloved by his father.

In addition, the proposed plan required a change in roles for mother and stepfather; that is, mother was to take over the behavior management and stepfather was to improve the emotional quality of his relationship with Vince. This change-in-role strategy is often very powerful in allowing family members greater behavioral flexibility; however, it demands continuous support. People rarely change their styles easily. In Vince's case both mother and stepfather needed some adjustment in their approaches to Vince, and Vince needed a strong male figure with whom to bond.

If the demands for change were too great, however, smaller modifications could be sought in each parent's behavior. Stepfather could be taught to "catch Vince being good" and mother taught to seek the stepfather's support in maintaining a consistent set of expectations for Vince.

CONCLUSIONS

The case of Vince has a number of interesting elements but is not dissimilar to hundreds of cases faced by school psychologists, resource teachers, principals, and counselors every day. A child who has ability but is not matching the school's expectations in academic or behavioral achievement may be the most common referral problem.

The time-consuming assessments done on such children individually must be paired with equally detailed understandings of the settings the children inhabit and the people who interact with the children. In Vince's case, most of his significant adult relationships were impaired, in part, due to deficits in adult behavior, attitudes, or expectations. Further, he was not achieving in academic areas because some of the tasks did not match his strengths or created anxiety reactions. This ecological analysis suggests that adults and tasks should be "modified" as well as children.

A shift in our assessment and treatment targets to include children's life spaces will be difficult. Primary reliance on a biophysical model is an obstacle to creating comprehensive treatment plans. Overreliance on narrow behavioral understandings can interfere with an appreciation of the effects of past emotional experiences and current cognitive strategy deficits.

An ecological framework is useful in considering all data as potentially useful and valid. Humans are remarkably complex and seem to resist easy theoretical explanations. Expert human ecologists are precise observers of what people do and sensitive interpreters of how people feel and process events. An openness to what may work for a particular child in a particular setting is far more important to the practitioner than implementing a prescribed treatment package.

It is also true that ecological interventions can be more complex and demanding than putting a child in a resource room or increasing the rewards and punishments a child receives. A practitioner's skill in motivating adults to take part in such interventions is a key element in predicting success. It's not hard to think of interventions, but it is hard to get others to cooperate. The practitioner must be as expert in understanding the life spaces of each adult as he or she is in understanding the child's situation. This necessary element in treatment implementation makes clear why assisting children with their life difficulties usually takes much longer than anyone has predicted or planned for. Establishing the resources necessary to support troubled children is a "case" that deserves adults' unending attention.

REFERENCES

Apter, S. J. (1977). Applications of ecological theory: Toward a community special education model for troubled children. *Exceptional Children, 43,* 366–373.

Apter, S. J. (1982). *Troubled children/Troubled systems.* New York: Pergamon.

Barker, R. G. (1978). *Habitats, environments, and human behavior.* San Francisco: Jossey-Bass.

Farris, R., & Dunham, H. (1939). *Mental disorders in urban areas.* Chicago: University of Chicago Press.

Gordon, E. W. (1982). Human ecology and the mental health professions. *American Journal of Orthopsychiatry, 52,* 109–110.

Hobbs, N. (1966). Helping disturbed children: Psychological and ecological strategies. *American Psychologist, 21,* 1105–1115.

Hobbs, N. (1975). *The futures of children.* San Francisco: Jossey-Bass.

Hobbs, N. (1982). *The troubled and troubling child.* San Francisco: Jossey-Bass.

Kounin, J. S. (1970). *Discipline and group management in classrooms.* New York: Holt, Rinehart and Winston.

Kounin, J. S. (1975). An ecological approach to classroom activity settings: Some methods and findings. In R. Weinberg and F. Wood (Eds.), *Observation of pupils and teachers in mainstream and special education settings: Alternative strategies.* Minneapolis: Leadership Training Institute.

Lewin, K. (1951). *Field theory and social science.* New York: Harper.

Rhodes, W. C. (1967). The disturbing child: A problem of ecological management. *Exceptional Children, 33,* 449–455.

Rhodes, W. C. (1970). A community participation analysis of emotional disturbance. *Exceptional Children, 37,* 309–314.

Swap, S. M. (1974). Disturbing classroom behaviors: A developmental and ecological view. *Exceptional Children, 41,* 163–172.

Swap, S. M. (1978). The ecological model of emotional disturbance in children: A status report and proposed synthesis. *Behavorial Disorders, 3,* 186–196.

Swap, S. M., Prieto, A. G., & Harth, R. (1982). Ecological perspectives of the emotionally disturbed child. In R. L. McDowell, G. W. Adamson, & F. H. Wood (Eds.), *Teaching emotionally disturbed children.* Boston: Little, Brown.

Thomas, A., & Chess, S. (1977). *Temperament and development.* New York: Brunner/Mazel.

Thomas, A., Chess, S., & Birch H. (1968). *Temperament and behavior disorders in children.* New York: New York University Press.

CHAPTER 11

Integrating Psychological Approaches to Intervention

Barbara A. Rothlisberg
Ball State University

The purpose of this text has been to engage the reader in an active exploration of the major psychological approaches used for intervention. Vince's case study—the common reference point—served as a basis of comparison among the theoretical positions. The chapter authors were challenged to discuss how their respective approaches might explain Vince's behavior as well as suggest strategies for behavioral change. Thus, the reader could gain insight into the nuances of each orientation and determine how each author interpreted the case material according to his or her theoretical premise. It was also interesting to note, at various junctures in the text, that the same bit of information could be viewed as serving very different functions depending on the author's orientation. For instance, both the Behavioral and Psychoanalytic chapters utilized historical data but with different intentions—one to gain information on patterns of behavioral consistency and the other to uncover the motivations underlying current behaviors.

The objective of this final chapter is not to judge the relative merits of any one of the theoretical positions expressed. Indeed, each author presented his or her case for a particular viewpoint in an insightful way—stressing the strengths that each position could offer. Instead, these final comments will try to generate thought and discussion by reviewing how the perspectives address behavior and the emphases of their prescriptions for intervention. It will be left to the discretion of the reader to determine which psychological perspectives offer him or her the most coherent and reasonable approaches for change in Vince's case. To provide some structure to this chapter, an analysis of the respective positions will be discussed relative to the following topics: stated objective of the approach, theoretical assumptions, types of data employed, and method of intervention. In each topic area, the variations in theoretical orientation will be discussed. See Table 11.1 (pp. 192–193) for a summary of this information.

STATED OBJECTIVES

As should be expected from texts dealing with intervention (see, for example, Gutkin & Reynolds, 1990; Maher & Zins, 1987; Prochaska, 1979; Prout & Brown, 1983), the major objective of each of the perspectives was change in behavior. However, it was interesting to note that even in this most basic area, the different authors expressed the necessity of change differently and weighed it with significantly different emphases. It seemed that chapters could loosely be considered to fall into three categories (or camps) of intervention; those whose approach seemed to focus primarily on observable performance differences, those that primarily emphasized internal (motivational) change, and those approaches for which intervention appeared to be a secondary issue resolved only after the diagnosis or identification of a specific problem area was completed (Hersen, Kazdin, & Bellack, 1983).

Those perspectives with a behavioral orientation (Behavioral and Cognitive-Behavioral) tended to stress observed behavorial change as the dimension of greatest interest and necessity. Generally, the suggestion was that inappropriate behavior should be the focal point of intervention with cognition either not considered or used as a mediating force to modify actions (Bellack & Hersen, 1988). Under such schemes, a methodical method of change was possible, with clearly demarcated intervention procedures and evaluative criteria. From this view, attention was given to the overt and measurable.

In contrast, internally oriented approaches (Psychoanalytic, Moral, Person-Centered, and Ecological) appeared more interested in the discontinuity between the individual's thought or affective experience and expectations for behavior than in overt action per se (Hersen, Kazdin, & Bellack, 1983; Prochaska, 1979). Within these orientations, behavior was inferred as simply an outward manifestation of Vince's internal state. To truly change behavior, Vince's thoughts and emotions must be made clear to him. Cognitive understanding must occur before change is relevant or owned by the individual (Kazdin, 1983). In this cluster of approaches, more effort seemed to be placed in deducing Vince's perceptions of the situation. Such deductions might suggest depression, anger, low frustration tolerance, poor motivation, or a plethora of other options as underlying Vince's reactions to situations. As a consequence of such inferences, each internally oriented position evaluated information based on its own theoretical terms.

A third category of approaches may be perceived as seeing problem identification as an initial area of focus with intervention as the critical second phase of the evaluative process (Brown, Pryzwansky, & Schulte, 1987; Maher & Zins, 1987; Rourke, Bakker, Fisk, & Strang, 1983). The Psychoeducational and Neuropsychological approaches might be seen in this diagnostic regard. Viewing Vince's performance in the context of a search for possible pathology and appropriate diagnosis, prescriptive statements result only when difficulty is specified. For example, it is unclear how either the Psychoeducational or Neuropsychological approach would handle case data if no evidence of pathology was forthcoming. Since the overriding assumption in these two perspectives is that formal diagnosis is a critical aspect of practice, the fact that they integrate the intervention strategies of other psychological or educational orientations suggested a more eclectic approach to change than that of the other positions.

TABLE 11.1 Intervention Plans for Vince*

Objective	Assumption	Data Employed	Method
		Behavioral	
Change in observable behavior.	Behavior is learned and situationally determined. Restructuring environment will modify behavior.	Direct observation and indirect sources from which behavior can be referenced are used.	Systematic monitoring and evaluating of behavioral responses. Retraining of Vince encouraged. Responsibility for change external to Vince. A broad-based approach.
		Psychoanalytic	
Facilitation of adaptive capacities.	Children may operate based on motivations outside of awareness. Symptomatic behaviors serve a function—to adapt to inner needs and external realities.	Focus most on information that discusses the relationship of Vince to others. Need to assess the child's capacity to regulate needs.	Psychotherapy. Discussing issues related to behaviors and increasing awareness of beliefs. Responsibility for change is Vince's. Individual understanding of subjective experience required.
		Psychoeducational	
Identification of educational need and subsequent remedial options.	Problem-solving strategy based on use of assessment techniques—particularly norm-referenced.	Full array available. Compares individual to normative group.	Eclectic. Tied to techniques derived from behavioral and cognitive orientations. Here, academic focus predominates. Responsibility for change primarily external to Vince.
		Neuropsychological	
Determination of quality of brain functions. Offers a rehabilitation program.	All behaviors mediated by cerebral function. Based on empirical evidence of brain-behavior relations.	Full array available. Used within context of identification of pathology. Concerned with etiology.	Eclectic. Derived from educational and behavioral orientations. Provides compensatory as well as remedial options for intervention. Responsibility for change external to Vince.

Moral Development			
Promotion of psychological maturity and reduction of negative emotions.	An individual will not reason in terms of a sense of justice higher than his thinking about role-taking will allow.	Interview information focusing on relationships. (Includes early history and test data related to relationships.)	Counseling that is morally directed. Responsibility for therapy lies with the relief of Vince's sense of injustice.
Person-centered			
Provide a climate that promotes actualizing tendencies.	Behavior determined by the individual's perceptual field.	Little, if any, of that provided. Must involve direct observation and reported self-perceptions.	Counseling that is defined by the individual's wishes. Responsibility for therapy lies with Vince.
Cognitive-Behavioral			
Employs cognitive and behavioral strategies to mediate behavioral change.	Maladaptive cognitions produce dysfunctional behavior. Behavior change accompanied by modification of thinking.	Uses most available data (norm-referenced tests, historical, and behavioral).	Combines cognitive and behavioral approaches in an intervention plan. Responsibility for change primarily external to Vince. A broad-based approach.
Ecological			
Establish congruence of the individual with his ecosystem.	Behavior determined by the interaction of the environment and the individual. Problems due to discordance in the system.	Sources that focus on Vince in interaction with significant others.	Uses existing techniques of intervention in an ecological manner. Responsibility for change shared by Vince and the systems with which he is involved. Systems-oriented.

*Interventions suggested for other clients may differ significantly from those identified for Vince.

The argument between viewpoints on the internal/external dimension of change may simply reduce to the idea that either change in behavior can affect thinking or change in thinking/perceptions can affect overt behavior. In any event, it appeared that no position could fully deny the interaction of internal and external states in describing or changing Vince's actions. Change options may be viewed in terms of a continuum along which the degree of internal or external influence on the individual can be described.

THEORETICAL ASSUMPTIONS

The underlying theoretical assumptions espoused by the various chapter authors defy placement on the basis of a single category such as an internal or external focus (Kazdin, 1983). Instead, the criteria one must use to view the varied conceptual frameworks must display the multifaceted texture of the theories themselves. The assumptions detailed in each chapter may explain behavior according to several dimensions and concentrate on several levels of analysis (i.e., individual, family, system). For example, the rationale for Vince's actions can be attributed to his personal perceptions or to the quality of the relationships he maintains with others. Likewise, the causative agent of the individual's behavior can be consigned to learning (as in the individual's reinforcement history) or to some type of intrinsic dysfunction (as in brain damage). In all, the diversity of opinion used to explain problematic situations seemed most obvious here, although reducing the theories to the essence of their respective views is difficult. It was apparent that looking at the theoretical assumptions explained the way in which alternative interventions may be structured.

Perhaps the most straightforward way to view the theoretical assumptions is in terms of their elegance or simplicity. Science tends to strive for the opportunity to interpret the observed in the simplest manner possible since too many exceptions to a rule make theory less generalizable (Kuhn, 1970). The Behavioral and the Person-Centered approaches appeared to offer the greatest implicit simplicity. The Behavorial position assumes that actions are learned and situationally determined. Knowing the environmental variables involved can help predict future performance. For the Person-Centered practitioner, behavior is determined by the individual's perceptual field (or perceived experience). The Behavorial system strives for objectivity and the purity of predictability while the Person-Centered approach embraces subjectivity and uniqueness. Because these perspectives explain actions along such clear lines, their respective strategies reflect this clarity and do not seem as prone to consider other intervening factors. In contrast, the other perspectives of behavior tend to integrate multiple levels of analysis into their assumptions for change.

In the context of many of the orientations, there seemed to be a "behavorial standard or norm" provided by society or by the individual's interpersonal relationships which mediated how behavior was interpreted. In the Psychoanalytic, Moral, Cognitive-Behavioral, and Ecological stances there seemed to be a greater inference that the individual's thoughts/behaviors are modified by societal forces interacting with the person. The value of current behavior is then judged against the backdrop of societal expectations (Stainbrook, 1965). For instance, the Psychoanalytic position would expect to define for the individual his or her unconscious as well as conscious motives. In a similar vein, the Moral Developmental view would evaluate not only the individual's level of thought but also compare it to societal expectations and parameters. Likewise, the Ecological approach accepted that discordance between the systems in the individual's life must be considered and adjusted. In all cases, the inferences used by the theories involved the blending of both objective and subjective analysis and included the suggestion that norms outside the individual determine what change is required.

How do the Psychoeducational and Neuropsychological schemes compare to the other approaches? They seem to be more related to assessment strategies than to psychological paradigms. Although the Neuropsychological perspective offers a view of intervention that includes compensatory as well as remedial principles, it appears more focused on etiology as the key to understanding behavior than on personality theory per se. Since brain–behavior relations are investigated, it would seem that change is geared to helping the person adjust to conditions that interfere with individual functioning. The Psychoeducational perspective is less a theory than a procedure. In a sense, to mention it with the other approaches is suggesting a unity of theoretical assumptions that this position does not seem to possess. It integrates the use of other theoretical orientations when attempting to treat behavior rather than just measure it.

TYPES OF DATA EMPLOYED

In the review of the case study, the chapter authors had access to a broad sampling of information about Vince and his family. Such a range of formal and informal data bases was provided to accommodate the needs of the various theoretical positions while offering the reader a chance to view Vince from several perspectives. Despite the fact that the amount of data exceeded that typically accessible, it was surprising that most of the authors still had to infer much of their analysis of Vince. For instance, both Moral and Person-Centered approaches seemed particularly hobbled by the indirect nature of the case. The Person-Centered orientation stated that direct observation and discussion were required while the Moral Development perspective would have been aided by interviews and instruments devoted to Vince's perception of his place relative to society and his reaction to ethical dilemmas. Perhaps the difficulties authors had in determining Vince's orientation to others, his view of self, and the quality of his thought affords a useful lesson in the evaluation of case data. Although the facts of an individual's case can be maintained in a written format, they seem two-dimensional when the practitioner attempts to capture the essence of an individual and situations in which he or she finds himself or herself. The authors were unable to actually test their hypotheses with the people involved; therefore, the matching of observation or prescriptive strategy to the real individual was hampered.

Certain of the positions made use of most of the data offered in framing the discussion of Vince. Not surprisingly, the Psychoeducational and Neuropsychological positions as well as the Cognitive-Behavioral approach addressed the full complement of information although with slightly differing agendas. For instance, the Psychoeducational and Neuropsychological positions viewed test results relative to normative standards to determine Vince's performance relative to his peers, while the Cognitive-Behavioral approach seemed to be looking for the associations among behaviors and cognitive strategies. Any information that could reflect the respective relations was employed.

The other theoretical orientations seemed much more selective in their actual data usage. While they might have acknowledged information about Vince's relative intellectual skills or achievement potential, Behavioral, Psychoanalytic, and Ecological theories tended to emphasize those data sources that were most relevant to their assumptions and objectives. Interestingly, both Psychoanalytic and Ecological positions concentrated on relational or interactional patterns although the former emphasized the individual's capacities to interact while the latter looked more uniformly on the concordance between the person and the system.

Depending on the practitioner's orientation, then, the range of data provided was more or less useful. Those positions which were psychometrically disposed seemed to benefit from the array of methods used. Data collection could be construed for these perspectives as a necessary precursor to the intervention process. In contrast, those psychological perspectives tied into the quality of Vince's thoughts and perceptions probably would have forgone many of the formal assessment procedures in favor of in-depth interviews and interpersonal exchanges. The use of such clinical interviewing among those positions may effectively blur the line between the phases of data gathering and treatment, allowing change to be initiated earlier in the intervention plan.

METHOD OF INTERVENTION

As one would expect, the issues focused upon in treatment were modified by the philosophical underpinnings of the various theoretical positions although the actual prescriptive suggestions indicated considerable overlap among perspectives in treatment techniques (Kazdin, 1983). The behaviorally oriented approaches concerned themselves with modification of the client's responses to situations just as the cognitively oriented perspectives attended to the thought processes and affective states that purportedly trigger behavior. However, what was intriguing was both the apparent focal point of change and the responsibility for change inherent in the chapter authors' prescriptive suggestions.

Almost uniformly, the primary focus of change was placed upon Vince. Although several perspectives acknowledged the need for system or familial alterations that would encompass the behaviors of others, Vince seemed to be the key to any intervention process. Perhaps this should come as no surprise; however, the emphasis suggested that, despite psychology's attempts to increase the accountability of the greater social and environmental system, the burden of change still falls upon the individual with his "deficits" or "faults" when the need for intervention is recognized. In a very real sense, this should be anticipated by the practitioner given the amount of power required to enlist the broader environment as a co-client in any prescriptive framework. Yet, it points out that in the individual/social exchange, the onus of behavioral accountability still rests with that individual. Coordination of change within the broader social environment may be beyond the scope of any theory's power.

Given the accountability for change with which the individual must grapple, it was something of a paradox to recognize that many of the psychological perspectives appeared to impose change on Vince. Relatively elaborate methods were suggested to promote increased academic skills, interpersonal skills, and a more defined sense of self. However, it remains a question as to whether Vince, himself, recognized that his behavior was problematic. Unlike cases of intervention involving adults, Vince did not refer himself for assistance; change was proposed for him and assumed to be in his best interest. Behavioral contracts, therapeutic counseling, and suggestions for changing the support system were all made with the intention of showing Vince (and other participants in his environment) the need for change. Consequently, prescriptive programs seemed designed to convince Vince that modifications of his behavior were necessary. It appeared that only the Person-Centered approach and selected aspects of others (e.g., Cognitive-Behavorial, Ecological, Moral, Psychoeducational) thought that Vince should actively control modifications of his behavior.

CONCLUDING REMARKS

As the reader worked through the various approaches to intervention, he or she should have been struck by the rich and varied nature of psychological thought devoted to understanding and modifying human behavior. Each author advocated his or her preferred position and what that philosophy adds to the sum of knowledge about behavioral change. It should be apparent that no one perspective holds the key to all the complexities inherent in thought, affect, and action or that prescriptive suggestions are unique to specific psychological approaches (Kazdin, 1983). Each position provided its best view of how to modify Vince's reaction to or interaction with his environment; interventions for another individual would undoubtedly display different elements in order to match treatment to the person's specific needs. Consequently, to capably tailor intervention to meet individual characteristics it seems critical that practitioners have at their disposal multiple strategies for change (Phillips, 1990). Rather than considering different psychological theories as rival positions, treatment may be better served by celebrating the complementary nature the various approaches demonstrate (Kazdin, 1983, Prochaska, 1979). By recognizing the strengths of the respective approaches to interpret different types of behavior or address different client concerns, the practitioner who can understand and integrate several views should be able to pattern intervention to best meet the individual's requirements for change. It is hoped that the material presented in this text will facilitate this integrative process.

REFERENCES

Bellack, A. S., & Hersen, M. (1988). *Behavioral assessment* (3rd ed.). New York: Pergamon.

Brown, D., Pryzwansky, W. B., & Schulte, A. C. (1987). *Psychological consultation: Introduction to theory and practice*. Boston: Allyn & Bacon.

Gutkin, T. B., & Reynolds, C. R. (Eds.). (1990). *The handbook of school psychology* (2nd ed.). New York: Wiley.

Hersen, M., Kazdin, A. E., & Bellack, A. S. (1983). *The clinical psychology handbook*. New York: Pergamon.

Kazdin, A. E. (1983). Treatment research: The investigation and evaluation of psychotherapy. In M. Hersen, A. E. Kazdin, & A. S. Bellack (Eds.), *The clinical psychology handbook*. New York: Pergamon.

Kuhn, T. S. (1970). *The structure of scientific revolutions* (2nd ed.). Chicago: University of Chicago Press.

Maher, C. A., & Zins, J. E. (1987). *Psychoeducational interventions in the schools.* New York: Pergamon.

Phillips, B. N. (1990). *School psychology at a turning point.* San Francisco: Jossey-Bass.

Prochaska, J. O. (1979). *Systems of psychotherapy: A transtheoretical analysis.* Homewood, IL: Dorsey.

Prout, H. T., & Brown, D. T. (1983). *Counseling and psychotherapy with children and adolescents: Theory and practice.* Tampa, FL: Mariner.

Rourke, B. P., Bakker, D. J., Fisk, J. L., & Strang, J. D. (1983). *Child neuropsychology.* New York: Guilford.

Stainbrook, E. (1965). Society and individual behavior. In B. B. Wolman (ed.), *Handbook of clinical psychology.* New York: McGraw-Hill.

Author Index

Subject Index